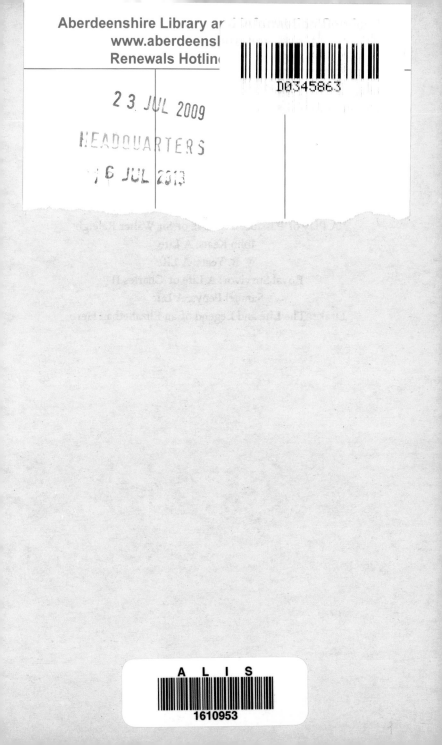

# NAPOLEON

## AND THE

# HUNDRED DAYS

*Stephen Coote*

**POCKET
BOOKS**

LONDON • SYDNEY • NEW YORK • TORONTO

First published in Great Britain by Simon & Schuster UK Ltd, 2004
This edition published by Pocket Books, 2005
An imprint of Simon & Schuster UK Ltd
A Viacom company

1 3 5 7 9 10 8 6 4 2

Simon & Schuster UK Ltd
Africa House
64–78 Kingsway
London WC2B 6AH

www.simonsays.co.uk

Simon & Schuster Australia
Sydney

A CIP catalogue record for this book is available from the British
Library.

ISBN 0-7434-4993-2
EAN 9780743449939

*For*
Jilly

# ACKNOWLEDGEMENTS

I would like to thank Bob Campbell who first suggested the subject of this book to me. During the writing of it I received help from many friends. I would particularly like to acknowledge Antonio Fong and Paul Morley. Among the scholars of the period I would like to record my indebtedness to the works of Anthony Brett-James, Henri Houssaye, Gilbert Martineau, Alan Schom and Norman Mackenzie.

# CONTENTS

# 1

## VIENNA

### 1815

## When the Dancing Had to Stop

It seemed that all of Europe was in Vienna: the great and the good, the movers and shakers, the leeches and chancers. Two emperors, four kings, one queen, three princes, two heirs apparent and two grand-duchesses were housed in the royal palace, while innumerable aristocratic mansions gave shelter to a barely countable number of hereditary nobles and distinguished diplomats along with their wives, mistresses, flunkies and friends. The men spent their days in the long-drawn-out, infinitely serious and endlessly devious business of setting the boundaries of a continent ravaged by the detested and defeated Bonaparte. They made little progress but, after the labours of the day, they could at least join their women and give over their nights to a seemingly tireless round of balls and feasts and routs.

Napoleon's own father-in-law, the Emperor of Austria, set the tone by throwing a carnival party at the Schönbrunn from where, after a sumptuous banquet and a performance of *Cinderella*, the guests, surrounded by an army of outriders, were driven home in gilded sleighs along roads lit by hundreds of torchbearers standing patiently in the falling snow. Then there were medieval tournaments, masked entertainments, hunts, shooting-parties, music and endless, endless dancing. '*Le Congrès ne marche pas, mais il danse,*' quipped the octogenarian Prince de Ligne before succumbing to the pace of it all and dying. His funeral was, as he had wished, yet another spectacle for them to enjoy. And still the glittering leaders of the old regime danced on – danced as only the victorious can in the heedless joy of the unassailable.

Prince Metternich was nearly always to be seen at these glittering occasions, his pointed brow and affable face hiding a mind as tensed and ruthless as a steel trap. The burden of the Austrian Empire was falling more and more on his shoulders as the ageing Emperor Francis, head of the most ancient royal house in Europe, devoted his time to hosting his guests, to tending his garden and to perfecting a recipe for his own brand of sealing wax. Altogether more attractive was Tsar Alexander, who had suggested Napoleon's exile to Elba. His thirty-year-old's face was still boyishly bright save when it clouded with melancholy and he talked in hushed, Slavonic tones about a Holy Alliance of the Great Powers. Nobody knew quite what he meant but, still, he was the Tsar of all the Russias and undoubtedly a hero. So too was Field Marshal Blücher with his ferocious face and eyebrows as heavy as his vast moustache. He was the barely literate general of the Prussian army and was said to keep up his fury on the battlefield by eating nothing but raw onions. And now there was a new hero to admire. The Duke of Wellington had just arrived fresh from triumphs in Spain and Paris, and was surrounded by young British officers who bore themselves with all the nonchalance of the known masters of the world. Only their imperiously handsome general with his great beaked nose and ruthless insistence on doing the business of the day in the day frightened them a little as the dancers whirled on.

But now, suddenly, the dancing would have to stop. The letter said it all. The young Madame de Périgord had been summoned in the dawn light to read it to her uncle while he lay in his bed. The missive was in Prince Metternich's tersest style and brusquely declared that Bonaparte had left Elba. It was a catastrophe. The prisoner had escaped, his exile was over, and Europe would soon be in flames again. 'O Uncle,' Madame de Périgord said quickly, 'what about my rehearsal?' From somewhere deep in his luxurious cocoon her uncle, his head suddenly buzzing with thoughts of the meeting Metternich had demanded, spoke reassuringly. He had brought his niece to Vienna to do the honours of his house and he owed her a debt of courtesy. 'Your rehearsal, Madame, will take place all the same,' he said reassuringly.

If the young woman was relieved, her uncle, realising he would have to stir himself into action, was not. Charles Maurice de Talleyrand-Périgord, Prince of Bénévent, was very fond of his bed and was rarely minded to leave it before eleven in the morning. When that uncomfortable hour came he rose and, swathed in a sumptuous muslin dressing gown, placed himself before his dressing table. There, surrounded by flunkies, began the long labour of preparing the great man to face the world. There was much waving of arms, much brandishing of ivory combs, as his two hairdressers set about shaping that coiffeur of wavy silver locks by which Talleyrand was known throughout the drawing rooms of Europe. The ministrations of his barber which followed ended in a cloud of expensive and fragrant powder before, altogether less attractively, another of the servants bent down to rub his master's lame leg with the foul-smelling Barège water that was supposed to strengthen it. Then, with this unpleasant duty completed, the head servant at last stepped forward to tie the Prince's stock into an opulent but finely judged knot.

The result, despite all these efforts, was not entirely pleasing. At sixty years old, Monsieur de Talleyrand was showing signs of age. His blue eyes which, over a long career, had watched a thousand deceits, were not so much cold as habituated to an expressionless glitter. The naturally fair flesh of his face was pale, sagging and dead. It fell in folds around a supercilious mouth which suggested at one and the same time satiated self-indulgence and utter disdain. Many thought of him as reptilian. 'When he approached me,' wrote one observer, 'with his limping gait, his heavy body, his flashing eyes, his snakelike mouth and jaw, his paralysing smile and his affected flatteries, I thought: "Nature gave you the choice between snake and tiger, and you chose to be an anaconda."'

Like that beast, Talleyrand could fascinate, hypnotising with his tongue. His extraordinary intelligence was matched by the dangerous brilliance of his conversation which, with a tireless subtlety, ensnared and won to his side those who could be of use to him. Women especially were appalled and confused as they felt themselves seduced by a man they knew to be reprehensible. Even the most exulted were mesmerised. 'The day he condescends to speak to you,' wrote Queen Hortense, 'he is already too kind . . . and you are fully ready to adore him if he so much as asks after your health.' Everybody knew about Talleyrand's immorality, about his insatiable lining of his own pocket, about his treatment of women, about his utter lack of scruple. Nonetheless, although 'one personally regretted having so many reasons for not being able to respect him', the fact was, declared the shrewd and delightful Marquise de la Tour du Pin, 'after an hour's conversation, all was forgotten'. Now, here in Vienna, the abilities that had charmed innumerable women were being exercised to give defeated France, disencumbered of her Napoleonic spoils, her rightful place at the heart of a peaceful Europe. Monsieur de Talleyrand was more than ever determined to remove from the world the last opprobrious traces of an empire which, for the previous two decades, he had served with assiduous and increasing deceit.

He shouldn't really have been in Vienna at all. It was not for the vanquished to sit with the victors, and a secret clause added by the triumphant allies to the Treaty of Paris forbade any representative of the French government from attending the Congress. Talleyrand had refused to accept this and, resolving to make himself indispensable, became so. Throughout the greater part of his career he had watched with increasing concern as Napoleon extended his seemingly interminable wars from the Spanish peninsula to Moscow.

Such ghastly havoc was not, Talleyrand believed, in the true interests of France. It would be far better for all concerned if the country were to stay contentedly within her natural boundaries – the Channel, the Rhine, the Alps, the Pyrenees – and forge alliances with the other mighty powers beyond them: Britain, Austria, Prussia and Russia. The generous terms of the Treaty of Paris which Talleyrand, as President of the Provisional Government, had helped secure after Napoleon's defeat by the Allies in 1814 recognised the wisdom of this and castigated Napoleon himself rather than the French nation as the enemy of Europe. Talleyrand, however, his infinitely devious mind finely attuned to the duplicity of others, believed that the public statements of the Allies hid a private wish to place France on the margins. 'Trained eyes,' he wrote, meaning of course his own, 'could easily detect in several of the principal plenipotentiaries the secret desire to reduce France to a secondary role.' To avoid this, Talleyrand's presence in Vienna was essential, his place at the discussion table of paramount importance.

The last was not something easily to be achieved, as he was well aware, and Talleyrand set about getting his way with the minutely practised guile of the finest diplomat in Europe. While Madame de Périgord helped him entertain the constellation of ambassadors gathered in Vienna, her uncle approached the representatives of the lesser states especially with all his accustomed charm. Slowly, expertly, he began to convince them that the domination of the proceedings by the Great Powers was unacceptable. Why should Britain, Austria, Russia and Prussia be the sole arbiters of Europe's future? With their resentments easily stirred, the plenipotentiaries of the lesser states began to group themselves around Talleyrand, and the man who might so easily have been a lone and unwelcome voice became the formidable spokesman of a disgruntled body of opinion that had to be heard. A reluctant invitation from Metternich was eventually forthcoming and a delighted Talleyrand at last found himself seated at the conference table.[1]

This was a triumph not to be spoiled by modesty or gratitude. So much was at once clear. The British Foreign Secretary, Castlereagh, opened the proceedings with the superior tone of one addressing a favoured dependant. 'The object of today's conference,' he told Talleyrand, 'is to acquaint you with what the four Powers have done since we have been here.' He then turned to Metternich and, asking for the protocol, bade him hand it to their new guest. The glittering eyes ran quickly down the page and fastened on the word 'Allies'. What did the word mean? Talleyrand asked with feigned incomprehension. Who were the Allies allied against? 'It cannot be against Napoleon, for he is defeated and on Elba; nor can it be against France, as peace has been achieved.' The Great Powers, embarrassed by the logic of this, began to realise the depth of their mistake in inviting the Prince to join them. Aware that they could hardly ask him to leave, they agreed to withdraw the document. Another was then produced. This made clear that the Great Powers – whether allies or not – were determined secretly to resolve all the more important questions between themselves before the official and public work of the Congress began. This, Talleyrand declared, was something new. He would have to have time to consider it before recommending such a proceeding to His Majesty King Louis XVIII of France.

It was exasperating, but the men who had subdued Napoleon could hardly alienate the representative of the man they wished to replace him, and Talleyrand's attachment to the grotesque figure of Louis XVIII was well known. The question of who should stand as the figurehead of France were Napoleon ever to be brought down had long exercised him and he had come to the conclusion that the agonies inflicted by the Corsican upstart could only be soothed by the plump hand of a legitimate king. Talleyrand now talked much about legitimacy. 'The first priority for Europe, its greatest need,' he declared, 'is to banish the doctrines of usurpation and to revive the principle of legitimacy, which is the sole remedy for all the woes afflicting it.' Legitimacy meant the ancient house of the Bourbon kings who had been swept away by the French Revolution. It meant in particular the Bourbon's hugely obese titular head, Louis XVIII, who, living in exile in England, had so gourmandised his way through the period of his disgrace that he was now barely able to move for gout. His time nonetheless had come and, in the words of the constitution issued by the Provisional Government: 'the French people freely call to the throne of France Louis-Stanilas-Xavier of France, brother of the last King – and after him the other members of the House of Bourbon in the old order.'

To secure Louis-Stanilas-Xavier his proper standing as a great European monarch required more than a patriotic flourish. It needed Talleyrand's second stroke of genius. He had inveigled his way into the councils of the Allies and, having proved that their representatives were no such thing, he now set out to divide them against each other. He played on their ambitions in order to diminish their power. It was perfectly obvious to him that they hated each other with a deep loathing born of territorial rivalry. Russia was determined to annex the whole of Poland, Prussia was resolved on grabbing the entirety of Saxony, while the Austrians were appalled at the ambitions of both. It remained to persuade Britain to play a part advantageous to France. The negotiations were as acrimonious as they were complex and Talleyrand, realising that the devil was in the detail, started goading him into work. 'He spoils, he plots, he manipulates in a hundred different ways daily,' wrote an observer.

The mutual rivalries of the so-called Allies were now mingled with exasperation. Before his arrival, Wellington sent angry letters insisting that the Congress concentrate on the big issues. Talleyrand suggested that if Prussia and Russia got their way then France would withdraw from the discussions and leave Europe in a feverish state which would sooner or later lead to war. A public reconciliation was no longer possible and a private agreement seemed the only resort. On 3 January 1815, the representatives of Britain, Austria and France signed a secret pact by which each agreed to send 150,000 men to defend the others should Russia or Prussia engage in hostilities. For Talleyrand, this was a personal triumph. The man who had come uninvited to the Conference had inveigled his way to its top, divided the nations that had defeated his own, and made France a great player of the international game. He wrote exultantly to Louis XVIII informing him that 'the coalition is dissolved, and dissolved for ever'. France was no longer isolated in Europe and would very soon be joined 'by all the states whose principles and politics are not revolutionary'. It was a triumph for legitimacy and the old regime. 'So great and so fortunate a change,' Talleyrand continued with sublime irony, 'can only be attributed to that protection of Providence which has been so plainly visible in the restoration of Your Majesty.' Now, it seemed, the whole elaborate edifice was about to be blown to pieces by Napoleon's guns. What could be done to save it would have to be decided at Prince Metternich's meeting.

## The Young General

The delegates of the Great Powers so hurriedly assembled for the early morning conference were well aware that the crisis they faced was made worse by the speed with which Napoleon was wont to realise his titanic ambitions. They had seen it before. In 1797, the twenty-eight-year-old general returned from his Italian campaign to tell the enfeebled leaders of the French government – the so-called Directory, which had hoped to put an end to the tumult of the Revolution – that he owed his astonishing success against the Austrian masters of the region to the fact that 'my troops have moved as rapidly as my thoughts'. That he could get them to march at all was among the most remarkable of Napoleon's early achievements. At the start of his campaign the little army of some 40,000 men was bright-eyed with hunger and as thin as rakes. On their heads they wore a motley collection of faded revolutionary bonnets, bald bearskins and battered helmets that had long since lost their plumes. Their variously coloured tunics were patched and frayed, their linen trousers were out at the knees, while the greater part of the men protected their feet as best they could in clogs or filthy rags. Nothing more pathetically proved Napoleon's dictum that an army marches on its stomach, and he at once disbursed the 8,000 gold livres he had been given to buy six days' worth of bread, meat and brandy. A hurriedly raised loan bought enough corn for a further three months' bread (provided this was eked out with nuts) and what was left over was spent on 18,000 pairs of boots. It was men so provisioned and bent down under the weight of their calfskin haversacks, cartridge pouches and long, heavy muskets that Napoleon led into Italy. There, in ninety-six hours of almost continuous mountain marching, he routed the Austrians and their Piedmontese allies in four strategically brilliant battles.

'He moves at the speed of light and strikes like a thunderbolt. He is everywhere at once and misses nothing,' declared *Le Courrier de l'armée d'Italie*, the newspaper with which Napoleon was careful to feed his troops' morale and impress his masters back in Paris. 'We do not march; we fly,' exclaimed General Berthier. Such speed was as novel as it was unique and was the untrammelled expression of Napoleon's own powers. His astonishing quickness of thought was equalled by a strategic intelligence that could always see a battle as a whole and by a memory so retentive that he could recall every detail of the disposition of his men and the terrain through which they were passing. He knew where every regiment, every service company and every baggage waggon was, when it had started out and when it should arrive at its destination. 'The topography of a country,' wrote the devoted Caulaincourt, 'seemed to be modelled in relief in his head.' Napoleon thus focused in himself the combined abilities of a general staff and was thereby able to realise his deep-seated wish that everything should move with the maximum of efficient speed and bear the imprint of his own genius.

It was a genius he was at pains vigorously to promote. During the Italian campaign newspaper reports hymning Napoleon's glories were supplemented by engravings that offered images extolling his leadership. The most memorable of these images is Gros's oil portrait, which is a study in youthful heroic resolve. The thrusting pose and the long hair blowing in the wind suggest turbulent energy, but it is the face that evokes the mastering intelligence and the will. The jaw line is firm, the chin strong, the nose proud, large and Roman. The mouth, by contrast, is curiously mobile. Its expression here is one of determination, yet it is easy to imagine it angry or broadening to a brief, chilly ironic smile. When Napoleon talked, his contemporaries observed, these austerities could melt to an uncommon expression of sweetness. The man of the battlefield was not afraid of the salon. Nor was he unfamiliar with the library. The observant very slightly short-sighted eyes, set beneath the firmly drawn brows, were blue-grey and intelligent. It was these last qualities that struck the English novelist Fanny Burney. Napoleon's face, she wrote, 'is of a deeply impressive cast, pale even to sallowness, while not only in the eye but in every feature – care, thought, melancholy and meditation are strongly marked, with so much of character, nay, genius, and so penetrating a seriousness, or rather sadness, as powerfully to sink into an observer's mind'.

Gros's portrait is of a broad-chested but not a large young man. That the power is contained in a relatively small frame seems to make it all the more vivid. Napoleon stood at just under 170 centimetres. His head was not large but its size was accentuated by his bull neck. His hands like his feet were small (the same was alleged about his privates) but the hands in particular had the refinement of a man whose artistic interests were important to him – a man who was also acutely sensitive to cold and to bad smells. Napoleon's health, by and large, was very good. During the Italian campaign he suffered briefly from piles, which he quickly if painfully cured by applying a handful of leeches, and throughout his adulthood he had repeated attacks of dysuria which meant that passing water could be a slow and tedious business. None of these less than heroic details however detracted from his exceptional physical resilience which was the basis of the energy – the sheer boundary-breaking forcefulness – that is the essence of Gros's portrait.

Napoleon was from the outset acutely aware of the value of propaganda images such as Gros produced (he was to make him his court painter) but he knew that their substance was the leadership of men – the necessary combination of charisma, force, subtlety and clear determination. No man was more fascinating than Napoleon when he chose to be and 'no woman was ever more artful than he in making you want, or agree to, his own desire when he thought it was in his interest to persuade you'. Napoleon would stop at nothing to win a man to his side and he once confessed to Caulaincourt that, 'When I need anyone I don't make too fine a point about it; I would kiss his arse.' Such language came easily to Napoleon and was relished by many of his officers, men who had risen up the ranks as the French Revolution opened the careers their talents aspired to. From modest Corsican origins himself, Napoleon had with him on his Italian campaign such generals as the eagle-eyed Masséna, an erstwhile smuggler who had fusted for many years as a sergeant major until the call of liberty, fraternity and equality allowed him to show his superior abilities. Kilmaine was one of many Irishmen who fled to serve with England's enemy, while the gutter language of Augereau was natural to a man who had once been obliged to sell watches on the streets of Constantinople and to scrape his way by giving dancing lessons. That their hero should be surrounded by such men was greatly encouraging to the mass of Napoleon's army. In a world where careers were now open to talent rather than to birth alone any man might rise to be their general's aide, and Napoleon encouraged the bravest by issuing them with swords inscribed with the words: 'Given on behalf of the executive Directory of the French Republic, by General Buonaparte to

Citizen . . .' This was a shrewd device, for it bound men to him by at once glorifying Napoleon's own reputation and harnessing it to another great inspiration that fired his men – love of *la patrie* and its institutions.

Nationalism and a growing sense of national identity were feelings of increasing importance to people in the late eighteenth century.[2] Frenchmen were beginning to talk about *'le génie François'*. Rousseau, whose works Napoleon had studied avidly in his early youth, had moved an idea of 'national character' to the centre of his political thought, and the French Revolution had hugely enhanced this idea of the French nation as a unique body free at last from centuries of old repression and driven now by an ideology of liberty. The French began to think of themselves as being a distinct ethnic community with shared ideals and shared memories of the struggle for freedom, members of *la patrie* who had come through a nationalist salvation drama and emerged into the modern world.

The rulers of the other nations of Europe were appalled at the bloodshed caused, by the chaos, the destruction of the old order, and by the threat it posed to them. They might yet have to fight to preserve their traditions. Few things crystallise nationalist sentiment more surely than the prospect of war and the thought of the nation taking on the other, the outsider, the enemy. To defend their new republic from the loathing and hostility of their all-surrounding foes the French, under a plan masterminded by Lazare Carnot, raised a citizen army to protect *la patrie en danger*. By the early 1790s it wielded 7,000 cannon and a million men, many of whom were galvanised by an aggressive nationalism and an ideology of freedom which they wished to spread to others, by force if necessary. Here, in all its terrifying novelty, was the nation in arms equipped and commanded by a centralised administration which soon had cause to fear what it had created. Napoleon was sent into Italy precisely because the leaders of the Directory, their reputations collapsing with their finances, saw the desirability of moving part of so massively dangerous and expensive a force beyond their own boundaries to win booty and glory abroad rather than wreaking havoc at home.

Napoleon's Italian army, relatively small but brilliantly successful, had risen from these circumstances to herald that new and terrible type of warfare which Napoleon himself was to perfect: a warfare of whole nations seemingly unhampered by limits of size or ambition, a warfare based on the struggles of entire male populations which, as the great philosopher of the subject Clausewitz wrote from bitter experience, 'marched over Europe, smashing everything in pieces'. This they did so surely and certainly that where they 'only encountered . . . old-fashioned armies, the result was not doubtful for a moment'. The might of this terrible leviathan was even now clear as Napoleon swept down through Lombardy, over the bridge at Lodi, and entered Milan in May 1796 before going south to Bologna, Ferrara and Tuscany, receiving the submissions of Naples and the Papacy, and then hurrying north again to defeat four more Austrian armies at Castiglione, Bassano, Arcola and Rivoli. From there the mountain passes led him to Trieste, to Klagenfurt, and to the outlying regions of Vienna itself which he reached by the spring of 1797. Here, in such astonishing success, was that hopefully inseparable companion of *la patrie*: love of *la gloire*.

This too was something deeply rooted in French national consciousness. It was at one and the same time flamboyant, aggressive and supposedly moral. Glory had been the guiding force of Louis XIV, who called it his 'dominant passion' and waged his seemingly interminable wars because of it. The concept of *la gloire* was then assimilated into the republic after the ferment of the Revolution, and men now wrote about the inspiring ideal of 'the courageous and ardent zeal of a citizen to expose the abuses which dishonour his nation and to contribute to its glory'. War was the most conspicuous way of winning *la gloire*, but it required extraordinary qualities on Napoleon's part to hold together a once ragged-trousered army that had so suddenly become a triumphant force of European importance. Personal example and personal courage were among the most important of them. That Napoleon was capable of immense daring is beyond question. The crossing of the bridge at Lodi in May 1796 is a supreme example. To storm a bridge under heavy fire was unprecedented. The officers and men grumbled that it was folly. Having ordered his cavalry to find a crossing higher up the river and prepare themselves to sweep down on the Austrians in a surprise flanking movement, Napoleon commanded 4,000 of his infantry into the town square. Riding along the ranks he began to berate the murmuring men. How could he achieve what he wanted with the likes of them? How could he have confidence in them? The rebuke stung and anger turned resentment to enthusiasm.

When their spirits were at a height, Napoleon ordered the men towards the bridge, drums and fifes shrilling out the anthem of the republic: *Allons, enfants de la patrie!* Austrian guns strafed the wooden bridge with terrible ferocity. Men fell. More were summoned onto the bloodstained planks. They inched their terrible way forward and, fifty yards from the other side, dived into the water, hoping to wade to the bank and seize the enemy guns. The Austrian forces rendered their heroism nugatory, and it was only the late arrival of the French cavalry, thundering down in a surprise attack, that gave Napoleon the bridge and the road to Milan. It was exhilarating, terrible and devastating – the proof of Napoleon's powers of leadership. Indeed, the taking of the Bridge of Lodi was a turning point in his life and thus in the history of Europe itself. 'It was only on the evening after Lodi,' Napoleon recalled many years later, 'that I believed myself to be a superior person and that the ambition came to me of performing the great things which hitherto had filled my thoughts only as a fantastic dream.' He believed he had learned that nothing was impossible to him. It was a moment of intoxication at one glorious and terrible. 'I already saw the world flee before me, as if I were being carried in the air.' Napoleon had become the eagle of his own imagination and very soon the shadow of his wings would be darkening the whole of Europe.[3]

Meanwhile the military triumphs of the Italian campaign continued. Napoleon had given his men victory with one hand. Now, with the other, he gave them loot. The ragged army could luxuriate in plunder from the fertile plains of Lombardy while Napoleon filled their pockets not with the paper money that none of them trusted but with true silver. More cash went back to Paris along with bulletins praising the young general's achievements. Nor was this all. The Directory were determined that the Louvre should have what the palaces of Italy no longer deserved, and Napoleon served them royally. Manuscripts by Galileo and crabbed, arcane treatises by Leonardo were put into wagons and, along with that serene vision of Arcadian peace that is Giorgione's *Concert Champêtre*, were sent to Paris so that the plunder of war should resound to the glory of France. And at the centre of the glory was Napoleon, the ruthless, disingenuously modest shaper of his own reputation. 'He says with simple dignity to those whom he respects,' declared the carefully supervised columns of the *Courrier*: '"I have seen kings at my feet; I could have amassed fifty millions in my coffers; I could easily have claimed to be someone other than what I am; but I am a citizen of France, I am the leading general of *La Grande Nation*; I know that posterity will do me justice."' In such ways as these Napoleon emerged as the figure he for the moment wished to be – the superman of the people.

Nor was it only republican France that was to breathe the clean air of democracy. The frowsty tyrannies of Italy too were to be swept away and replaced by new, modern rational states based on French ideals. In the squares of captured towns the leaves of the newly planted 'trees of liberty' waved in the fresh breeze and symbolised the rights of man. Beneath them the newly liberated citizens could refresh themselves, read the newspapers that now came from the free press, relish the fact that they no longer had to pay feudal dues, watch the soutaned priests scurry more humbly about streets where superstition was now depreciated and moan about the high cost of supporting the army that had liberated them. There were those among the Italians themselves who even doubted if they were 'worthy of the reign of virtue' and the liberty forced on them by Napoleon's newly created Cisalpine Republic.

Set up along French lines, this was a bicameral institution under five directors chosen by Napoleon himself with a view moderating the influence of liberals and conservatives alike. In fact this was colonisation in all but name and shared many of colonialism's characteristics. A new form of government had been imposed on the people by a foreign and culturally very different state. There was little if anything about the new system that was indigenous, and even the new territorial borders paid scant attention to the boundaries in which the people had previously lived. The newly liberated inhabitants were thus given an imposed, factitious freedom, and very soon their states would be mulcted to provide men and cash for Napoleon's imperial ambitions. Nonetheless, the founding of the Cisalpine Republic was, Napoleon himself declared, an act of the highest altruism on his part and one designed to foster political maturity. 'Divided and bowed under tyranny for so long,' he told the delegates, 'you could not have won your own freedom; left to yourselves for a few years, there will be no power on earth strong enough to take it from you.' Those who resisted the opportunity were summarily shot.

It was not just in Italy, however, that democracy grew out of the barrel of a gun. The enfeebled leaders of the Directory, so wary of the genius they had unleashed that they plotted to curb him, were now faced by the altogether more immediate horror of finding that the people had elected to their body a majority of right-wing politicians eager for a royalist restoration. Their efforts apparently spelled the end of Napoleon's ambitions and he despatched the foul-mouthed Augereau to Paris. There he surrounded the government in the palace of the Tuileries, arrested the conservatives, voided the election of the royalists, silenced the press and reduced the

Directory to a rump subject to the army and its all-conquering hero. It was to a body so cowed, and amid prodigious pomp and acclamations hyperbolical, that Napoleon returned home and presented to the people of France the greatest prize of his Italian campaign: the Treaty of Campo Formio, which he had concluded in October 1797. By its terms Napoleon redrew large parts of the map of Europe. Austria ceded Belgium to France and, in return for Istria, Dalmatia and Venice, acknowledged France's rights over Bologna, Modena, Ferrara, Romagna, the Ionian islands and parts of Albania. Thus, with unerring and terrifying speed, the young general of a once starving army returned in triumph as a shaker of thrones and a divider of kingdoms – the hero who was in every Frenchman's eyes 'a pure and mighty colossus of glory'.

## The Egyptian Campaign

An empire was in the making but across the Channel, France had a mighty enemy. The victorious young general was, on his return, at once made 'commander of the army against England'. A quick reconnoitring of the northern French ports convinced Napoleon that the Directory's plan of invasion was as illusory as its power. The fleet was small, the recruits raw and the officers inexperienced. Amphibious landings on an enemy coast are among the most hazardous of operations and the Channel is a dangerous waterway. Disdaining 'to risk *la belle France* on the throw of a dice', Napoleon determined instead to bring down the mercantile power of industrialised Britain by a plan that was neither original nor new but whose sheer grandiosity seemed to promise much. Napoleon would invade Egypt and then, in alliance with Turkey and Persia, strike at India, which was Britain's richest possession.

Here once again was that refusal to be circumscribed by the limits of the possible. In Napoleon's own phrase: 'the word "impossible" is merely the hobgoblin of the timid and the excuse of fools.'

Besides, success in such an undertaking would make Napoleon a new Alexander, a new Caesar, and his renown would be given moral substance by freeing the native Egyptians from the servitude imposed on them by the feudal Mamelukes. They would become citizens of the modern world, even as their ancient civilisation would be unravelled by the battalion of scholars that was to accompany the army. Napoleon had already discussed the plan with the Foreign Minister of France, and Monsieur de Talleyrand, realising the advantage of having Napoleon and his troops out of the tottering state, gave his assent and promised with blithe disingenuousness to go in person to Constantinople and negotiate the necessary alliance with the Sublime Porte.

The magnificent folly of the entire enterprise was evident from the start, but under no circumstances whatsoever would the British sit idly by and watch the scheme disintegrate through sheer vaingloriousness. They recognised that it was intended as a threat to their trading empire and were determined to do something about it. British commerce had already been badly damaged by the loss of the fledgeling United States of America nearly twenty years before and strenuous efforts had since been made to guarantee the Indian market especially. Besides, industrialisation was now making the country the workshop of the world, and Britain needed to be able to import and export in comparative safety as it underwent its astonishing metamorphosis and became the most developed nation in the world. She would not let France — and Napoleon in particular — get in her way.

The effects of this process of driving Britain forward with the thunderous power of steam were as prodigious as they were novel. The great industrial areas of central Scotland, the North-east, Yorkshire, Lancashire, the West Midlands and South Wales were already employing a rising population in manufacture rather than agriculture. Cotton and woollen textile factories especially, made ever more efficient by advances in technology, roared and belched with mass production. Economic growth and, with it, cities and huge concentrations of workers involved in an extraordinary range of manufacturing, mining, transport and commercial activities led to an accumulation of capital, to further expansion and to changes that affected every aspect of life. Radical stirrings among a workforce inspired by the French Revolution were severely repressed by a government determined to defend property and the old order against reform. Even to talk of changes to the constitution became a matter for punishment under the Treasonable Practices Act. Technical innovation flourished as such reactionary measures were passed and, while steam and muscle powered the engines of trade, the laissez-faire doctrines of Adam Smith drove the ambitions of a rising class of manufacturers. Men of initiative could thrive as never before. Aristocrats exploited the natural resources of their land while Dissenters especially, barred by their beliefs from public office, embraced the new technologies and the new skills of marketing to a mass public. Government revenues rose, helped especially by the introduction of income tax in 1799, and paid for the ships by which Britannia ruled the waves and the world's commerce with a mighty and often ruthlessly cunning hand. Napoleon was now to discover precisely what it could mean to pit his might against a nation of shopkeepers.[4]

In May 1798 he sailed to Egypt from Toulon with an Army of the Orient consisting of 35,000 men. When he had disembarked his forces and made for Cairo, a detached squadron of the British Mediterranean fleet, under the command of Nelson, found his flotilla of seventeen ships anchored off Aboukir. In a movement of exceptional daring Nelson sent five of his vessels between the French and the shore. Bombarding the enemy from both sides, he destroyed thirteen of their warships. Despite such heroic incidents as the efforts made by a lad to stand by his dying father aboard *L'Orient* – an episode immortalised in the ballad 'The Boy Stood on the Burning Deck' – *L'Orient* exploded and a triumphant Nelson, having by the so-called Battle of the Nile cut Napoleon off from essential supplies, reinforcements or the hope of a seaborne withdrawal, sailed away to Naples where he was soon to win another type of reputation in the arms of Lady Hamilton.

Still shocked by the disastrous news of the loss of his fleet, Napoleon marched into the wastes of Syria. His campaign on land had already proved itself to be less than the triumph he expected. Although in July 1798 he destroyed the Mameluke forces at the Battle of the Pyramids and, in characteristic fashion, sent home engravings of the triumph that inspired little boys like the poet Lamartine 'to feel the first sensations of *la gloire*', the newly liberated Egyptians were less than enthusiastic about freedom offered by infidels at the price of forced loans and the savage suppression of discontent. Turkey had, besides, declared war on France (Talleyrand, true to form, had preferred the delights of Paris to the rigours of Constantinople) and it was to counter the Turkish threat that Napoleon marched with only 15,000 men towards Syria. Repeated disasters now revealed a fundamental side of his character: a wholehearted embracing of ruthless realpolitik when it came to matters of survival and his own reputation. Two thousand hapless prisoners were shot after the capture of Jaffa, while in early 1799 Napoleon was prepared to sacrifice nearly half of his own men during the disastrous siege of Acre which he recklessly undertook without the necessary artillery. He limped back to Cairo, repulsed a Turkish landing, but had already learned from the newspapers of disasters altogether more terrible than those he had recently endured.

Turkey, Naples, Austria, Russia and Britain had formed a coalition against France, where peasant risings had forced the government to withdraw its forces from significant parts of Italy. A combined force of Russians and Austrians now occupied Milan. The Russian army had advanced on Switzerland. The French forces on the Danube had been defeated, and an invasion of *la patrie* seemed imminent. The reputation of the Directory was in shreds and, with his recent triumphs apparently destroyed, Napoleon, convinced that he alone could salvage all he stood for, resolved to leave Egypt and abandon his army to the mercy of the sands. After landing at Fréjus in October 1799 and spending the night in the Chapeau Rouge he made straight for Paris where he met with Talleyrand, who was now working to destroy the government that employed him. The Directory itself was crippled by financial problems, by the growing cynicism of the electorate, by a lack of able men, and the constant friction generated between the five executive Directors and the two legislative councils of the Elders and the so-called Five Hundred, the latter being men elected by a highly restricted property franchise. Talleyrand's ally, Joseph Sieyès, erstwhile revolutionary and now a cantankerous old bachelor living in his apartment with no more company than a wax profile of Voltaire, saw the need to strengthen the executive against the legislature if anarchy were to be avoided and declared that two things were necessary – a head and a sword. Believing that the head should be his own, Sieyès reluctantly accepted that the sword should be Napoleon's. Together they planned the coup which Napoleon himself was privately resolved should make him supreme.

Later, with the easy half-truths of a successful man, Napoleon presented his role in the coup of Brumaire during 9–10 November 1799 as a triumph of manipulation in which, listening to radical Jacobins and reactionary Bourbon agents alike, he caught everyone in his nets but only emerged in public when he judged that they all would come running to him and build some special hope on his success. The truth was rather different. Seizing the initiative from Sieyès along with control of the troops in Paris, Napoleon persuaded the two Councils of the Directory to remove themselves to Saint-Cloud. There, after a long delay, the Elders deprived Napoleon of his hope that they would elect a committee to decide on a new constitution. Furious, he marched into the richly frescoed room and, addressing the men gathered there in their absurd would-be classical red togas and scarlet toques, he delivered an oration and was told to leave. He was, the Elders said, a dictator.

Napoleon's fate when he addressed the Five Hundred was yet more humiliating and he was only saved from the pandemonium of an angry crowd when five soldiers bungled him, his face bleeding, out of the door. He was rescued by his brother Lucien who, quietening the Council and playing for time, sent a message telling him he had ten minutes in which to act. Lucien then informed Napoleon's troops that there was a Jacobin plot afoot to overthrow the government. The doubtful men were only won over when Lucien, seizing the dramatic moment, swore to run his brother through 'if ever he interferes with the freedom of Frenchmen'. The guards then ran into the chamber. The greater part of the members fled and the docile remainder, surrounded by bayonets, signed an order making Napoleon the senior of three new Consuls. Thus ignominiously began one of the most remarkable periods in French history.

## The First Consul

First Consul Napoleon Bonaparte, dressed in his red velvet double-breasted uniform with its gold braid, moved himself and his beloved Josephine into the Tuileries where, surrounded in the Grand Gallery by statues of conquerors from Alexander to Frederick the Great, he enjoyed a power as extensive as any Bourbon. The new constitution, passed by three million votes to 1,500 a month after the coup of Brumaire, appointed Napoleon and his two consultative assistants to their offices for ten years. Napoleon himself approved a Senate of some sixty men which, in turn, chose one hundred representatives from the national body of 6,000 *notables*, or men deemed suitable for public office. This Tribunate could talk but not vote and was shadowed by a Legislature that could vote but not talk. Real power, however, resided with the Council of State whose members were chosen by Napoleon and of which he was president. It was now under his direction that legislation was proposed and all officials, both national and local, were appointed. Napoleon was minded to say that the Revolution had terminated in him and he now claimed to embody the general will in his own person. Armed with such powers and such principles, Napoleon set about reforming the country at home and settling its problems abroad.

The hero of the battlefield brought his magnificent organisational abilities to his office in the Tuileries.[5] He woke early and, after a long, hot and luxurious bath, shaved himself with razors he had specially imported from Birmingham. Then, scented with cologne and dressed in white stockings and breeches, a linen shirt and the green frock coat of a colonel of the chasseurs, Napoleon entered his office promptly at nine. The room was so arranged that he could walk up and down constantly as he worked. There was a round mahogany table for signing letters, a desk for his secretary (the only other person automatically allowed in the room) and a sofa. Nothing else was permitted to distract Napoleon's phenomenal powers of concentration and will to work. Practically everything was done by dictation and with an undivided focus on the matter in hand. Every issue, every problem raised by the myriad of mighty matters there were to deal with he grabbed 'by the neck, by the arse, by the feet, by the hands, by the head', wrestling with it until it conformed to his will. Only then did he pass on to the next. In such a manner Napoleon set about reforming the nation's finances, its legal and educational systems and the relationship between Church and state.

The practical and intellectual scale of Napoleon's proposed reforms was truly colossal and it took a colossus to achieve them. Napoleon was refashioning his nation's identity, and his admired Rousseau pointed the way. 'It is neither boundaries nor men which constitute la patrie,' Rousseau had written, 'it is the laws and customs, government, constitution and way of life that results from them.' Napoleon was determined to recast all of these in a new, modern, rationalist mode. He would create a civic state with shared historical myths and memories of the revolutionary ideals that had given birth to it, provide common legal rights and duties for its citizens and foster a generally shared culture and educational system along with a common economy. Through such things the French could newly identify themselves with *la patrie*. Nothing less was required than a wholesale overhaul of the administration, the economy and the French way of life. Centralised bureaucratic control from Paris was Napoleon's chosen means.

Money was the first priority. The financial situation Napoleon inherited from the Directory was both disastrous and chaotic. He set about rectifying it at once. Loans were raised for the short term and paid officials were appointed under the auspices of the Treasury to ensure the regular and efficient long-term collection of taxes. The spending ministries were then scrupulously monitored, usually by a naturally thrifty Napoleon himself. Rectitude and parsimony were the order of the day, while the new spirit of efficiency and initiative led to the founding of the Bank of France, a steadily rising stock market and trust in the new gold coinage which bore Napoleon's portrait even as its largest denomination – the twenty-franc piece – bore his name. So much was necessary, but the subsequent imposition of heavy indirect taxes on such staples as tobacco, alcohol and salt suggest the deeper purposes of Napoleon's policies. Indirect taxation raises substantial sums but hits the better off far more lightly than the poor. Napoleon was determined to foster the interests of the property-owning classes, who emerged as his staunchest supporters. Their profits were only lightly taxed but the financial institutions they used were strong, even if economic progress in the commercial, industrial and the agricultural spheres lagged far behind Britain's. What mattered in the short term, however, was the fact that a solid phalanx of the bourgeoisie could be induced to support Napoleon's regime, be incorporated in its structures (administrative, financial, judicial and increasingly military) adhere to its image and profit by promoting its values.

Financial stability had to go hand in hand with order at home, and of all Napoleon's reforms his overhaul of the legal system is perhaps the most famous. Again he found chaos and again he left a large measure of centralised order that leaned heavily in the direction of his conservative supporters. Property rights, freedom of conscience and choice of work were all instituted, but the liberal aspirations of the erstwhile revolutionaries were overshadowed by the adoption of principles from Roman law and Napoleon's own bias in favour of patriarchal family life. He believed a woman owed obedience to her husband in return for his protection and both she and her children could be imprisoned if they jibbed excessively at his authority. Divorce existed but only at a high cost and usually at the instigation of the man. Illegitimate children had no automatic rights of inheritance. With extraordinary energy well over 2,000 articles of the Civil Code were drafted between July and December 1800, and the prominent personal part played in this by Napoleon himself justifies it bearing his name. The Code Napoleon is a famous work of jurisprudence, but the changes made to the criminal and penal codes suggest the more sinister underpinning of Napoleon's regime, the first hints of a police state. Trial by jury was now severely restricted, hard labour and branding were restored, while the means of arbitrary imprisonment for political crimes were gradually made more accessible as a myriad of state informers proliferated under a ruthlessly efficient policing system.

The need for bureaucrats burgeoned with the state and an overhaul of France's education system was necessary to provide them. Here, once again, the emphasis of Napoleon's reforms was on the careers of his natural supporters. Basic primary education was not a right under the Consulate. The aim was to train boys from the middle classes as soldiers and administrators and to ensure that they were citizens 'attached to their religion, their ruler, their *patrie* and their family'. Like most creators of new states, Napoleon realised that civic education was fundamental and existed for *la patrie* more than for the individual. Boys would become citizens and, in so doing, win approval and eventually position. They would, it was hoped, mature by the absorption of their common culture. They would find and define their individuality in terms of the state. Mathematics, Latin, blue military uniforms and musket drill were the means of instilling the values espoused by the newly founded *lycées*. The failure to teach science was to have the predictable deleterious effect on the nation's industrial competitiveness, a shortcoming made worse when the *Polytechnique* where brighter students received their tertiary education was placed under the management of the War Ministry and concentrated on the skills required of soldiers. It was not deemed necessary to provide extensive public education for girls at all since it was inconceivable they would ever enter public life. It was Napoleon's view that they could not be better brought up than by their mothers.

Despite this state provision for the brighter sons of the better off, parents often preferred the traditional education offered by the Church, and here lay danger. The Catholic establishment was the natural ally of the Bourbons, and the First Consul's relations with the Papacy centred on prising the Church away from royalist sympathisers. Although brought up as a Catholic, the influence of the Enlightenment had made Napoleon himself a Deist and it was his belief that 'the gospel writers offer no facts that can be substantiated'. Having read the Koran on the way to Egypt, he seems to have nursed a greater sympathy for Mohammed than Jesus, but he realised the grip that Catholicism had over perhaps the majority of the nation and the importance of its enormous powers of social control. Some sort of agreement had to be reached and, by dint of careful preparation, a concordat was brokered whereby bishops nominated by the government would, like the reduced number of parish priests they could appoint, be paid by the state which the Papacy both recognised and agreed to obey. Such an agreement was inherently unstable. The Church chaffed at its status as a public servant and did its best to tighten its grip over education, even as the middle classes who had profited from the seizure and sale of Church lands held onto their gains. They had much to be grateful for. It now remained for Napoleon to consolidate their loyalty by winning victories abroad. These would at one and the same time enhance their feelings of national prestige, ensure that their property was not threatened by a royalist resurgence and swell their profits through military contracts and the flow of loot.

## Crossing the Alps

The bourgeoisie were very quickly given what they wanted. The incursions made by the confederation of Allies into French gains in Italy especially needed to be driven back and, when the Austrians refused offers of a settlement, Napoleon raised capital for a plan of astonishing daring. Once again here was no such word as impossible. While part of the French army would be active on the Rhine, Napoleon would personally lead 40,000 men over the ice-gripped passes of the Alps and descend with terrifying surprise on the Austrian army besieging Genoa. The plan required heroic powers of courage, improvisation and sheer dogged strength. Getting the cannon across the St Bernard Pass during May and June 1800 called on all three. The pass was 8,000 feet high, the paths a mere eighteen inches wide, the cannon weighed in the region of 2,000 lbs apiece. It was decided to dismount the cannon from their carriages, place them in hollowed-out pine trees and order a hundred men to drag each one along the slippery ground with ropes. Encouraged by the roar of martial music and the thunder of drums the men, disdaining extra pay, sweated and groaned through ice, snow, storms and avalanches. Each cannon took two days to make the journey before going on to the perilous descent into Italy. Despite the hardships, and because of the men's morale, the strategy worked. The bewildered Austrians were scattered across the plains of Lombardy and Napoleon, re-entering Milan and now reinforced by troops from the Army of the Rhine, advanced to rout his enemy at Marengo in June 1800.

His famous victory was one of his least deserved. Through Napoleon's mismanagement what was now a small, divided and uncharacteristically slow battle force operating in territory insufficiently reconnoitred was forced into confused retreat. Only the arrival of reinforcements under the heroic Desaix, who died in the attempt, the frantic procurement of more gun power and a sudden charge by Kellermann's 400 cavalry saved Napoleon's reputation. This was then grossly inflated in the bulletins that reached Paris. The credulous were in ecstasy. The Cisalpine Republic had been re-established and the Church sang Napoleon's triumphs and treated him as a sovereign. 'A campaign so short, so brilliant and so decisive has never previously been witnessed,' it was said. The laurelled victor returned to his capital a new Caesar able to boast that he came, saw and conquered. The subsequent Treaty of Lunéville, amplifying the gains originally agreed at Campo Formio, broke the coalition united against France and there now remained only the matter of pacifying a still-hostile Britain.

Napoleon considered that Russia, so recently his enemy, might help here. He persuaded Tsar Paul I, peeved as he was over the British capture of the nominally Russian island of Malta, to close the Baltic ports to Britain and so cut off vital naval supplies as well as grain during a time of bad harvests and social unrest. Nelson put paid to the plan by winning the Battle of Copenhagen early in 1801, but his country was still ready to negotiate at least a temporary peace with France. The representatives met. Each side publicly promised to reduce its recent territorial gains while privately resolving to hold on to them for as long as possible. The Peace of Amiens was then drafted and signed in March 1802 by the French who had no intention of limiting their ambitions, and by the British who were resolved never to tolerate them. The Peace of Amiens was thus no more than a temporary truce between the two powers who were soon to be principal players in a war of continental proportions. For the moment, however, each had what they wanted. The French people voted Napoleon Consul for life. The British gained time.

## Perfidious Albion

The loathing nurtured by the two states was mutual, profound and increasingly acrimonious. In an age of savage cartooning 'Boney' was depicted in Britain as a monster mounted on the devil and spewing forth armies, cannon and all the horrors of war. There were those who still regarded him as 'a clever, desperate Jacobin, even a terrorist', while the wits in London high society passed round the Marquess of Buckingham's quip that the Corsican upstart was 'Sa Majeste très Corse'. Napoleon, for his part, saw the British as the fount and origin of all the Continent's miseries. Writing in Le Moniteur, he declared that 'for the sake of indulging her malignant and all too powerful passions, England disturbs the peace of the world, wantonly violates the rights of nations, tramples on the most solemn treaties and breaks her pledged faith – that ancient and eternal faith which even savage hordes acknowledge and religiously respect'. France, 'victorious, moderate, prosperous France', was thereby shown as obliged to defend herself against irrational evil.

Diplomacy was bound to suffocate in an atmosphere increasingly poisoned by invective and acts on both sides which could only cause mistrust. Meetings between Napoleon (who had now annexed Piedmont and Switzerland) and the British who, contrary to the terms of the Treaty of Amiens, refused to surrender Malta, became increasingly acrimonious. Lord Whitworth, the haughty British Ambassador in Paris, was summoned to meet the First Consul. 'It was,' Napoleon declared, 'a matter of infinite disappointment to him that the Treaty of Amiens, instead of being followed by conciliation and friendship . . . had been productive only of continual and increasing jealousy and mistrust.' The British had evacuated neither Malta nor Alexandria, the latter of which fell to them when they defeated Napoleon's Army of Egypt. 'I was going to instance,' Whitworth continued, 'the accession of territory and influence gained by France since the treaty, when he [Napoleon] interrupted me saying, "I suppose you mean Piedmont and Switzerland; *ce sont des bagatelles.*"'Napoleon's language was actually rather more blunt and forceful than Whitworth chose to remember. It was clearly not the speech of a gentleman but of a man the English newspapers were beginning to caricature as some monstrous hybrid: 'an unclassifiable being, half-African, half-European, a Mediterranean mulatto.'

The venom became more poisonous as diplomacy collapsed. The ideological hatred became more pronounced. Edmund Burke spoke for those on the British right who thought of republican France that 'her intercourse, her example, the spread of her doctrines are the most dreadful of her arms'. France was a moral and political sewer. As the result of such pollution 'it is not the enmity but the friendship of France that is truly terrible'. Peaceful coexistence with what others called 'a tiger let loose to devour mankind' was clearly impossible and war the only alternative. These were desperate measures but, as a spokesman of the increasingly vociferous British war party declared: 'I cannot help considering the keeping of France engaged in a Continental war as the only *certain* means of safety for us.' Britain would try to exhaust the country. Even George III seemed to agree. When Napoleon wrote to him personally suggesting peace George rankled with all the unquestioning certainty of an offended member of an ancient German house and declared it was 'impossible to treat with a new, impious, self-created aristocracy'.

The proffered olive branch had withered and Napoleon prepared to attack. British goods were excluded from France and her dependent territories in a move all too successfully designed to lighten the purses of British entrepreneurs. The embargoing of

British goods through French-owned Antwerp was particularly serious. Less effectively but altogether more frighteningly the French war machine was geared up for an invasion. On a clear day it was possible to stand on the cliffs at Dover and watch the preparations through a telescope even as Napoleon himself, riding sometimes five to eight hours a day, made his tours of inspection. The reports sent back to Paris were exhilarating, the reality less so. A flotilla of 2,000 gunboats and flat-bottomed barges was to be readied at lightning speed to transport 64,600 men and 600 horses, along with munitions, food and other necessaries. A fleet of requisitioned merchant vessels would convey a further 12,940 men and over 5,000 horses. 'Perfidious Albion' would indeed be crushed.

This was as ambitious as it was ridiculous. There were neither the shipyards nor the skilled workers in France, neither the materials nor the seamen to ready and man such an expedition. Delays caused postponements that were in turn drawn out by winter weather, a reality almost as disillusioning as the fact that even if it had been possible to complete the preparations it was unlikely that all the vessels could have been launched on a single tide. The Lords of the Admiralty meanwhile, sitting in high conclave, resolved on sending Nelson to blockade Toulon, Pellew – since Spain was now an ally of France – to do the same off Ferrol and Cadiz, while Cornwallis patrolled the Channel and Keith kept the nation's reserve of ships safely off the Downs. So much for Napoleon's boast that he was only waiting for 'a favourable wind in order to place the Imperial Eagle on the Tower of London'.

## The Emperor in Glory

That the eagle was indeed imperial was a recent innovation brought about partly by the unintended consequences of British actions. Faced with what appeared to be one of the most terrible threats to the country since the Spanish Armada, the British were resolved to rely on more than their wooden walls. Even as the French were preparing their invasion, a little band of their disillusioned countrymen was waiting for a ship in the tiny coastal town of Hastings. There had already been at least one previous attempt to assassinate Napoleon. The effort had failed because the coachman driving the somewhat reluctant First Consul to the first Paris performance of Haydn's *Creation* was tipsy and hurtled so quickly past the cart with its waiting incendiary that it blew up and destroyed the Rue de la Loi only after Napoleon himself was out of danger. The perpetrators were arrested but the ringleaders escaped to England where, on windswept Romney Marsh, a Goliath of a Breton peasant named Georges Cadoudal ran a training camp for conspirators which was funded by the British government.

Now his hosts gave this hideous if useful devotee of the Bourbon cause letters of credit and a passage to France. There he and his fellow conspirators would win over malcontents in the army, attempt a successful assassination of the First Consul and restore Louis XVIII to his throne. Such were the efficiency and resourcefulness of the French police, however, that not only was the plot discovered but Cadoudal himself was seized by officers as he got into a cabriolet in the vain hope of changing his hideout. Under interrogation he confessed to the plan and to the reason why he had not yet acted. 'I was to attack the First Consul only when a prince came to Paris,' he said. 'And the prince hasn't yet arrived.' The police believed he was on his way. They had received reports from Brittany where it was whispered among the royalists that 'the ci-devant Duc d'Enghien would soon be returning to France'. The young Bourbon aristocrat arrived more suddenly than supposed. At Talleyrand's prompting, Napoleon sent a band of kidnappers to Germany where, in March 1804, they surrounded the Duke's house, grabbed him while he was asleep and hurried him to Paris. There he was found guilty of plotting against Napoleon's life and summarily shot. An apoplectically angry Napoleon shouted that 'the House of Bourbon must learn that the attacks it directs against others can come down on itself'. The courts of Europe went into mourning. This was no ordinary judicial murder, for the victim was one of their own. Echoes of the revolutionaries' tumbrels rattled through their fevered imaginations and even the Foreign Minister, Talleyrand, recognised the gravity of the situation. What had happened was 'worse than a crime', he whispered, 'it is a blunder'.

The blunder was to have extraordinary consequences almost at once. The threat to Napoleon's life made plain as perhaps nothing else could how precarious was his hold on his immense power. It could be ended by a bullet or a bomb, and the republic would plunge back into the anarchy that would inevitably follow the return of either the Jacobins or the Bourbons. Some way needed to be found, as one of Napoleon's supporters rather airily expressed it, to 'make him immortal'. A campaign to immortalise him began to gather momentum. Pamphlets circulated, one suggesting that the only reward due to so great a man as the First Consul was to proclaim him Emperor of the Gauls and, for all that Napoleon and Josephine had no children, to make the title hereditary.

The suggestion grew louder with its popularity. It was expressed and re-expressed in newspapers, speeches and letters to the government. The quick ears of the police heard more and more people declaring that imperial power was 'a sure means of establishing peace and quiet in France'. Even the Tribunate spoke in its favour but, while the Tribunate could not vote, the political nation at large might yet be allowed to. A plebiscite was held, and the hopes of the 3,000 people who were opposed to the idea of an immortal Napoleon were swept away by the votes of the more than three and a half million who welcomed it. The Napoleon who roundly declared that 'it is I who embody the French Revolution' was being wished into imperial office. He accepted. Thus the career open to talent. Only a handful of his erstwhile admirers were appalled. Beethoven, who was working on the most revolutionary of symphonies yet to be composed, heard the news and, tearing up the dedication to the *Eroica*, reascribed it to 'the memory of a great man'.

But there seemed much to be gained from accepting the imperial crown – much more than the gratification of increasingly monstrous egotism and the wish to found a dynasty. As Emperor of the French, Napoleon could perhaps be thought of as making a concession to royalists at home while he certainly hoped he might pass as an equal among the other monarchs of Europe. This latter bid for respectability conspicuously failed with the British at least. Napoleon was and remained in their eyes an arriviste. George III did not take kindly to being greeted as '*mon frère*' and the patrician officials of his government always referred to their enemy as 'General Bonaparte'. But it was above all the great body of French opinion that Napoleon needed to impress with his new dignity, and his coronation was designed to be an event of medieval magnificence – the installation of a new Charlemagne with his newly created court and military aristocracy of marshals, his newly incorporated subject states and his official images of his own magnificence to which all had to conform.

Napoleon was driven to Notre-Dame in a gilded coach drawn by eight bays with red morocco harness. Josephine sat beside him on the white silk cushions wearing diamonds in her hair. Napoleon himself was dressed in a white silk shirt, breeches and stockings, and wore a purple cape lined with ermine and embroidered with golden bees. These last were a deliberate attempt to create an ancestry for the parvenu, an effort to link France's new emperor with her most ancient past. Metal bees had been found in the sixth-century tomb of Chilpéric, King of the Franks (in fact they almost certainly came from the robe worn by his wife), and were now adopted as Napoleon's personal emblem. When he descended at the palace of the Archbishop of Paris, Napoleon donned a black velvet cap ornamented with enormous swaying ostrich feathers and was further dressed in a huge purple train decorated with branches of olive, oak and laurel surrounding the letter N. He was fully aware of the potential for looking ridiculous. 'Swaddled in all those robes,' he had declared, 'I shall look like a dummy.' It was partly to avoid such embarrassment that the ceremony was held in the dark medieval interior of Notre-Dame.

There his sumptuously arrayed court was waiting for him along with his fractious family. The whole purpose of raising Napoleon to the purple was to ensure the future of his dynasty but, for the moment, he had no children. His brother, the urbane Joseph Bonaparte, jockeyed to be named his heir but, having only daughters himself, was passed over and made plain his dissatisfaction. The irascible and rebellious Lucien was equally unacceptable as he had contracted an irregular marriage which Napoleon, ever the conservative in family matters, thoroughly disapproved of. The incapacitated and taciturn Louis had a son, but Napoleon's preferring the boy to the father led to a row and the whole matter had to be dropped. Meanwhile the women squabbled as if the occasion were a family wedding. The wives of Joseph and Louis were now to be called 'Highness'. Napoleon's sisters, Caroline and Élisa, seethed with so rancorous a jealousy that even Napoleon was obliged to submit to their demands. Having achieved royal status, the thought of carrying Josephine's train at once became demeaning to them and the sisters were only quietened when they were persuaded that they were required merely to 'hold' the train rather than 'carry' it. Thus, partially reconciled at least, the new imperial family progressed down the nave of Notre-Dame amid the tumult of a military band vying with the shouted greetings of the immense congregation.

Pope Pius VII anointed the imperial couple, recited the first part of the mass and, after the gradual, turned to bless the regalia. He then handed Napoleon his orb, following this with a symbolic hand of justice on a bejewelled pole, a sceptre and a sword, all of which were modelled on those possessed by Charlemagne. Then, alone, Napoleon walked up the steps to the altar. Taking the waiting golden wreath in his hands, he raised it in the air before placing it down on his own head in an astonishing assertion of his self-created majesty. '*Vivat Imperator in Aeternum*' sang the choir as Josephine then stepped forward and, kneeling before her husband, received her crown at his hands as the final affirmation of Napoleon's dynastic glory – a moment frozen forever in David's heroic painting of the scene. The long service then continued (Napoleon stifling a yawn of boredom) until, at its end, a herald announced that 'the most glorious and august Napoleon, Emperor of the French, is consecrated and enthroned'. The people of France finally had their emperor and the Emperor had his wars. Nothing, it seemed, was impossible to either them or him in the pursuit of *la gloire* and *la patrie*. The eagle could fly where he would.

## The Eagle Triumphant

There were, however, means by which that flight could be made more difficult. The English Channel having foiled his hopes of an invasion, English gold now obliged Napoleon to march east towards the Rhine. Resentment of Napoleon's ambitions had fuelled young Tsar Alexander's hostility to France and, in April 1805, this led to the signing of an Anglo-Russian Convention. When Napoleon established the Kingdom of Italy the following month and was enthroned in Milan, the aggrieved Austrians, realising that he once again wished to destroy their hold over Italy, joined with the Allies in what became known as the Third Coalition against France. A land war on an unprecedented scale was about to commence. The military forces Napoleon had raised for the invasion of England were rapidly transformed into the *Grande Armée*, and the Austrians, deluded into thinking that the action would take place principally in Italy, learned to their horror that nineteen infantry battalions, supported by 286 field guns and six light cavalry divisions, were marching towards them at lightning speed, the total of some 200,000 battle-hardened men pillaging as they went. Here indeed was the nation in arms, the force that Clausewitz had described with such grim, rigorous horror and which was now, under Napoleon's command, to reveal its full and pitiless strength.

The Austrians were caught unaware, while the commander of their army, General Mack, was a soldier who stood high in no one's estimation save his own. The English despised him, and Napoleon called him 'one of the most mediocre men I ever met'. Mack was vain and conceited. Worst of all, he was unlucky. He was certainly no match for an emperor leading a huge and hugely patriotic army, an emperor who not only planned with rigour and spent hours each day on his horse as he watched, encouraged and scolded his men, but who was also a military genius. Mack believed that Napoleon would advance from the Black Forest. He was wrong. In a brilliant tactical manoeuvre Napoleon totally outwitted Mack by wheeling round to the Austrian rear, surrounding his enemy and then crushing him at the Battle of Ulm in October 1805. Mack and over 30,000 of his men were obliged to surrender to a grim-faced but exultant Napoleon who, through eight days of heavy rain and snow, had not found time to change his boots and who now stood before them a victorious if bedraggled figure in a muddy grey coat. 'I have fulfilled my goal,' he wrote to Josephine, 'I have destroyed the Austrian army by simple marches; I have taken 60,000 prisoners, 120 cannon, more than ninety standards and more than thirty generals.' Now, he added, 'I am going after the Russians.'

He did so by a ruse. For all the Russian General Kutusov's warning that they should wait until their full forces could assemble, Francis II and Alexander believed they knew better and, having unsuccessfully tried to persuade the Prussians to join them, were lured by Napoleon's feigned retreat into strategic disaster. On the eve of the Battle of Austerlitz in December 1805, Napoleon told his expectant troops that 'the positions we are occupying are formidable, and while [the enemy] marches to outflank our right they will present their flank to me'. Thus it transpired and, at the conclusion of the battle, the enemy army was caught between three fires. Thousands were slaughtered or captured while, as those who fled threw down their weapons and ran desperately over the frozen ponds, Napoleon brought up more cannon and ordered them to fire at the ice and thereby send another 2,000 men to a cruel and ghastly death. A third of the Russian army had been destroyed and Tsar Alexander, who barely escaped capture himself, felt that his once heroic confidence in his own abilities was shattered. As a result of the treaty that followed, Austria lost her remaining possessions in Italy and was obliged to recognise various Germanic states as independent monarchies. Forty-five enemy standards were sent to a jubilant Paris where they were displayed in Notre-Dame.

Prussia was rewarded for neutrality by gaining Hanover but, hearing whispers that he might lose it again, the vapid Prussian King Frederick William began to listen to the voices of the anti-French faction about him led by his wife. He acted with uncharacteristic decision. Succumbing to overtures from Russia, he opened his North Sea river mouths to British ships, thereby breaking Napoleon's trade embargo. He was rewarded with promises of British money with which to mobilise his army. This was a suicidal folly for if the Prussian army could be effectively mobilised it could not be speedily modernised, and it currently languished as a vast and ludicrously outdated shadow from the days of Frederick the Great. It was partly in the hope of reviving those days that the Prussian generals, otherwise at each others' throats and wholly unfamiliar with the techniques of modern war, vowed to go into battle against the finest army in Europe, marshalling to their side 150,000 men armed with obsolete muskets and drilled in an antediluvian stiffness that was made the more ponderous by their being supplied from slow and creaking wagons. The result was as ghastly as it was predictable. Defeated at Jena and slaughtered at Auerstadt in October 1806, the fleeing remainder of the Prussian army was decimated by the French cavalry. General Blücher was on the run while, in addition to the usual trophies (captured standards, captured men and a prodigious number of captured cannon), Napoleon profited from captured cash, horses, food, drink, munitions and so much plundered British merchandise that his entire army was given new uniforms from the cloth alone.

Napoleon was determined that Britain should suffer more. The smoke from her factories would never besmirch *la gloire* and *la patrie*. If Napoleon was unable to invade he might yet crush her in his eagle's claws, and he now issued orders that France and its dependent states should refrain from 'all commerce and all correspondence with the British Isles'. This is what became known as the Continental System and it exemplified Napoleon's belief that the business of the greatest commercial and industrial power on earth could be stifled and his enemy brought to its knees by poverty. Social upheaval and even revolution might follow and, where there was chaos, he could impose order. Although the Continental System could and indeed would cause great hardship in Britain it was ultimately unrealistic for many reasons. Chief among these was the fact that Britain was a maritime commercial power and Nelson's victory at Trafalgar in the very month of Napoleon's victory at Austerlitz annihilated the joint French and Spanish navies.[6] It was a moment of enormous national pride and relief. Nelson's genius and daring ensured that British naval superiority was and would remain overwhelming. As the Prime Minister, Pitt, declared to the great and the good assembled amid the sumptuousness of that year's Lord Mayor's Banquet: 'England has saved herself by her exertions and will, as I trust, save Europe by her example.' The last remained to be seen, but Napoleon realised that if his Continental System were to have any chance of success then it was necessary to block every European trading outlet to British ships. The ports of Russia in particular had to be closed by bringing Russia herself to heel.

Such a decision could only have been made by the commander of the *Grande Armée*. That army had had its origins in revolutionary enthusiasm but now the French nation in arms was, as commanded by Napoleon, a Behemoth of undisguised and unabashed imperialist aggression. Belief in the omnicompetence of force, and trust in the effectiveness of violence unleashed on an unparalleled scale, had moved to the iron heart of Napoleon's thinking and, in order to subdue Russia to his will, he now ordered his troops to overwinter in Poland. What though the bitter extremes of a Polish winter made its virtually unknown terrain a living hell? The army would endure it. What though French supply lines were hugely drawn out and Poland itself inadequately provided with provisions to plunder? They would survive somehow. What though most of his men had no winter uniforms and their boots might only last a further ten days? The matter would be seen to. And what about keeping up numbers? It was not a problem. France was richly supplied with suitable young men. Napoleon could call up 100,000 now and summon more from his dependent states. Poland herself had promised 30,000 men in return for becoming a kingdom independent of the Tsar. Let *les grognards* – the 'grumblers' in the army – mutter. Their complaints meant nothing. All that mattered was a bridgehead on the Vistula.

The bloody and indecisive battle fought in depths of freezing mud against the Russians at Pultusk showed what could be expected. And all the while the French army was obliged to live on potatoes plundered from the surrounding fields. 'My position here would be very beautiful,' Napoleon wrote, 'if I had some provisions.' He himself took comfort in the arms of Marie Walewska, an exceptionally beautiful twenty-year-old Polish countess married to a septuagenarian. Marie talked enthusiastically about Polish nationalism, partnered the besotted emperor at dances and made his bed the sweeter by soothing his doubts about his virility. Only the necessities of war tore them from each others' arms, and to terrible effect. In February 1807 the indecisive Battle of Eylau was fought in a snowstorm so ferocious that vision was reduced to fifteen yards. When the storm eased a little many wished that what they saw could still be hidden from view. 'Never were so many corpses cramped into so confined a space,' wrote a French army doctor. The fallen snow was red with blood, while that which was still gently tumbling tried to cover the carnage with a freezing shroud. Thousands of the Russian dead were piled up behind the clumps of fir trees. Mounds of hundreds more were hidden behind the hills. Thousands of abandoned muskets, caps and breastplates littered the roads where wounded and crippled horses barely had the strength to stand as they waited in freezing agony to fall down dead from hunger. Even the tobacco-chewing and fiercely loyal Marshal Ney, at thirty-eight the veteran of many battles and widely known as 'the bravest of the brave', shook his head of red hair and whispered in appalled bitterness: *'Quel massacre! Et sans resultat!'* Here was the full dreadful carnage of the nation in arms analysed by Clausewitz and such scenes were now among Napoleon's principal gifts to millions of people across Europe. When they were repeated five months later at Friedland, they brought Tsar Alexander to the conference table.

Napoleon was charmed by him. The two men met on a pavilioned raft moored in the River Niemen off Tilsit. The French Emperor at once declared of the Russian: 'Were Alexander a woman I think I would fall passionately in love with him.' Napoleon then made his overtures with all the very real charm of which he was capable and, in less than an hour, the boyish young Russian's prejudices melted away to leave him with only his vanity, his idealism and his bravado. He listened with a charming smile as his new hero talked of dividing the world between them and then confessed how much he hated the British. 'In that case,' Napoleon replied, 'everything can be speedily settled between us and peace is made.' So, it seemed, it was. While Frederick William's defeated Prussia was humiliated – 'a nasty king, a nasty nation, a nasty army', Napoleon declared – Alexander was obliged to cede only the Ionian Islands and, in a secret clause, agreed to make war on Britain if the British refused to make peace with France. With the uncountable barbarian hordes of Russia now apparently at his beck and call Napoleon stood at the very summit of his power.

## The Spanish Peninsula

There remained only *l'Albion perfide* with her mighty navy and her thunderous factories to subdue. If victory against her by sea and land was out of the question there still remained the possibility of economic warfare. Napoleon set about developing his previous trade embargo into the fully fledged version of the Continental System. From now on virtually the whole of Europe would be closed to British merchants. By the terms of the Treaty of Tilsit, Russia, Austria, Denmark and Sweden were added to those places where trading in British goods was forbidden. This hurt and hurt badly, but the British economy was too strong to be brought easily to its knees, and economic stress did not foment rebellion. It was a hollow boast of Napoleon's that his enemy, growing old and weak like the increasingly insane George III, would decline as France herself revelled in 'the vitality of youth'. The goods Britain produced or transported were urgently needed by those to whom they were denied. Grumbling French manufacturers were deprived of essential raw materials as they watched the French economy being supported less by their own efforts than by the plunder and taxes which streamed in from conquered states – states which were, in their turn, increasingly resentful of the hardships they were obliged to endure because of Napoleon's France First policy. Smuggling on a huge scale was rife, while the very means Napoleon was now obliged to take in order to ensure the success of the Continental System led to its being progressively undermined.

It seemed particularly irksome to Napoleon (indeed rather absurd) that little, backward Portugal was reluctant to subscribe to his plan to crush Britain. In fact the country was Britain's oldest ally and continued to allow the Royal Navy and British merchant ships access to her ports. Here was the back door into Europe and it was essential that it be firmly closed and locked. By 1807, Napoleon was casting his conqueror's gaze on the Iberian peninsula. He saw that the regent of Portugal was a nonentity and that the Spain of Charles IV was in the hands of the queen and her lover Godoy. It appeared a relatively easy matter to subdue these priest-ridden and seemingly somnolent nations, kept down as they were by the worst excesses of the old regime while being lulled by memories of their own long-gone imperial past. All that was required was high-handedness, deceit and a large army. These were available. Napoleon arranged with Godoy that 25,000 men of the *Grande Armée*, led by his great friend the impetuous General Junot, should move through Spain and occupy key fortresses in preparation for the military humiliation of Portugal. Spain in the meantime would be annexed through cunning. Knowing that Charles IV faced a plot encouraged by his son Ferdinand, Napoleon offered to mediate. Summoning the Spanish royal family to Bayonne, he forced Charles to resign and Ferdinand to renounce the succession before proclaiming his own brother, Joseph, King of Spain and providing him with another army led this time by Murat. The peoples of the Iberian peninsula would be liberated from their past whether they liked it or not.

They did not. Portuguese resistance confined the French largely to Lisbon, and the Bishop of Oporto, heading the *junta* there, appealed to Britain for help. This came in the form of a general exactly of an age with Napoleon who had recently returned from subduing large swathes of India.[7] Sir Arthur Wellesley was the son of an impoverished and long undistinguished family from the Anglo-Irish Protestant ruling class. His time at Eton suggested that he too had acquired his fair share of the Wellesley family's characteristic traits, and it was only when his mother spotted her still unemployed son in a London theatre and realised that he might as well become 'food for powder' that the young man's true qualities began to emerge. Sent to India with the 76th Regiment, Wellesley rankled at the graft and greediness he found among his compatriots and disparaged their self-indulgent lifestyle. He lived moderately, drank little and studied much. An iron self-discipline was beginning to become one of his most salient characteristics and everyone noted that the mature man was stern, grave and taciturn, remote and difficult of approach. It also soon emerged that he was a commander of genius. His seizing of the fortress at Seringapatam and even more the brilliance with which he won the Battle of Assaye against overwhelming odds showed his true qualities. Unwilling to delegate, unquestioningly brave, always in the heart of the action, at once cunning and supremely commonsensical, Wellesley won the absolute respect and even the grudging love of his men.

An imperialist by conviction and a High Tory by temperament, Wellesley nonetheless loathed the fury of party politics and declared: 'I serve the public and not any administration.' As a High Tory he regarded Napoleon as a bully and a thief and often compared the Emperor to the notorious English highwayman Jonathan Wild. Wellesley however retained a great respect for Napoleon's abilities as a soldier. These last he had considered deeply and he believed himself to be more than a match for his great rival. Just before his departure for Europe, musing over the after-dinner port in his dining room in Harley Street, Wellesley declared that his die was now cast and that while the French might overwhelm him they would not outmanoeuvre him. He gave two characteristically concise reasons for this. 'First, because I am not afraid of them as everyone else seems to be; and secondly, because, if what I hear of their system of manoeuvres is true, I think it a false one against steady troops.' Here was professionalism of the highest order.

Napoleon for the moment thought he had little to fear. The Royal Navy might be the greatest in Europe, the British army was not. As Wellesley's 9,000 men arrived in Portugal it seemed certain that they would add one more item to their fifteen-year catalogue of frequent ignominious bungling. And who was this 'Sepoy' general anyway? Junot was now to discover. Within three weeks of Wellesley's landing Junot – incontestably brave but too wild to be a great commander – was obliged to surrender his 26,000 men after their defeat at Vimiero in August 1808. Wellesley and his newly augmented army had been neither overwhelmed nor out-manoeuvred, and his steady troops, brilliantly deployed, had won a famous victory. They did so in a manner that was to become characteristic. Their line of well-trained and fiercely disciplined soldiers, two men deep, could maximise an altogether more terrible firepower than the advancing column of the French which was hemmed in on itself and broken before it could fan out and deploy. Napoleon was never to take this tactic properly into account, but what he had for the moment lost on the battlefield he appeared partially to regain at the peace table. Wellesley's newly arrived superior officers concluded that absurdity known as the Convention of Cintra whereby no French prisoners of war were taken and the Royal Navy agreed to return home Junot's surviving army along with the huge amount of treasure it had looted. There was a public outcry in Britain followed by a public enquiry. Wellesley, who was no more afraid of a committee than he was of an enemy army, skilfully acquitted himself of responsibility for what he called the 'very extraordinary paper' that was the Convention of Cintra and then retreated to Ireland.

There Napoleon's nemesis might have remained but for the actions of Napoleon himself. The Emperor now appeared personally in Spain with 100,000 veterans, many of them those so recently evacuated by the British. He was bent on revenge, for the French battalions already in Spain had been humiliated by forces altogether novel to them. Only a small number of the Spanish intelligentsia had welcomed the equality so dubiously offered by the French Revolution and their chattering had easily been drowned by the combined voices of monks, priests and the landed gentry who inveighed against atheism and clung to their property. The opinions of their masters became the thoughts of the people which eventually boiled over on 2 May 1808, when they rose across Madrid and killed

150 of Murat's soldiers before being crushed and subjected to the devastating mass executions which are the subjects of Goya's horror and pity in two of his greatest paintings. Fury and nationalism now burned across the dry Spanish plains where a thousand *juntas* raised men and women to fight those savage little engagements they called *guerrillas*. Spurred on by feelings of a religious intensity they inflicted ghastly revenge, burying dozens of Frenchmen alive at a time and mutilating and murdering thousands more, sometimes leaving only one earless victim to tell the tale. Forty thousand Spanish troops and partisans slaughtered 9,000 French recruits at Baylén, and Napoleon determined on vengeance. He defeated the Spanish at Tudela, a victory that also necessitated a fighting retreat by the British army to Corunna from where, after the death of its commander Sir John Moore, it was evacuated by the Royal Navy. 'My business in Spain is finished,' Napoleon roundly declared as he set off once again for Paris.

## Securing the Bonaparte Dynasty

The suddenness of his departure was not a display of confidence but of deep concern. For all Napoleon had tried to bind the Russians to a promise that they would restrain the Austrians from attacking his eastern flank while he was so busy in the west, Tsar Alexander had not prevented Joseph from mobilising his forces. However, if Napoleon saw the likelihood of yet another foreign war, he was altogether more immediately troubled by the actions of two men at home. Talleyrand and the police chief Fouché – the one the habitué of the gilded salon, the other the familiar of the plotter's dingy tenement – had joined forces in an unlikely alliance to place Murat on the imperial throne. Napoleon's anger was boundless, venomous and ultimately impotent. Fouché could not easily be sacked. He knew too much. The same was true of Talleyrand, who was nonetheless summoned to the Tuileries, reduced to the nominal position of Vice-Grand Elector and told he was a thief, a coward, a traitor and a turd wrapped up in a silk stocking. Aware of his value to the true interests of France, Talleyrand said nothing, contenting himself on his way out by muttering that it was a shame that one so mighty should be so ill-bred and then going on to sell the nation's secrets to Metternich for a suitably enormous sum. As he did so, Napoleon prepared for his war against Austria, and Wellesley returned to Portugal.

There were by now three French armies on the Iberian peninsula. Wellesley decided to drive Marshal Soult out of Oporto first. The enemy had blown up the bridges and seized most of the available shipping but, learning of the presence of four empty wine barges, Wellesley ferried his men across the river at a rate of about 600 an hour, seized the town and with it seventy enemy guns. Northern Portugal was his despite the difficulties he faced with supplies and the cantankerously incompetent Portuguese general who was supposed to be his ally. By the closing days of July 1809, the dreadful Battle of Talavera had confirmed the seriousness of the British presence. Despite losing over 5,000 men – a quarter of his army – Wellesley's tactics prevailed. Three thousand of his soldiers manned the thin red line that drove back 10,000 French in an encounter that was, in Wellesley's own word, 'murderous'. Nor was the engagement itself the only horror. As the battle was ending, the summer grass caught alight and the wounded scattered across it were burned alive. Such was the cost of driving the French back to Toledo, but Wellesley's victory was treated with rapture in Britain. Hero-worship was the mood of the time and every conceivable item – pots, clock faces and doorstops – were decorated with the distinctive profile of the newly ennobled Viscount Wellington.

Wellington had won his victory by the brilliance of his tactics and was now to consolidate it by the ruthless inventiveness of his strategy. He ordered the construction of the Lines of Torres Vedras: 165 redouts mounted with 628 cannon were built high along the miles of mountainous terrain between Spain and the Portuguese hinterland. It was an achievement on a heroic scale that made Lisbon virtually impregnable while defending nearly 40,000 British troops who could be evacuated by sea if the Lines failed and be supplied by the Royal Navy if they did not. The French in the meantime would starve. As Wellington retreated behind his bulwark he instituted a savage 'scorched-earth' policy on the fields he crossed. The French, used to living off the lands they invaded, would find those lands barren. The policy proved as terrible as it was effective, and won even Napoleon's grudging admiration. He was reported to have said that only Wellington or he was capable of such ruthless measures.

Napoleon himself heard news of Wellington's victory at Talavera as he was negotiating the settlement that concluded his campaign against the Austrians. His feckless brother Joseph presented the encounter as a French triumph but Napoleon, tossed on a sea of misinformation, preferred to learn his facts from the English press. 'What a fine opportunity has been lost!' he fulminated in a letter. 'Thirty-thousand English at 150 leagues from the coast in front of 100,000 of the best troops in the world! My God! What it is to have an army without a chief.' But such anger was for private consumption. The delicate negotiations in the Schönbrunn required that Talavera be seen as another victory to be added to the one Napoleon himself had recently won at Wagram.

The Austrian campaign had been no easy triumph. Napoleon sent 300,000 men into the field but the sheer force of which he was so enamoured and on which his plans depended contained within it the limitations that threatened to undermine it. For all Napoleon might boast that he could expend 30,000 men a day, those men were no longer of the calibre of his earlier armies. The number of battle-hardened veterans was inevitably declining, the new recruits were raw and even untrained, while their numbers were made up by men conscripted from reluctant vassal states. A vast army so seriously weakened did not move forward of its own volition, and it was Napoleon's personal presence that led it to victory. Even then victory was far from assured. Mistakes were made. At Aspern–Essling

Napoleon seriously underestimated the Austrians' strength and news of his forced retreat and heavy losses echoed around Europe. Nor was Wagram a triumph in the old type. The battle cost Napoleon heavily and, if Austrian losses were even heavier, they were still able to withdraw a force of 80,000 men and demand an armistice. Its terms were punitive. Austria had to pay huge indemnities, face losing millions of her subjects and shackle the trade of the Habsburg empire to the Continental System. Metternich considered that, for the moment, the price was worth it and he had, besides, a trump card to play.

The machinations of Talleyrand, Fouché and Murat had come to nothing but had shown Napoleon how insecurely he sat on his throne. He had no legitimate son to be his natural heir. The fact that he had fathered a child by Countess Walewska proved he was not impotent, and Napoleon now turned his still loving eyes on the forty-year-old Josephine and realised she was barren. He ordered a divorce, and the question was now as to where he should remarry. A sister of Tsar Alexander's was adroitly removed from his grasp and Metternich waited with his own Emperor's daughter on his arm. Marie-Louise was neither very bright nor very attractive but she was only eighteen and came of prodigiously fecund stock. Her marriage to Napoleon was celebrated in April 1810 and Europe sighed as it saw Austria and its empire apparently lost to its hopes of freedom. 'The Austrian marriage is a terrible event,' wrote Wellington, 'and must prevent any great movement on the Continent for the moment.'

This was no less than the truth, for in 1810 the greater part of Europe was shackled by the iron band of the Napoleonic empire, the influence of which now stretched from the Atlantic borders of Spain to the western limits of Austria, from Denmark to the toe of Italy. It comprised 70 million people who were to profit from the liberalising of their ancient ways and to pay for this with men, money and an enforced enrolment in the Continental System. Napoleon meanwhile concentrated immense power in his own hands. France, extended now to include Belgium, Savoy, much of

Italy, Corsica and the lands around the left bank of the Rhine, was his bailiwick. Among his client states were Switzerland, Denmark, Prussia, the German principalities that made up the Confederation of the Rhine and Austria. In other regions Napoleon devolved much of his imperial responsibilities on his family. The bickering little group at his coronation were now European princes to be ordered about like schoolchildren when necessary.

Napoleon's letters suggest that such orders were often necessary. Only his stepson Eugène de Beauharnais, sent to Italy as viceroy of the newly augmented Cisalpine Republic, proved himself a model Bonaparte prince. He balanced his books, revitalised his army, reformed education, patronised the arts and packed his Council of State with his cronies. Napoleon ordered him to take 'France First' as his motto and set the tone of his imperial designs when he informed Eugène that 'Italy must not make calculations independent of the need to assure the prosperity of France; she must combine French interests with her own; above all, she must avoid giving France a motive for the annexation of Italy, for if France decided to do so, who could stop her?' Eugène did his best, as did Napoleon's sister Élisa. Plain and masculine, she showed her abilities by reviving the industries of Lucca and the marble quarries of Carrara before becoming Grand-Duchess of Tuscany.

Napoleon often wished his other siblings were as useful. Joseph was sent to Naples to replace the unfortunately favoured Ferdinand the Nose who, barely able to read, had ordered the public burning of Voltaire's works in the intervals of ringing a little bell which he had acquired from Loreto as a known defence against thunderstorms. Leaving Ferdinand to play with his collection of relics, Joseph wiped out the state's massive debt by secularising the monasteries and freeing five million of the poorest people in Europe from feudal overlords who were sometimes minded to prevent them from building houses so that they might be herded at night like cattle into barns. Corruption, stagnation and the Church were all too powerful forces of inertia, however, and Joseph was sharply ordered to 'levy a contribution of thirty millions from the Kingdom of Naples; pay your army generously, re-equip your cavalry; have shoes and uniforms manufactured'. Such things were needed for the suppression of the rest of Europe and 'so far as I am concerned, it would be too ridiculous if the conquest of Naples did not bring comfort and well-being to my army'. Napoleon then added: 'If you do not make yourself feared from the beginning, you are bound to get trouble.' In fact this came later. The rather dull Joseph, wanted in Spain where he proved himself singularly inept, was replaced in Naples by the hot-headed Murat. Married to the manipulative Caroline Bonaparte, Murat tended to ignore his brother-in-law's orders while playing to the Neapolitans for his own dynastic ends.

The bonhominous Louis Bonaparte was even more friendly towards the Dutch he was sent to rule. He refused to enforce conscription and only imposed a mild version of the Continental System on a people whose wealth was so vested in its trade that they escaped ruin solely by 'King Lodewijk' turning a blind eye to their illicit activities. A rodomontade came from Paris. Louis would 'find in me a brother, provided that I find in you a Frenchman; but if you forget the ties which attach you to our common country, then you will not be unpleasantly surprised if I forget the natural affinity between us'. And that is precisely what happened. Napoleon accused his brother of becoming nothing more than a Dutch cheese dealer, which Louis said was just what a king of Holland should be. He lost his throne and with it his place in the family firm – a fate that very nearly swept up Jérôme Bonaparte too.

With Jérôme, the glitter of the playboy masked the steel of the autocrat. Napoleon sent him to rule the north German region of Westphalia, writing him a letter once he was installed there which began: 'You will find enclosed the constitution of your kingdom.' Despite this tone, the ideas in the letter are liberal. 'The benefits of the Code Napoleon, public trials, the introduction of juries, will be the distinctive features of your rule,' Napoleon continued. The Germans of the region would enjoy an unprecedented degree of modern freedom. Despite Jérôme's prodigal nature – he had ninety-two carriages, two hundred horses and spiralling personal debts – he set to work with a will. While only reluctantly following the Continental System, he so geared the Westphalian state to providing his brother with fearsome Hessian soldiers that the otherwise moribund economy slipped towards bankruptcy even as its people began to feel the first stirrings of nationalism and pride in an identity that owed nothing to France.

Such feelings were particularly marked among German-speaking intellectuals, especially in that erstwhile patchwork of princedoms Napoleon had refashioned into the Confederation of the Rhine.[8] Here, in the worlds of thought and emotion, were weapons quite as powerful and dangerous as cannon. The people increasingly felt their sense of shared cultural identity affronted by Napoleon's imposing on them a cosmopolitan regime that demeaned their historical traditions. A sense of what it meant to be German was ever more strongly opposed to what it felt to be a French colony. There were increasing numbers who believed that what should have been recognised as the German nation had, like every other people, its particular genius, its unique guiding spirit. 'Let us follow our own path,' the cultural philosopher Herder had declared, 'let all men speak well or ill of our nation, our literature, our language: they are ours, they are ourselves, and let that be enough.' Living under an alien imperial regime that seriously threatened the integrity of their common culture and their economy, such people found themselves drawn into an ideological movement that sought unity, identity and direction on the basis of nationhood. Fichte, lecturing in a Berlin occupied by French soldiers, spoke for all his fellow-countrymen when he declared: 'it is only by means of the common characteristic of being German that we can avert the downfall of our nation, which is threatened by its fusion with foreign peoples, and win back again an individuality that is self-supporting and quite incapable of any dependence on others.'

The consequences of such ideas are all too familiarly chilling. Few things inspire them more than military defeat, and few nations had been more humiliatingly defeated by Napoleon than Prussia. After the catastrophe of Jena, Prussian nationalism began to express itself in terms of brutal efficiency. The archaic aristocratic system that had helped bring the state down was swept away so that it could march anew. The internal arrangements of the nation were strengthened along with its economy by emancipating the serfs, restructuring the tax system and introducing municipal self-government. In the meantime the War Office purged the old men from the military academies and created a new and terrifying army through recruitment, the encouragement of the talented rather than the merely high born, by education and by a fierce training in modern techniques of war. This was to be the core of Blücher's army. The most autocratic of German states was being created as a direct response to all that Napoleon had done to it. In 1810 this did not seem excessively dangerous. The size of the Prussian army was still restricted to 42,000 men by the terms of the Treaty of Tilsit. It seems nonetheless that, aware of the diverse strains within his empire, Napoleon's thoughts were moving increasingly in the direction of an ever more centralised imperial government. Early in 1811 the future of both his empire and his dynasty seemed assured when Marie-Louise gave birth to his son. Here was the future ruler of Europe and, to suggest his imperial destiny, Napoleon named him the King of Rome.

## The Russian Campaign of 1812

Of the states outside Napoleon's empire, only the British, the Russians and the Ottomans were of real significance. Napoleon still hoped that Britain might be brought down by the Continental System while Russia appeared tied to France by the Treaty of Tilsit. Those terms might however chafe and those bound to them seek to break free. When it became clear to Tsar Alexander that Napoleon had no interest in furthering Russian plans to make war with the Ottomans, other causes of discontent also began to rub. Russian merchants were all too painfully aware that the terms of the Continental System were insupportable. They created a balance of trade deficit so serious that the exchange rate plummeted and the paper currency was depreciated. Alexander had to act. Talleyrand was already whispering flatteries in his ear which suggested that he should resist Napoleon's plans not simply for the sake of Russia but for the sake of Europe. The young man could indeed have a role on the world stage. On the last day of 1810 Alexander withdrew from the Continental System, claiming that he wanted to encourage his poorly developed home industry, balance his books and raise his peoples' morals by curbing the excessive import of luxury goods by land. The duty on French wine was doubled, while goods arriving by sea – British goods carried in neutral American ships – would not be so penalised. Napoleon reckoned that by August 1811 some 150 American ships had carried British goods to Russia and so he prepared for war.

Napoleon's Russian campaign of 1812 was his most devastating absurdity, a folly even more destructive than his incursion into the Iberian peninsula. It was ill-conceived, impossible of fulfilment, ruinously expensive and doomed from the start. It was to prove the greatest refutation so far of his belief that the word 'impossible' was the hobgoblin of the timid and the excuse of fools. The astonishing arrogance – the megalomania – of Napoleon's ambition was contagious all the same. As Captain Fantin des Odoards, one of the grenadiers in his treasured Old Guard, wrote when the army was about to set off: 'it's going to begin, this new campaign which will greatly increase the glory of France.' Glory had now become an end in itself and force its means of attainment. The *Grand Armée* appeared invincible. 'Its august leader has so accustomed it to fatigue, danger and glory,' the deluded captain wrote, 'that a state of repose has become hateful.' So enamoured of the myth was he that he declared: 'with such men we can conquer the world.'

All of this was quite simply untrue. The unprecedentedly large army of 600,000 men that invaded Russia was drawn from every reach of the empire. Much of it was an untrained and unwilling polyglot horde. One general wrote of his corps consisting of a Prussian contingent 'and a division formed by three Polish regiments, one Bavarian and one Westphalian; my staff was French'. Such factors made communication difficult and badly affected discipline. This was a problem exacerbated by the difficulties of the march into Russia. Napoleon, now a pot-bellied man of nearly forty-three, rode in a green four-wheeled carriage drawn by six horses. This was fitted up like an office, and all day long reports would be received or sent out from it in the intervals of the emperor studying his maps. The vastness of Russia was all too evident from these last and from the endless, agonising vistas through which the army stumbled. It had been Napoleon's plan to lure the Russians towards him and then split and defeat their forces. Alexander had other ideas. 'The system which has made Wellington victorious in Spain, and exhausted the French enemies, is what I intend to follow — avoid pitched battles and organise long lines of communication for retreat.' A 'scorched-earth' policy would ensure that the French army, lured ever deeper into enemy territory, would be reduced to starvation. Such a strategy would indeed help to defeat Napoleon in Russia even as it did in Spain. The weather would do the rest.

The conditions were already terrible. 'The advanced guard lived quite well,' wrote Caulaincourt, 'but the rest of the army was dying of hunger. Exhaustion, added to want and the piercingly cold rains at night, caused the death of 10,000 horses. Many of the Young Guard died on the road of fatigue, cold and hunger.' So vicious was this starving army in its attempts to seize such food as was available that the embittered Russian peasantry organised themselves into guerrilla bands that were quite as cruel as those in Spain, the depredations they inflicted being made worse by savage surprise attacks mounted by the Cossacks. Despite these conditions, the

*Grande Armée* managed to prevent the two Russian armies meeting up at Vitebsk and obliged them to retreat to Smolensk. The effort and the exhaustion were such, however, that Napoleon found it necessary to halt for a fortnight before obliging the Russians to fall back to Moscow. Here their army was put under the command of General Kutusov, a one-eyed warrior of sixty-eight and such enormous girth that he found it necessary to campaign in a *droshky* rather than on horseback. Napoleon called him 'the dowager', unaware that Kutusov's natural ruthlessness had been honed by his desire to wreak revenge for his experiences at Austerlitz.

Kutusov drew up his army of 120,000 men at Borodino where Napoleon was obliged to give battle. He was not well. He had caught a feverish chill and was suffering once again from dysuria. Worse, he had just received news of Wellington's victory at Salamanca. Both ends of Napoleon's would-be empire were in turmoil and the crushing weight of his self-made difficulties was all too evident. He and his vast army were deep inside hostile terrain and he had already lost as many men as if he had fought two battles. Now it was evident that he had not only to face Kutusov but that he had been humiliated by Wellington whose small army of well-trained soldiers had already defeated 130,000 of the French at Busaco before successfully fighting a long campaign for the fortresses along the Spanish–Portuguese border. The English had captured Cuidad Rodrigo and Badajóz. Now they had defeated Marmont at Salamanca and were advancing on Madrid. The need for a decisive victory was paramount.

It was not to happen. The Battle of Borodino was one of the most bloody Napoleon ever fought. Twelve hours of incessant bombardment, two million French musket rounds and 40,000 Russian dead were insufficient to end Russian resistance. Kutusov and 90,000 of his survivors retreated in good order while, in Moscow, where the Tsar had proclaimed 'a national war . . . in defence of Mother Russia', the authorities ordered that the immense and ornate wooden city be burned to the ground, partly by criminals specially released from prison for the task before being shot. Tsar Alexander claimed that it was by the light of these fires that he glimpsed the workings of God in history. Certainly the sacrifice was ghastly, but its effects were worse. There were still luxuries available in the ruined city – vast supplies of champagne, for example – but few if any necessities. When the French went to pillage the surrounding countryside, concealed peasants emerged to slay them, leaving those who escaped to the mercy of the Cossacks. It seemed the only thing the French could do was fall back on Smolensk. They did but there was no food in the place and now it had started to snow. Worst of all, the Russians had decided to annihilate the French army as soon as it was forced to retreat.

Turning back along the terrible route that had brought them to this humiliation, the French army was obliged to witness sights of unbearable ghastliness. The battlefield at Borodino was uncleared and littered not just with debris but with 30,000 corpses half-eaten by wolves. 'The troops and the Emperor passed by rapidly, casting a sorrowful glance at this immense tomb,' wrote one observer. Worse was to come as the snow deepened and temperatures fell to a terrible and rarely equalled –17°. Starving, freezing men got detached from their columns and fell a prey to the laughing Cossacks who stripped them of everything. The luckier ones were killed outright. Some were buried alive. The rest, mother-naked, were left to perish of hunger and cold on the deadly highways. Desperate men turned to cannibalism. When the remains of the army reached the River Beresina they found that the Russians had destroyed the bridges, and it was only by dint of building two pontoons across an icy ford while under Russian fire that the greater part of the army escaped, many nonetheless dying when the larger of the two pontoons collapsed. Those who survived lived in hell: naked, shivering, starving and waiting to be released from their agony by a throat-slitting peasant or a Cossack horseman. A few days later Napoleon told his generals that he had to abandon them and make speedily for Paris. He would travel disguised as

Caulaincourt's secretary. It was utterly humiliating. Napoleon had abandoned an army for a second time. *La gloire* had been destroyed and now it seemed *la patrie* (or Napoleon's empire at least) was in danger.

## The Eagle Chained

The reason for Napoleon's flight was a threat to his dynasty. In Paris a lunatic by the name of Malet had escaped from his asylum and was claiming he had been given provisional government of the country after Napoleon's death in Russia. The ravings of a lunatic could do little to harm even a defeated emperor. What mattered was the fact that the French did not seem unduly concerned that Napoleon's reign was apparently over. The empire had no substance to outface calamity, no eternal root in *la patrie*, and now *la gloire* had all but shrivelled away. The people had suffered terribly. There was hardly a family that had not lost a father, a brother or a son in Napoleon's interminable wars. Paris, once a capital in a constant carnival mood of victory, became dreary, frightened and preoccupied. The inhabitants watched the imperial bees dying in the winter cold. The Emperor was no longer invincible. His armies were perishing in Russia and in Spain where Wellington was soon to triumph at Vitoria. Napoleon's enemies were stirring elsewhere too. Austria was at best a shaky ally. Prussia would almost certainly show its reformed strength soon. Britain would send her diplomats and her gold to the courts of Europe to encourage resistance there. The most wily could see that the game was already up. When Talleyrand was asked to resume his position at Foreign Affairs he refused, telling Napoleon to his face that the Emperor's ambitions were contrary to the true glory and happiness of France.

Napoleon would not accept this. He would not accept that the alliance between Russia and Prussia that now forced his troops into central Germany presaged the Treaty of Kalisch which would in turn rouse the German-speaking peoples to a war of liberation. He would not accept that the withdrawal of the Austrians from the *Grande Armée* suggested the true direction of Metternich's devious diplomacy. He would not accept that he had lost in Spain, where Wellington forced Joseph to flee and Soult to fight a hopeless campaign. He would not accept any of this. He would fight. Napoleon threw himself into the campaigns of 1813 with all the resolve and terrifying efficiency that was characteristic of him. But Europe neither could nor would march automatically to the beat of his drum. Half the 500,000 soldiers Napoleon enlisted melted away. France was ransacked for supplies, but urgently needed horses could not be found in sufficient numbers. And still he pressed on. He would push the Allies back over the Elbe. Magnificent manoeuvres culminating in victories at Lützen and Bautzen seemed to show that his genius was not dimmed, but the failure on both occasions to pursue his fleeing enemies was a sure indication of his material weakness. The British in the meantime stiffened the resolve of the Allies with more gold. Sweden was induced to join them with promises that she would be given help to capture Norway. Metternich was persuaded that Russia could be trusted. Prussia was carefully harnessed to the Allied juggernaut whose 800,000 men now included well over 100,000 of Blücher's newly trained recruits. Wellington would very soon be pushing with his army across the Pyrenees.

In the meantime, first Dresden and then Leipzig became the focus of operations. Vast armies tramped the lands between the two cities, avoiding for a time a major confrontation but weakening each other piecemeal: 95,000 Prussians, 120,000 Swedes and Pomeranians, 240,000 Austrians and 300,000 Frenchmen. The obvious might of the Prussians enthused the princes of Germany, and Napoleon's waning army was eventually pushed back to Leipzig. His 200,000 men now faced a combined force of nearly 300,000. Thus the nations of Europe in arms. Thus the appalling cult of force embodied in Napoleon himself. But, at this climactic moment, he hesitated and lost. He failed to destroy the Austrians decisively and, as they were joined by the other Allies, part of his own army defected and he was heavily outnumbered at the 'Battle of the Nations'. Afterwards he was forced to retreat with his decimated army back to the traditional borders of France. The battle was now for *la patrie*.

It was very nearly won. The fractious Allies were held together largely by British gold and diplomacy while desperation fired Napoleon's genius with all the incandescent energy once ignited by *la gloire*. Even as the French economy slumped, subordinates defected and taxes were hiked as the legislature groaned and was prorogued, so Napoleon raised yet another army. Youths barely into manhood were pulled from the fields and veterans were summoned from their firesides. One hundred and twenty thousand soldiers rallied to the eagle. Napoleon's principal concern was to use them in the defence of Paris. With the enemy now on French soil, speed and brilliant tactics – the flair Napoleon had shown in his early Italian campaigns – was of the essence. For a while he was remarkably successful. Three times he led his army against Blücher's and three times he defeated him. He drove the Austrians back from the Seine. He moved his army behind the enemy, hoping to lure them away from his capital. But, in the end, it was all to no avail. The British Foreign Secretary, Castlereagh, coaxed and begged the fractious Allies into maintaining the cause. Tsar Alexander urged them on to Paris where the citizens put up only a token resistance before surrendering to the armies that would liberate them from their own. With the surrender of Paris, Napoleon's position was hopeless. Even now he would not recognise the fact. Only when his leading marshals told him that they would not fight on did Napoleon realise his career was at an end. But his dynasty – did that have to go too? He asked to be allowed to abdicate in favour of his son, but the infant King of Rome exercised no great appeal and was unacceptable to the Allies. They were determined on a restoration of the old regime, on the return of Louis XVIII and, after considerable discussion, resolved that Napoleon should be exiled to Elba, an island off the Italian coast.

Now, as they haggled over his empire, Napoleon himself had escaped and was loose in the mainland of Europe once again. The representatives of the great powers gathered in the grey light of an early Viennese morning realised the gravity of the situation. Talleyrand gave it as his opinion that Napoleon would make first for the Italian coast and then fling himself into Switzerland. For once he was wrong. 'He will go straight to Paris,' Metternich declared. The important thing was to stop him and prevent the unchained eagle from darkening the skies of Europe once again.

# 2

## ELBA

### 1814

## The Wounded Eagle

Napoleon kept the poison in a little leather bag tied with a black taffeta ribbon. It was probably a mixture of opium, belladonna and white hellebore. Dr Yvan had prepared it for him as he was leaving for Russia but throughout the whole of that ghastly campaign, while tens of thousands died in agony, it stayed unopened. The contents remained unexamined through the following terrible months as the armies allied against Napoleon marched inexorably towards Paris: Wellington and the British from the south, Schwarzenberg and the Austrians, Blücher and the Prussians, Alexander and the Russians from the north. Now they had closed the circle and Paris was theirs. It was unendurable. Napoleon spent the evening of 12 April 1814 talking moodily with Caulaincourt at Fontainebleau. The world he had fashioned in two astonishing decades had collapsed and now on the desk in his study, not yet signed, lay the document that would determine his fate. It was Napoleon's acceptance of the fact that he who had ruled the greater part of Europe was now to be the king of tiny, dirty, backward Elba. It was all too dreadful to contemplate. When he was finally on his own Napoleon wrote a letter to his wife Marie-Louise and went to bed. His sleep, if he knew any, was fitful and after a few hours he got up, disturbing one of his valets as he poured himself a glass of water, tipped the poison into it and resolutely swallowed.[1]

The agony was slow to start but, as the valet became increasingly alarmed, he sent for the ever loyal Caulaincourt. By the time he arrived the scene was appalling. The sometime Emperor lay writhing on his tiny bed with his back arched, his eyes bulging and his limbs slowly going numb as the poison attacked his vitals. His body told him to vomit but his mind refused the command. The terrible, self-destructive iron will was reasserting itself, that iron will Napoleon had shown when, returning defeated to his capital as the Allies advanced, he had stopped at a post-house near Juvisy and learned the degree of his humiliation. 'What are you doing here?' he had shouted at an officer who was leading some bedraggled men through the dark. Where was the enemy? Where was the King of Rome? Where was the Empress? The unfortunate man was required to tell Napoleon the bitter truth. Paris had surrendered and his wife and son had fled with two of his brothers. Napoleon's fury was titanic. 'Everyone's lost their heads,' he bellowed. 'That's what comes of trusting people who have no common sense and no energy!' He stormed up and down vowing to save Paris and his own fortunes while inveighing against those who had caused him to lose both.

But events were moving quickly and against him. The people of France and the army especially were exhausted. Their loyalty to what now seemed to many to be Napoleon's factitious empire was all but worn out. 'The need for rest,' Caulaincourt wrote, 'was so universally felt through every class of society, and in the army, that peace at any price had become the ruling passion of the day.' Napoleon himself was the butt of all resentment, and even his marshals realised that the army they had served was disintegrating and that their careers and even their lives might soon be in peril. The victorious Allies in the meantime were resolute in their determination to remove Napoleon utterly from the scene of European politics. 'Our objective is to make sure that our children have years of peace and that the world has some repose,' declared General Schwarzenberg, voicing the opinion of many on both sides. 'The Emperor Napoleon had shown all too plainly of late that he desires neither of these things,' Schwarzenberg continued, adding, 'with him, there is no security for Europe.'

The politicians knew this quite as well as the soldiers and realised, like them, that their careers and their lives might also be in danger. Talleyrand had long determined on the restoration of the Bourbons, but the Bourbons were not widely popular. It had taken a revolution to remove them, and twenty-five years of exile had endeared them to few other than die-hard royalists. What Talleyrand wanted was a constitutional monarchy which might satisfy most of the people while assuring his own continuing power and influence. These last were now exercised as he set about getting his way. The Senate was summoned and was persuaded to sign a resolution blaming Napoleon for the devastated state of *la patrie*. The Emperor was personally responsible for all its woes and the Senate declared him removed from his throne. The King of Rome would not be permitted to succeed him (such a move, Talleyrand assured them, would put Napoleon back in power within months) and Louis XVIII would be asked to reign as a constitutional monarch. Most subtly of all, Talleyrand persuaded the Senate to free the army from its oaths of allegiance. Men of every rank could now in good conscience change sides and, rather than marching with their sometime ruler, could prosper under the restored regime. There was even talk of disguising some thugs as cavalry officers and sending them off to assassinate Napoleon. If Talleyrand toyed with this idea it came to nothing, and it was altogether more satisfying to watch Napoleon's leading generals waver and then come over to his side as he sent letters urging them to avoid fomenting the horrors of civil war.

War meanwhile – and the recapture of Paris in particular – was the one fixed point in Napoleon's widely fluctuating moods. He reviewed the Guards in the great courtyard at Fontainebleau and encouraged by their shouting 'To Paris! To Paris!' went off to draft a plan of attack with the strains of the *Marseillaise* ringing in his ears. The hopelessness of his fantasies never occurred to him. He believed he could move the world by the resolve of his own will. He had done it before and he would do it again. He told the bewildered marshals gathered about him: 'We will save France, redeem our honour and then I will accept a moderate peace.' It was in vain he was told that the state of his troops was so poor that any attempt to regain Paris might well result in that city suffering the same fate as Moscow. 'A last effort,' Napoleon insisted, 'and then we can all relax after twenty-five years of struggle.' But that last effort could not be made. His troops were fast melting away. Tsar Alexander had declared that the only thing Napoleon could do was surrender unconditionally. If he abdicated then there might yet be some discussion as to his personal future. Napoleon hesitated and, fearing to fall into the hands of the Allies, lost more of his supporters until he was obliged in the end to depend on the mercies of those who had defeated him. There would be no assault on Paris but, Napoleon warned, there would be no peace for those who had made it impossible either. They would lie uneasily on their feather beds, a prey to constant fears of enemy attack. But this was the ranting of a cornered bully and decisions were now in other hands.

There were those who were determined to make their mark with the new powers, even at the cost of the most conspicuous disloyalty to their old cause. Marshal Ney, 'the bravest of the brave', was one such. He had criticised Napoleon more outspokenly than any of his peers and was now determined to profit from being on the right side. He went to Fontainebleau and roundly told his former master that there was no hope for him. Napoleon would have to abdicate unconditionally. Ney even wrote to Talleyrand assuring him of his success. He thought that very soon he would himself be returning to Paris with the tyrant's letter of abdication in his hand. The Allies would then be able to set about winding up the Bonaparte dynasty for good. The Allies themselves in the meantime squabbled about where Napoleon should be sent. It was, wrote one British diplomat, 'somewhat theatrical generosity' on the part of the Tsar that Elba was determined on. The Allies were aware of the dangers, aware of the island's proximity to the European mainland and wondered 'whether Napoleon may not bring the powder to the iron mines of Elba'. They would have to hope he would not. Talleyrand certainly disapproved of the choice and so did the British, but the Tsar had pledged his word and the situation was an extremely delicate one. Too great a humiliation of Napoleon was still unwise. Sending him to Elba, for all that it failed to make adequate provision against his possible return to France, seemed the only way to end matters diplomatically. It was hoped that there would be peace and, for Napoleon himself, some very small measure of honour.

The Treaty of Fontainebleau set out what were believed to be the precise terms for Napoleon's future. In return for his unconditional abdication, he and his family would retain their titles, pensions and possessions. Napoleon would have 'full sovereignty and property' over the island of Elba. He would be given help to fight off the Barbary pirates who regularly made life such a misery there. He would have a naval corvette at his beck and call and be allowed 400 hand-picked men from the Imperial Guard to defend his kingdom when necessary and march about in rather silly little displays when it was not. Napoleon would also have a pension of two million francs a year from the French government. None of this was ungenerous and it could perhaps be hoped that Napoleon would live out the rest of his days as the toy ruler of a petty island. What was not clear, however, was whether he would be able to have his wife with him. What was a suitable position for the daughter of the Emperor of Austria now that her husband was defeated? It was a question that would take a long time to settle.

In the meantime it seemed that the man at the centre of these enormous issues was dying. Spasms and brief moments of calm alternated with violent retching while, all the time, Napoleon sweated profusely. Caulaincourt was barely inside the bedroom before he realised the gravity of the situation and sent for Dr Yvan. Could it really be suicide? His master had often spoken forcibly against it, dismissed it as a coward's trick, but now he listened to his muttered fears about his disgrace and how he feared he would never reach Elba alive. 'Soon I shall be no more,' Napoleon muttered ominously. Caulaincourt was made to promise to send his last wishes to Marie-Louise and his blessings to their son. The arrival of Dr Yvan confirmed Caulaincourt's worst fears. Napoleon begged him to mix up a draught strong enough to bring his sufferings to an immediate end. The good doctor was appalled. He was no assassin, he blurted out as he dashed from the room and made for Paris. Caulaincourt was once again alone with his master. Only the gradual increase of Napoleon's railing against the monarchs, friends and family who had misunderstood and deserted him convinced him that there was hope. Napoleon was recovering his strength. The poison was not strong enough to kill, and with returning strength came returning confidence. 'I shall live,' Napoleon declared, 'since death is no more willing to take me on my bed than on the battlefield.' Now, as daylight flooded the room, he wrote his name boldly across the treaty confining him to Elba. As the morning wore on he began to talk of the arrangements for his journey there.

## The Journey to Elba

These arrangements, like everything else, had been decided by the Allies.[2] Each of the major powers was to provide the exiled Emperor with an escort. The Russians sent General Shuvalov, the Austrians General Köller, and the Prussians Count Truchess-Waldbourg. Castlereagh picked the British escort with particular care. His name was Colonel Neil Campbell, a mature and handsome man of thirty-eight with dashing whiskers who had enjoyed a good if not outstanding career in the army and was currently a military attaché to the Tsar. Campbell was not abashed by royalty, having met the crowned heads of Sweden and Prussia along with a host of the minor princes gathered in Paris. He had even glimpsed Napoleon at the Battle of Bautzen. He had fought too in the battles the Allies waged as they moved in to surround Napoleon and, at Fère-Champenoise, Campbell had been mistaken for a Frenchman and seriously wounded by the lances and sabres of the Russian hussars. Now, as he made his way to Fontainebleau, his arm was still in a sling and his left eye covered by a bandage. His convalescence meant that he knew little more of what was going on than could be gleaned from the newspapers, but he had found Castlereagh's offer for him to escort 'the late chief of the French government' something that provided 'so many points of interest' – Campbell was a dry Scot – that he could not turn it down.

In fact his role was to be far more than ceremonial, a mere token presence. In public Campbell was to preserve, Castlereagh informed him, the highest standards of courtesy towards Napoleon and to call on 'any of His Majesty's officers by land or sea' should their help be necessary. Once a British ship had transported its passenger to Elba, Campbell was also to consider that 'the presence of a British officer can be of use in protecting the island or his person against insult and attack'. In other words the French-speaking Campbell was to be the British government's confidential agent whose care for Napoleon's well-being was also their means for watching his every move and ensuring that he was neither rescued nor tried to escape from Elba and cross the Mediterranean where the Royal Navy was constantly on patrol. It was a very British solution and it famously didn't work.

Campbell arrived at Fontainebleau to find Napoleon in a state of high anxiety. For days now he had been in the most perturbed state of mind, rubbing his forehead with his hands, stuffing his fingers in his mouth and chewing his knuckles raw. He was, Campbell noted, like a caged beast. He was unshaven, he had not combed his hair and there were thick traces of snuff scattered over the breast of his uniform. The man who had waged war against Europe was genuinely frightened at the thought of being captured by the pirates that infested the seas off Elba and was secretly scared of being assassinated by royalist thugs on his way there. One of the Frenchmen who was to accompany him, Henri Bertrand, the fussy manager of the imperial household, had clearly caught the mood. Did they really have to go to so ghastly a place as Elba he asked Campbell. It was so ill-provided, so uncomfortable, so uncouth. It was also dangerous. If they really had to go wouldn't Campbell please go with them as a warranty of British protection?

So far, things were going well. They appeared to get even better as the wet-eyed Napoleon paid tribute to British achievements and to Wellington in particular. He was 'a man of energy in war', he declared, but then 'yours is the greatest of all nations'. He himself was no longer Britain's greatest enemy, he opined. And could they have a British frigate to sail with the promised French corvette? It was all rather grating and besides there were those in France who were still devoted to Napoleon. Their numbers were small but the danger they posed was considerable. General Cambronne had already marched off to prepare for Napoleon's arrival in Elba with 600 volunteers from the Imperial Guard. This was 200 more than was allowed. Meanwhile, in the forests around Fontainebleau, there lurked several thousand more loyal troops who might act desperately of their own accord or even be led away by Napoleon himself if he escaped the ministrations of Campbell and his fellow escorts. And there was, besides, the famous and dangerous Napoleonic charm that might yet be exercised to gull those charged with watching him.

They needed to move quickly if they were to avoid these dangers. In the meantime, Napoleon's anxieties apparently became ever worse. Every rumour seemed to frighten him. Every old associate was an enemy. Apparently it was being said in Paris that Fouché, the erstwhile police chief Napoleon had eventually sacked, was saying that Elba was no place to send such a man. It was far too close to Europe and far too easy to escape from. He was whispering, apparently, about Siberia. The region later infamous as the Gulag was the place for Napoleon. And what about royalist assassins? Louis Bourrienne, Napoleon's old school friend and disgraced erstwhile secretary, had held a meeting of the men who ran the post stops along the chosen route south. Perhaps they had been briefed to assassinate him. Perhaps there would be violence in the Midi. The route would have to be changed. When Caulaincourt went to discuss the matter with the Allied chiefs in Paris their exasperation was evident. They had far more important things to worry about and only rather wearily agreed to Napoleon taking a more westerly route than originally planned, a route that would take him by the 600 Imperial Guard who were waiting to see him pass, and then close to other French units in the Loire and near Lyons.

By the time they set off in the wet dreariness of dawn on 20 April 1814, everybody's patience was frayed. At the last moment Napoleon made things worse by saying that he was not even sure he was going. There were too many matters still unresolved, too many insults to his reputation still unappeased, too many dangers. His private funds had been seized. French army stores on Elba had been cleared so it seemed he would be unable to protect himself once there. And still there was the question of his wife and son. Would they be joining him? Napoleon had written to them earlier telling Marie-Louise that she could always count on 'the courage, the composure and the kindness of your husband' and then adding 'a kiss for the little king'. Now it seemed all he might have of them was his memories and the little travelling portrait of mother and child painted for him by Isabey. His moods alternated between anger and whining. He launched a tirade at Köller, the Austrian escort, and pleaded with Campbell to be allowed into exile in Britain. Campbell made a suitably obtuse reply to this last request and Napoleon, seemingly reassured, went down to the courtyard where grenadiers from the Old Guard were standing to attention.

Napoleon addressed them in a manner that had become second nature to him and in words which he probably believed were true. They could have won their last campaign, he said, but at far too great a cost. That above all was what he had wanted to avoid and now he would bare the cost himself. The twin themes of *la patrie* and *la gloire* were sounded again. 'I have sacrificed all my rights,' Napoleon declared, 'and am ready to sacrifice myself, for all my life has been devoted to the happiness and glory of France.' It was stirring stuff and there was more to come. 'Bring me the eagles which have led us through so many perils and so many glorious days.' His command was followed, and as the birds of war and empire perched before him seemingly for the last time so Napoleon lifted the silk square hung below one of them and, for a full minute, buried his face among the names of battles embroidered in gold upon it. Tears had begun to trickle down the faces of the Old Guard and now, as he bade them farewell, many were openly sobbing.

A little before two, the equipage pulled out of the gates of Fontainebleau. The procession was relatively modest even for a defeated emperor. A troop of cavalry was followed by the carriage containing those officers who had volunteered to accompany Napoleon to Elba. There was the coach in which Napoleon himself and Bertrand were to sleep. This was followed by fifty more cavalry, a carriage for each of the Allied commissioners and nine more for the household Napoleon was taking with him. The men of the Old Guard watched it roll out of sight and then, in a final ritual of brotherhood, burned their flags and divided the ashes among themselves.

The equipage covered a great distance in the first day and, when it was at an end, it seemed that all the crowds had shouted '*Vive l'Empereur!*' Napoleon was briefly elated by the magic he believed still clung to his name. Indeed, so intoxicated was he that the following day he airily waved away the detachment of Austrian soldiers waiting to accompany him, saying that he didn't need foreign protection to ride through France. But if he thought that he still embodied the aspirations of the people and their revolution events were quickly to prove him wrong. Arriving at Moulins, a large crowd swarmed about the equipage shouting, '*Vive le Roi!*' They sported the white cockades of the Bourbons. Here were the people of the French countryside whose families, fields and petty fortunes had been ransacked for Napoleon's wars. Now they were expressing their true feelings. Napoleon, who hated and was even afraid of unruly civilian crowds, ordered the equipage forward, refused to stop for dinner and hurried on his journey until after midnight. What he thought of as the treachery of the people made him think once again of his own safety and he insisted that Campbell ensure that he be transported to Elba in a British man-of-war. He felt more secure with his enemies than with his erstwhile subjects. It was a feeling that was to return. Even now Napoleon ordered the procession to move on with the utmost speed. Those who were riding in carriages were to sleep in them.

But it was not only the ordinary people of France who were showing how they had turned against Napoleon. His marshals had too. At Valence he met the foul-mouthed Augereau coming with his men in the opposite direction. Here was the man who, in the high and palmy days of the first Italian campaign, Napoleon had ordered back to a turbulent Paris where he had surrounded the Tuileries and reduced the enfeebled Directory to a rump subject to the brilliant young general fighting his victorious way through Europe. Now Augereau had issued a proclamation to his men denouncing Napoleon as a tyrant 'who after sacrificing millions to his cruel ambition had not the heart to die like a soldier'. There were many civilians who agreed with such sentiments and some soldiers – but not all. Large parts of the army had an atavistic attachment to the man who had for so long personified all their deep, uncritical feelings about the glory of their homeland. Still they cheered Napoleon. Still they pressed as close to him as they could. 'If you had 20,000 men like me,' declared one cavalryman, 'we would release you and set you at our head again.' Such an unforced statement could make a very deep impression, and the voice of the army was the voice Napoleon knew best.

It would echo in his head as much louder noises surrounded him. The people of Provence, whipped up to a fury by their royalist leaders, were summoned out to bray at him. The citizens of Avignon waited all night for his carriage to appear. No efforts of the mayor could quiet them nor could the local militia stop them throwing stones. Their leader, Colonel Mollot, came up to Napoleon's coach waving his sword. A groom threatened the colonel with his pistol, while the quick-witted coachman whipped his horses in order to drive Napoleon at full speed round the walls of the town. It was frightening, but more painful humiliations were to come. Outside Orgon, Napoleon saw a makeshift gallows with his own image dangling from it. It was smeared with blood and bore a placard that read 'Sooner or later this will be the Tyrant's fate!' Even the Russian General Shuvalov was moved to indignation, shouting to the crowd: 'Leave him alone. Look at him, and realise that contempt is the only weapon to use against a man who's no longer any danger.'

The terror inspired in Napoleon by such displays brought him near to abject humiliation. He could face no more. He resolved to disguise himself as a humble courier and, dressed in a blue coat with the Bourbons' white cockade in his hat, he and a groom rode pell-mell through the rising mistral, stopping only when they reached La Calade. There, at a roadside inn, the landlady began viciously to denounce Napoleon and all his works. She had lost her son and nephew in his wars and, unaware of whom she was addressing, let her anger pour out. 'I think the people will murder him,' she said, 'and in my book the bastard deserves it.' The rest of Napoleon's procession, when they caught up with him, found him with his head in his hands and crying his eyes out. He would not eat. The food might be poisoned. Every noise frightened him. The fact that there was an iron grille over the window made him blanch.

The servants made him tremble, and his voice was hoarse and broken when he begged to be allowed to take another, safer route to the coast. This was refused and Napoleon left the inn at midnight dressed in a motley collection of bits of Austrian, Russian and Prussian uniform – a scarecrow image of the armies who had defeated him.

Napoleon had arranged to meet his sister, the glamorous and feckless Pauline Borghese, at a farmhouse near Le Luc. He was disappointed to find her too ill to travel with him to Elba but was encouraged by her promise that she would come later and by the thought that she was both loyal to him and well placed to communicate with their brother-in-law, Murat the King of Naples. One never knew. What had the soldier said? Twenty thousand like him and Napoleon would be returned to his throne. But such fantasies were for the moment swept aside by the altogether harsher demands of the journey before him. With a self-lacerating sense of symmetry Napoleon begged to be allowed to make a small change of route and make for Fréjus. There he had spent the night when he came careering back from Egypt. From there he had set out the following morning on the road that took him to the Consulship and the Empire. Here, too, he would spend his last night on French soil. This was allowed, and Campbell ordered Captain Ussher to sail the frigate *Undaunted* across to nearby Saint Raphael from where they would depart the following morning. Still deeply concerned about his own safety, Napoleon opted to sail on the British ship rather than on one of the two French vessels that accompanied it. This too was allowed, as was the twenty-one-gun salute Napoleon required to be fired in tribute to his status as 'Emperor and Sovereign of the Island of Elba'.

It seemed that the Emperor might indeed now leave for his new, minuscule empire. He had already written a letter asking that his subjects be told he had chosen their island as his home 'on account of their pleasant manners and the excellence of their climate'. He had also made it clear that he wanted the French munitions on the island to remain where they were. At eight the following evening the party was ready to leave. The angry crowds in the streets still agitated Napoleon. They were, he told Ussher, a weathercock. His mistrust of them was such, as several British officers noted, that he had preferred to vest his safety in the Royal Navy rather than a French ship. Now, with the moon shining brightly down on the town and the hussars marshalled around Ussher's barge drawn up on the beach, Napoleon felt the feint, balmy sea-breeze on his face. He boarded the waiting barge and British sailors rowed him steadily across to the *Undaunted*. In the first light of dawn other sailors began to fire the twenty-one-gun salute.

Once aboard the *Undaunted*, Napoleon was treated with the utmost courtesy by the officers if not by the weather. The crossing, which should normally have taken two days, lasted for nearly 120 often storm-tossed hours. The effect seemed to raise Napoleon's spirits. With Campbell's help he chatted with the men. Feeling safe at last, Napoleon was in a mood to talk. Ussher in particular listened to him with polite wariness. What did Napoleon mean, he wondered, by saying that if the British imposed a commercially punitive peace on France then 'the Bourbons will be driven out in six months'? It was a deeply suspicious comment and Ussher considered it was his duty to report such remarks to his senior officers. Campbell was even more concerned. He believed that Napoleon was not always in command of his tongue when in an unbuttoned mood, 'and although at Fontainebleau he expressed his desire to pass the remainder of his life at Elba in studying the arts and sciences, he has given frequent proof of the restlessness of his disposition, and his expectation of opportunities arising which will give scope to the exercise of it in France'. For the moment this seemed little more than dangerous fantasy. 'He persuades himself,' Campbell continued, 'that the greater part of the population in France is favourable to him, excepting in the neighbourhood of the coast.' Such heroic delusion was dangerous all the same and needed to be watched. Now, however, as the Bourbon flag flew over Elba and the *Undaunted* sailed into Portoferraio, it seemed that the newly restored regime was safe.

## The Bourbons Return

On the very day that Napoleon disembarked on Elba, Louis XVIII entered his capital in a state coach powdered with heraldic Bourbon lilies. It had not been easy to get him so far. A severe attack of gout had held the King up for several days in his English exile at Hartwell, and it was only on 24 April that Talleyrand met him at Compiègne. The enormously large man for whom Talleyrand had plotted and connived for the greater good of France was, at fifty-eight, as orotund in his speech as he was in his body. 'I am pleased to see you,' Louis said to Talleyrand. 'Our houses date from the same epoch. My ancestors were the cleverer; had yours been, you would say to me today: "Take a chair, draw it up, let us talk of our affairs." Today it is I who say to you: "Be seated, let us converse."' Thus the public tone of the man who was secretly determined that Talleyrand himself should have as little as possible to do with the government of France. After their first encounter the King and the diplomat continued their way south and Louis, having been presented to the Senate at Saint-Ouen, made his way to his capital. He did so amid crowds who for the most part had never seen him before and were unfamiliar with the reality of hereditary monarchs. When he arrived in Paris, the choir in Notre-Dame dutifully struck up the *Te Deum* but, as Metternich recalled, the thousands gathered outside were not of one voice, divided as they were between those who shouted '*Vive le Roi!*' and those who looked on in sullen silence.

The French who most enthusiastically supported Louis formed the small, mutually suspicious group of the powerful. Napoleon's marshals had defected to the Bourbons almost to a man. The hereditary aristocracy also believed their royalist dreams were being realised. Women like the formidable Duchesse d'Angoulême were haunted by the guillotined ghosts of their parents and saw blood dripping from the hands of anyone who had served the republic or Napoleon. Now their nightmares might be less frequent. Aristocratic menfolk in the meantime could gather together as the Chevaliers de La Foix and raise their royalist enthusiasms with a mystic cocktail of extreme Catholic sentiment and medieval imaginings. The unlikely Charlemagne who was the focus of their hopes was not, however, a figure to inspire. Those who talked to Louis as he was moved around the Tuileries in a wheelchair found him sometimes witty, occasionally wise and invariably frightened of hard work, debate or making decisions. 'Do attend to it, please,' was his favourite request to his aides, men of such diverse opinions that, in Wellington's phrase, there were ministers in Paris but no ministry.[3]

It was on such a foundation that Louis exercised the rights given him by the newly drafted constitution. He was to be the sole initiator of legislation, the one man who could appoint or sack ministers and the single figure who could supposedly control the army and the judiciary. Louis also had the right to appoint an unlimited number of life members to the Chamber of Peers and, while the Chamber of Deputies had to approve fiscal legislation, the right to vote for the men who made it up was severely restricted by royal prerogative to about one in 300 of the richer members of the population. The Deputies themselves had to be substantial figures and over forty years old but, even so, they were not to prove agreeable to Bourbon taste. They soon acquired the unfortunate habit of expressing their opinions. They drew public attention to matters others thought were best hidden inside their own beautiful ormolu desks. The Deputies urged the freedom of the press, for example, but a monarch who had suppressed that liberty felt he could easily do without their advice and, at the close of the year, the Chamber of Deputies was prorogued for four months.

If Louis had alienated the political nation he also succeeded in losing his support among significant numbers of the rest of the population. His natural adherents among the old aristocracy were bitter when the bizarre processions of their perruqued and powdered country cousins came to the Tuileries, petitioned for the return of their lands and were told they could not have back what had already been sold. They began to mutter among themselves that a king restored by charter and functioning (in so far as he functioned at all) through an administration stocked with liberals and sometime Bonapartists was really no king at all. The bourgeoisie, who by and large had done well under the empire, were doubtful of Louis's staying power, suspicious of his cronies and more than a little angry when they heard that at a grand dinner in the Hôtel de Ville the municipal representatives of Paris had had the honour to serve the King and his family with napkins over their arms for all the world as if they were waiters. Such matters were made worse by the ruinous state of the country's economy. Napoleon's wars of 1812 and the disastrous defensive campaigns of the following years had been cripplingly expensive. The national debt was astronomical. Economies had to be made and these, of course, fell hardest on the poor. Parisian labourers waiting hopelessly for work on the Quai de Gesvres muttered menacingly against the Bourbons. Out in the countryside their brothers feared the reimposition of feudal dues on their ravaged farms and livelihoods.

King Louis's contribution to the crisis was the mean-minded folly of refusing to pay Napoleon his pension, something particularly disastrous in the light of the fact that heavy cuts also had to be made to the army Napoleon had raised and which still contained many men who were loyal to him. The standing army of half a million was more than halved and a horde of unemployed soldiers and some 12,000 out of work officers were a grave threat in a country already badly run down. Neither those men still serving nor those thrown back on their own resources could root their loyalties among the Bourbon lilies. Louis XVIII personified their ignominy: the collapse of the empire, the victory of foreigners, the throwing down of their idol, the humiliation of their country, the corroding of its glory.

Louis was, besides, a ridiculous figure to a military man. 'That's a fine king who needs to be carried by six porters!' was one of the more repeatable jibes levelled at a man too gross to ride a horse and too pusillanimous to command a regiment. Those who wore his white cockade all too often carried a tricoloured one in their knapsacks. When their disaffection was joined to that of those civilians who secreted portraits of Napoleon into their bonbonnières the position was grave indeed. So much was becoming obvious. 'The Parisians love for their King,' wrote one young observer, 'has so died down that barely a spark remains.' The restoration of the Bourbons could seem tenuous at best.

## The Emperor of Elba

While Louis XVIII believed he was settling into his new kingdom in France, Napoleon was trying to do the same on Elba.[4] Before his arrival he had learned from his reading what he might expect to find there. It was not encouraging. The traveller Thiébaut de Berneaud described how the Elban mountains 'present only a mass of arid hills which fatigue the senses and impart sensations of sorrow to the soul'. Rough and badly maintained roads wound their way through them and goats grazed between the brightly flowering shrubs. Many of the cottages were deserted ruins, the hamlets were wretched, and Portoferraio, the capital, was a rundown and disease-ridden little Mediterranean port that could boast only one insanitary inn. The entire island was a mere sixteen miles long and rarely more than seven in width. 'Well,' Napoleon declared ruefully a week after his arrival, 'it's certainly a very small island.'

His arrival had not been without incident. The 12,000 or so inhabitants – tough, illiterate and poor people for the most part – had for centuries been the victims of a savage history of invasion, and the appearance of Napoleon seemed only one more example of this. Many did not want him there at all. A matter of days before he set foot on Elba they had risen in half-hearted rebellion against the French, sought British protection, and would have got it by a ruse had not General Dalesme, the commanding officer, seen through the plan. Now Dalesme discovered that the island he guarded would be subject to the Bourbons until the formalities of handing over were complete and the people would once again be ruled by Napoleon. It was all like some frightful and confusing dream.

Preparations had nonetheless to be made for the realities of waking life. When Napoleon's letter of accession had been read to the local dignitaries aboard the *Undaunted* and their new ruler had promised 'to consecrate himself to the welfare of the Elbans', the men hurried back to the island to ready a welcome. The local people, with the cunning of peasant farmers and the encouragement of their vicar-general, rapidly sank their political hostility in hopes of the new wealth that would surely come to them with Napoleon's arrival. The Mayor of Portoferraio, in the meantime, borrowed furniture to make the upper rooms of the town hall into a suitable lodging for the new Emperor and, while sending out men to ensure crowds for the following day, gave orders for the construction of a dais covered in gold paper on which an old sofa would serve as a temporary throne. The following day the crowds gathered, the guns fired their salutes, the Mayor of Portoferraio stepped forward to present the town keys (actually the keys to his own cellar that had been painted with gold overnight since there were no others to be had) and then, in an access of stage fright, forgot his speech of welcome. The party moved on to the local church, decorated as if for a saint's day, and then on once more to Napoleon's hurriedly furnished apartments in the town hall where, from his sofa, he held his first reception with all the dignity he had once mustered in the Tuileries. When it was over he retired to his private rooms and began to realise what daily life on Elba might mean. His lodgings were small and there rose up through their windows the raucous sound of the celebrating citizens mingled with the putrid odour of their filthy gutters.

Reforms and modernisation were clearly essential, and the following days saw Napoleon swept up in what Campbell called 'perpetual motion'. His old energy was returning. He exhausted everyone around him as he examined the island's defences, which thankfully were adequate against the threat of pirates, and then looked for a house. He eventually settled on I Mulini, which was named after the windmills that had once stood by it. He visited the iron works which, along with the tuna fisheries and the salt pans, provided the exports that helped Elba's precarious balance of payments. Napoleon so charmed and impressed Pons de l'Hérault, the manager of the mines, that the man rapidly agreed to enter Napoleon's service and divert the profits of the business from the pension fund of the Legion of Honour which they had once fed to the Emperor's own use. Having settled that important matter, Napoleon then ordered that his new imperial flag – white with a red diagonal on which were imposed three golden bees – be hoisted in every village to symbolise his rule. This would be celebrated with a public holiday. He then wrote to his wife. He was he told her in the pink of health. 'What I want is news of you, and to know that you are well, for I have heard nothing since your courier reached me at Fréjus. Goodbye, my dear. Give a kiss to my son.' But the observant Campbell detected beneath this calm if busy surface the workings of discontent and even ambition. He was suspicious and he remained on his guard.

And still Napoleon's planning for both Elba and his own exiled way of life went on. The builders were instructed to improve I Mulini 'at the least possible expense', and Napoleon furnished the house from his sister's palace at Piombino by requisitioning such items as the faded drapes and hangings his agents found there. Napoleon himself lived on the ground floor of I Mulini in a suite of rooms that included a bedroom, where for many weeks he slept on his camp bed, a study and a library where he kept books brought from Fontainebleau and elsewhere. These included sets of classic French authors, scientific, military and historical works and a

1. Napoleon at the Bridge of Arcola

2. Napoleon as First Consul

3. Napoleon as Emperor

4. Napoleon in his study

5. Napoleon on the battlefield of Eylau

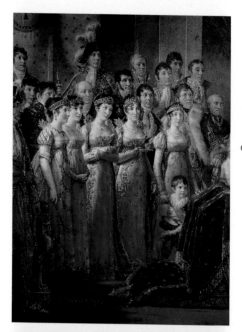

6. Bonaparte family and Court at the Coronation

7. Coronation of Josephine

8. Countess Marie
   Walewska

9. Marie-Louise
   and the King of
   Rome

10. Talleyrand

11. Fouché

12. Louis XVIII

13. Marshal Ney

14. Alexander I

15. Field Marshal Blücher

16. Duke of Wellington

collection of fairy stories in no less than forty volumes. A large room divided from the rest of the house by a moveable partition could be used for concerts and for dinner parties, though the fact that these last were attended by such modest people as the seamstress who repaired his uniform suggested to Campbell at least the 'ridiculous nature' of the exiled Emperor's ambitions.

The house was overstaffed with men sometimes less than qualified for the tasks they were supposed to perform, and a number of them, such as Captain Deschamps, one of Napoleon's grooms of the bedchamber, were rough if affable men hardly suited to a courtier's life. Of the four chamberlains, three were Elbans of little personal quality, despite their claims to gentility, who were nonetheless appointed to the Council of State along with various other notables of equal indistinction. It was all rather factitious and rather sad, but it seemed to impress the people of the island, who believed that extraordinary advantages would soon accrue to them. Certainly, Napoleon's plans for their welfare were ambitious. The little nearby island of Pianosa, for example, would be brought back to life, to profit and to serving the general security of the state by no longer being an area for wild horses but a place where the peasants would till the soil and the fishermen land their catches under the protective gaze of soldiers manning it as defensive outpost. The forests on the main island were to be better attended to, and a proper survey would reveal more ground suitable for growing the wheat which the islanders currently imported in uneconomic quantities. An engineer would see to the repair of the roads and modernise matters at the salt pans. Mulberry trees would be planted, rainwater conserved and the stinking gutters of Portoferraio cleansed. To some like Pons de l'Hérault such projects 'directed to the greater Dignity of Man, displayed in a radiant light the supreme creative power of genius'.

There were also the necessary defences to be looked to. Napoleon's Elban navy, constantly undermanned as it was, consisted of the 300-ton *Inconstant* with its sixteen guns and requirement of about 100 men. In addition, Napoleon himself bought the fast little three-masted *Etoile*, and there were also the twenty-six-ton *Caroline*, a couple of feluccas and three small vessels with oars. But the army, as ever, was of altogether greater interest to him. Napoleon's band of volunteers from the Old Guard had marched swiftly south with an unabashed display of their tricolours, passing through towns and over mountain passes with his baggage wagons. At midnight on 25 May he could just see through Ussher's telescope the ships that were now bringing them to Elba. Their disembarkation was a moment of high emotion on both sides. 'I have passed many bad hours waiting for you,' Napoleon declared as the soldiers landed, 'but at last we are reunited and they are forgotten.' Many of the soldiers themselves were weeping, and it was with intense feelings that they marched forward with their beating drums to their billets in the monastery of San Francesco and elsewhere.

Campbell looked on with particular interest and wrote to the Foreign Secretary asking for instructions. 'I am to desire that you will continue to consider yourself a British resident in Elba,' Castlereagh replied, 'without assuming any further official character than that in which you are already received.' It was an invidious position for Campbell to be at once an unofficial protector and an unofficial spy. Worse, the task promised to drag out endlessly. Nor was the position of the man he was observing any more comfortable. The changes Napoleon was putting in place were expensive and the cost of maintaining his army was high. He had a reserve of four million francs. He had his revenues from the underdeveloped Elban economy, and he had – he hoped – the pension promised him by the Bourbon government. Without this last matters would be impossible for him, and even now the efficiency with which he taxed the people of Elba was causing growing resentment. Campbell feared an uprising but Napoleon had other things on his mind. On the feast of San Cristino, the patron saint of Portoferraio, he attended a mass designed to celebrate his assumption to the imperial throne of Elba. It was a very modest affair compared to the great occasion in Notre-Dame when he had placed the imperial diadems on his own and Josephine's heads. She had written to him recently – a still loving if divorced wife who even offered to join him in his exile, and she extended her sympathies to him in deep, heartfelt phrases. Now, however, even as Napoleon was sitting through the mass, Josephine lay dying in her gilded swan bed at Malmaison – a victim of diphtheria.

## Josephine

Memories of Josephine were woven tightly around memories of the empire Napoleon had lost. Their courtship, their marriage, their assumption of the imperial crown, their divorce were all part of the nation's history. To think of Josephine was to think of France and of all Napoleon himself had apparently now to forego. It was to think too of his own youth. The couple had first met at a time of high national peril in which Napoleon, as a graduate of the *École militaire* in Paris, played a significant part. At first there was still something of the youthful gaucheries of the cadet about him which Josephine claimed she found mildly intriguing. Napoleon had entered the military academy as a King's scholar and left it a confirmed revolutionary, albeit of a particular cast attractive to Josephine's circle. He had not been popular at the school. His fellow students found him moody, arrogant, violent and a lone wolf, critical of the system and much given to solitary walking 'at a rapid pace . . . his arms crossed, his head lowered'. These traits were still evident when he found his way to Josephine's salon, and she would describe 'her funny little Corsican' to her sophisticated friends as '*drôle*'.

Napoleon had come thus far in Parisian political and social circles not because of his polish but because of his drive. For all he had passed out of the military school an undistinguished forty-second out of fifty-eight candidates, his examiners shrewdly recognised his qualities. They too found him reserved and studious but added that he was also 'capricious, arrogant, extremely inclined to egoism, speaking little, spirited in his answers, quick and harsh in his replies, having much pride and boundless ambition'. They added that 'this young man deserves to be encouraged'. Napoleon was commissioned in the elite *Régiment de la Fère* and, during his generous periods of leave when he was expected to be courting a future wife, schooled himself in hard work. The autobiographical hero of a novella he wrote after the break-up of his sentimental affair with Eugenie Désirée Clary is described as having 'thought out the principles of the military art at a time when those of his age were running after girls'. The same was true of Napoleon, and the young officer's self-imposed regime was Spartan in the extreme. Napoleon went to bed at ten, rose at four, ate modestly and devoured works on tactics, history and classical and modern philosophy, filling thirty-six notebooks with his observations. By such means he remained largely ignorant of women while fashioning a well-informed image of military glory and a political philosophy that disdained wholesale democracy and revelled in the principles of a rational system of government that would open up huge possibilities to men of real talent.

The outbreak of the Revolution saw Napoleon in Auxonne, suppressing food riots and developing his fear and loathing of undisciplined crowds. The same period saw Josephine in mortal danger. She was a seductive Creole of French parents who, at sixteen, had married the Vicomte de Beauharnais, been deserted by him, reconciled to him, shared his imprisonment during the Terror and barely escaped his fate on the guillotine. Now she was living on her wits and her lovers in a Paris where a still desperately poor Napoleon had had his political prejudices confirmed when he witnessed the people's second storming of the Tuileries. Eight hundred lay dead or dying in a lake of blood while the market women committed obscenities on the corpses of the Swiss Guard. Turning to his friend Bourrienne, who was later to be his secretary,

Napoleon asked: 'Why have they let in all this rabble? They should sweep off four or five hundred with the cannon and the rest would set off fast enough.' In the voice of the youth spoke the man.

Events and his own abilities were now to propel Napoleon towards Josephine and her circle. Bored with imposing French rule in Corsica, he wanted to join the French army in Italy. While on his way he passed close to Toulon where the workers in the important naval base had rebelled against Paris and the revolutionary regime and allowed British and Spanish ships into the port. Napoleon shrewdly used such contacts as he had to win his first taste of *la gloire*. He was given command of the artillery, drew up a plan and, after a four-month siege, gained control of the harbour and forced the enemy fleets to evacuate. It was an operation that showed not just his daring originality and concentration on the matter in hand, but his utter command of logistics and his exceptional ability to inspire loyalty in otherwise disillusioned troops. Promotion, helped by his writing a pro-Jacobin pamphlet, swiftly followed. The circle round the dreadful Robespierre's brother welcomed the new brigadier-general and the dangerous hand of the powerful Barras was extended to him, ushering him by day towards the office where Napoleon was to plan the operations of the Army of Italy and later by night towards the luxurious mansion where he would meet Barras's mistress, the alluring Josephine.

This last invitation was won by an event that transformed Napoleon's life. Barras, the newly appointed President of the Directory, faced the first of that feeble government's crises when 25,000 of the National Guard poured onto the streets of Paris vowing to bring the assembly down. Barras called desperately for loyal republican officers, and Napoleon – 'his puny figure and statuesque face, his untidy dress, his long lank hair and his worn-out clothes' still betraying his poverty – appeared in Barras's office and at once threw himself into action with all the ruthless efficiency of which he was already master. He made the chance appearance of the young Joachim Murat the key to his success, ordering him to go and seize the cannon in the Sablons military camp. The tactic others had failed to put in operation when the mob stormed the Tuileries was now Napoleon's own. As the bedraggled National Guard was eventually urged to march on the Rue Honoré, Napoleon opened fire and, with what he was pleased to call 'a whiff of grapeshot', slaughtered swathes of the advancing men and stupefied the rest who were left to the mercies to Murat's cavalry. By destroying Frenchmen and turning the streets of Paris into rivers of blood Napoleon became the saviour of the state, the toast of the salons, the well-paid commander of the Army of the Interior and the object of Josephine's intense interest.

Her thirty-two-year-old charms were beginning to pall on Barras and, realising this, she realised too that the twenty-six-year-old Napoleon might be inveighed into becoming her protector. He was invited to her modestly furnished little house in the Rue Chanteraine where, smiling in a way that hid her blackened teeth and claiming she was four years younger than she actually was, Josephine and her two teenage children began to find him a regular visitor. Eventually she invited him into her bed as she had so many others and received passionate declarations of his rapture. 'I awaken full of you,' he wrote to her after a night of passion, 'my senses have no respite. Sweet and incomparable Josephine, what is this strange effect you have on my heart?' Her anger, her sadness or her troubles would shatter his soul, he said. He would find no peace. 'But I find none either,' he continued in the same vein, 'when I succumb to the profound emotion that overwhelms me, when I draw from your lips, from your heart, a flame that consumes me.'

He was genuinely and hopelessly smitten. Why? The question can never be satisfactorily answered. Josephine had the appearance of style and class but she maintained these on precious little money. She was to Napoleon, at least, infinitely alluring and defeatingly passive without his being fully aware that she was also extremely experienced in the ways of the world. She was feminine, too, and gentle and warm when she chose to be, and there had been few enough places like that in his life. Perhaps, above all, Napoleon was now ready for such things, and Josephine encouraged him and was pleased as she easily caught him by allowing him to play the role of the great lover before both her eyes and his own. In fact it seemed that all concerned might do rather well out of the affair. Napoleon had his woman, Josephine had her protector and, when Barras appointed Napoleon to the Army of Italy, his erstwhile mistress was provided for and the Army of Italy itself had a general who would transform it even as he satisfied his own inordinate ambitions. That Napoleon chose to marry Josephine – which he did at a Paris register office in March 1796 – was none of Barras's business. Neither was the fact that Napoleon arrived late and, two days afterwards, set off for Italy and his first great campaign.

## The Empire and the Empire Style

In the early days of their marriage Josephine basked in Napoleon's reflected glory, slept with her other lovers, ran up huge bills and read her husband's turbulent and almost indecipherable letters. The brilliant young general discovering his genius was also a newly married man deeply in love with his wife, and Napoleon's letters to Josephine from this time overflow with emotion. 'In the midst of affairs, at the head of the troops or going through the camps, my adorable Josephine alone is in my heart, occupies my mind, absorbs my thoughts,' he wrote to her. She delayed replying for some days and, when she did, called him '*vous*'. He exploded with hurt and indignation. And why had she taken so long to write? 'What were you doing, since you were not writing to your husband?' Matters did not improve. His letters were passionate, hers dilatory. Napoleon's suspicions grew, but he had no means of getting at the truth and was, for the time being, spared it. Josephine had been brought up in a world where such romantic possessiveness as Napoleon showed was considered déclassé and she was now consoling herself in his absence in the arms of a dapper little lieutenant of hussars called Hippolyte Charles. He was yet another who had profited from the career open to talent for he was a draper's son from Valence who owed his success with Josephine to the fact that he had, in the words of one of his detractors, a 'pretty face and the elegance of a hairdresser's assistant'.

The crisis, when it came, was thunderous and pitiful. Napoleon had learned of Josephine's unfaithfulness to him while in Egypt, sworn to divorce her and very publicly taken as his mistress the wife of a lieutenant of chasseurs who had stolen into north Africa in one of her husband's uniforms. Returning from the Egyptian campaign to save France, Napoleon had also to save his own marriage. In his current mood the one was more congenial than the other. He locked himself in his study and condemned Josephine to a long and agonising night of weeping and imploring outside his door. Only when a maid suggested she join with her entreaties those of her children, of whom Napoleon was fond, did he agree to turn the key. The reconciliation made a pathetic tableau with a red-eyed Napoleon embracing Josephine's son while mother and sister clasped his knees. 'What was there to say?' Napoleon commented later. 'One cannot be human without being heir to human weaknesses.'

Was it human weakness that made the couple's responses to each other now change so markedly? It is hard to say, but the changes were profound. By Napoleon's showing his anger and vulnerability Josephine had realised at one and the same time that she might lose him and that she loved him. Her light-hearted cynicism was gradually replaced by the deepening response of a maturing woman. For his part, Napoleon sensed that the relationship had changed too. The scales had fallen from his reddened eyes and his expressions of adolescent ardour were replaced by something considerably more realistic and often more genuinely tender. The new balance was far from perfect but it was altogether more adult and it was very largely from it that there flowered the cultural world of Napoleon's court that has come to be called the Empire Style.

It was one of his most influential creations – one of his important contributions to European civilisation – and can be seen most agreeably at Malmaison, the three-storeyed and slate-roofed chateau outside Paris that Josephine had bought while Napoleon was in Egypt. Typically, she ran up huge debts in refurbishing it and Napoleon's settling of these was part of their reconciliation. The gardens, the fabulous collection of roses in particular, were Josephine's domain where she developed the original of the modern tea rose. Napoleon's contribution to the garden was largely confined to occasionally knocking the heads off the blooms with his riding crop and to taking pot shots at the swans. The interior of the house, however, reflected his military aspirations and did so in a way that is full of light and charm and grace. Napoleon agreed enthusiastically with his designers, Percier and Fontaine, that the imagery should suggest a modern Caesar and borrow its motifs from Pompeii. In the Council Room striped fabrics were fashioned into a tented ceiling. The doors, painted with trophies on a dark ground, were flanked by mahogany and gilt-bronze poles topped with eagles. Such graceful austerity was offset by the sumptuous ormolu chairs with their red upholstery. If the gold suggested the frogging on an officer's uniform and so carried on the military idea, the whole was designed to reflect not just glory on the battlefield but the new wealth of France and the skill of her luxury manufacturers.

Napoleon took this concern with the image and well-being of France into every detail. Dress became a particular concern. He liked his women to wear white, but both his patriarchal attitudes and his concern for French trade were roused to indignation by the flimsy dresses of the Directory designers, made as they were out of fabrics from British India. In order to encourage the use of French materials Napoleon once ordered the fires at a reception to be stoked to an unbearable temperature – the scantily dressed women must be cold, he said – and if Josephine or her daughter offended by wearing English muslin they were promptly ordered to tear the offending garment in two. And what was true on the small scale was true on the large. The public buildings of Paris were to reflect the glories of the Consulate and the Empire while, at the same time, encouraging French arts. The Rue du Rivoli and the Rue de la Paix were the last and very refined word in Parisian chic, their dignity guaranteed by strictly enforced laws against shop signs and the sounds and smells of manufacturing. The four triumphal arches planned for the city were designed to exalt the achievements of the army but were also intended, in Napoleon's words: 'to subsidise French architecture for ten years to the tune of 200,000 francs . . . and French sculpture for twenty years.' The Arc de Triomphe, heroic in size and original in its disdaining the use of columns, was intended to outdo the dominance of ancient Rome while being plain, majestic and modern. It succeeded magnificently.

French opera may not have been in a golden period but was nonetheless generously encouraged. Napoleon, who loved the form almost as much as his favoured heroic tragedy, whistled tunes from Paisiello and *La Vestale*, while his army marched and fought to orchestrated numbers from Grétry and Dalayrac. Publishing was encouraged, despite the imposition of censorship. Redoute's illustrations of Josephine's flowers are a high point of the genre as are the plates in the ten folio volumes of the *Description de l'Egypte* created by Napoleon's archaeologists. Even authors were supported, Napoleon himself taking great pains to assist that obstinately reactionary genius Chateaubriand. Indeed Napoleon, a voracious reader himself, had an acute critical sense of modern literature. When *The Sorrows of Young Werther* was making Europe weep he roundly told Goethe that his tale wasn't true to nature.

All the arts received Napoleon's attention. Canova's monumental marble statue of the Emperor nude may be considered a risible monstrosity (it served Wellington's humour by ending up in the stairwell of Apsley House) but sculpture and painting flourished at a high level in France at this time. Napoleon's favourite Gros developed the methods of heroic military painting, just as Ingres and David invented an iconography for Napoleonic imperialism.

Nothing shows this more clearly than Ingres' heroic portrait of the Emperor crowned.[5] For all Napoleon could, when the mood took him, airily dismiss a throne itself as nothing more than a piece of wood covered in velvet, its real emotional meaning to him – its deep, complex, obsessive appeal – is nowhere more powerfully suggested than here. Indeed, this vast tableau of power personified is one of the most enduring images of the whole Napoleonic idea, frozen as it is into a rigidity and coherence of purpose that circumstances in fact ensured the Empire and its ruler never possessed for very long at a time. It was an aspiration. Here is Napoleon crowned with the golden laurel wreath of a victorious imperial Roman. There are strong suggestions of the 'divine Augustus' and even of Jove about him. His power is godlike and from him flow the force that is invested in the army he commands and the justice embodied in the institutions of the civic nation over which he reigns. This Roman theme is important for, just as Augustus transformed the republic into the empire and remodelled the iconography of power, so Napoleon, achieving the same political feat, required his artists to extend their use of images taken from the past beyond the limits of the Republican heroes favoured by the revolutionaries into the altogether more heady realms of imperial glory.

But Ingres' image of Napoleon does more than this. If it completes and concludes one cycle of ideas it also skilfully explores another. The staffs of power Napoleon holds, the sword at his side and the golden bees on his robes refer deliberately, as we have seen, to the French Carolingian past. Divine Augustus is also Charlemagne and so plays on a whole repertoire of indigenous myths happily dating from a time long before the Bourbons. Napoleon is the medieval French emperor who, after thirty years of military campaigning, brought order to Europe through a vast empire which comprised not only France itself and modern-day Switzerland, Belgium and the Netherlands, but large parts of Italy, Germany, Austria and Spain as well. But there is one difference. Charlemagne was crowned on Christmas Day 800 by the Pope in Rome. Napoleon was famously crowned by himself in Notre-Dame. Ingres presents his subject as pre-eminently Napoleon, the man who could say to the novelist Benjamin Constant: 'I wanted to rule the world, and in order to do this I needed unlimited power . . . the world begged me to govern it; sovereigns and nations vied with one another in throwing themselves under my sceptre.' This was nonsense, but it was very potent nonsense and was supported in France at least by a densely woven but untimely flimsy fabric of social relations.

The warrior Emperor needed a warrior aristocracy and, from 1804, Napoleon set out to create one. In that year he invested eighteen marshals of France as 'Grand Officers of the Empire' and provided them with massive fiefdoms and enormous incomes of anything up to a million francs to support their new status.[6] Some were to rise even further – and very far indeed from their lowly origins. A fully fledged new aristocracy required a galaxy of princes, dukes, counts and barons, and among those to benefit from this were such figures as Marshal Lefebvre, the son of a washerwoman and a police clerk, who became Duke of Danzig. Napoleon's purpose in elevating such men was not only to provide a continuity with the revolutionary past and show that the career open to talent provided golden vistas but, as he himself said, it was 'the only means of uprooting the traditional nobility'. Quite as much as this, Napoleon's system of honours was also designed to reward loyalty and ability, and tie these firmly to his regime. This was made clear when the legislation introducing the honours was presented to the Senate. 'Such titles,' it was stated, 'will henceforth serve only to mark for public recognition those already noted for their services, for their devotion to the prince and the *patrie*.'

Here, supposedly, was *la gloire* in all its glittering carapace of money, lands, splendid uniforms and durability. The titles were dished out with a relatively generous hand – by 1814, over 3,000 citizens and their wives could insist on being addressed by them – and the titles could also become hereditary provided their original possessor had sufficient money to ensure his heirs could maintain the family's status. Where he could not, Napoleon was sometimes minded to make up the deficit with enormous gifts from his *domaine extraordinaire*. The riches of the far corners of the Empire swole the pockets of such men as the former regicide Théophile Berlier, who profited from assets in Swedish Pomerania and factories and rents in the provinces of Illyria. Such a sense of hereditary permanence was supposed to be the foundation of a worthy tradition for 'the memories that it transmits are the substance of honour'. It was a questionable idea nonetheless. In 1814 the same Marshal Lefebvre who had risen to the dizzy if factitious heights of the dukedom of Danzig was not minded to stand by his patron in the Emperor's hour of need. 'Did Napoleon believe that when we have titles, honours and lands, we would kill ourselves for his sake?' The new Napoleonic aristocracy was rooted in thin soil, and loyalty was even less to be trusted among those members of the old aristocracy Napoleon courted, often assiduously, to join his parvenu nobility.

Napoleon also sought to win the *haute bourgeoisie* to his side. He believed that the *notables* or the conspicuously wealthy were particularly important in binding the regions to the centre because it was these people who 'by the triple influence of example, discourse and expenditures, determine (when times are calm) general opinions and dispositions'. In other words their employees, tenants and relatives would, along with the tradesmen and lesser professionals they used, follow their masters' loyalties in the hope of a reasonably secure livelihood. Because of the relatively undeveloped state of French industry the possession of landed wealth was a key element here and it was members of this traditional elite (their wealth often enhanced by properties bought from the estates of aristocrats who were either dead or fled) who enjoyed the very limited political rights extended to them. These gave them some largely illusory status and were, in effect, a part of the Emperor's plan to depoliticise the country as far as he could. It was clear to him at least that a strong central executive was an altogether better guarantee of domestic tranquillity than the ballot box, and it was the loyal Prefect of the department of the Seine Inférieure who expressed the policy best when he wrote how the local population 'has an excellent public spirit, because there reigns here a great political immobility and a great movement towards domestic concerns'. There was no fear in such a place that the militantly revolutionary sans-culottes – the artisans who promoted the Reign of Terror – would upset the reign of Napoleon Bonaparte. They had been stigmatised, demonised and hopefully exorcised. Where they had not, they could be constantly observed by the secret police.

The police were everywhere in Napoleon's France and in Paris especially: listening, noting, following up.[7] They infiltrated the kitchens of the Tour d'Argent and cocked an ear to the grumbling of the porters and *plongeurs*. It didn't amount to very much. 'The conversations were trivial, a few complaints about the inactivity of commerce; but no remarks were heard that suggested trouble.' This was not always the case elsewhere. It was believed that sedition was being spread in the fashionable cafés of the Boulevard des Italiens, and the café owners were instructed to spy on their customers and to hire waiters who could be trusted to listen in to conversations. If they did not their establishments would be shut. This actually happened elsewhere. A café in Sancerre was closed when the proprietor was insufficiently firm with a customer who said he didn't give a damn about Emperor Bonaparte. Three cafés in Nîmes were told to pull down their shutters so as to frighten the seditious regulars. The establishments were only allowed to reopen when new and appropriate waiters had been found.

All of this activity was directed to several ends: the prevention of crime, the censorship of the press, the suppression of plots, the monitoring of rumour. Mere suspicion was often enough to trigger activity that was invariably efficient, and, where paid officers were lacking, the creeps and the snoopers by nature willingly offered their services. 'As I see a lot of people,' wrote a retired army officer in 1804, 'I can sometimes provide you with information with no ulterior motive than my gratitude to His Imperial Majesty who, since he gloriously took hold of the reins of power, has provided decent people with peace of body and mind and paid bondholders and pensioners, of which I am one, on time.' Spying on their neighbours allowed such people to feel important and that they belonged to the Empire and even to Napoleon himself.

Nor were such activities limited to the lower levels of society. When one of his guests observed that Admiral Decrès, the Minister for the Navy, employed a very large number of servants the host turned to him and said: 'I can afford to, my dear sir, for I don't have to pay them since you do.' Perhaps the bloodless face of M. Fouché, the head of the secret police, was briefly lit by an almost lipless smile. This was just the sort of thing he wanted to hear and, in his memoirs, he congratulated himself on how well he had organised it. 'I was certainly shrewd to spread it about and have everyone believe that wherever four people were gathered together then there were present also eyes to see and ears to hear, all paid for by me.' Forever ferreting out information, blessed with a tenacious memory and a total lack of moral scruple, Fouché's innumerable eyes and ears allowed him to play with supreme adroitness his favourite game of sidling up to every leading political figure in order to betray them all.

There was one other force of incalculable importance in the Napoleonic empire – the army.[8] The civilian attitude to the Napoleonic army was deeply and powerfully ambivalent. On the one hand its existence resulted in increasingly oppressive levels of personal and financial suffering, on the other the *Grande Armée* was the terrible instrument of patriotic glory. It was very largely a conscript force and the figures involved were astronomical. From about 1806 onwards some 80,000 young Frenchmen were annually required to sign up. There were various ways of getting out of this. Draft-dodging and desertion were not unknown, but the efficiency of the police made this a decreasingly effective option. Marriage was another means of evading service, as were illness, self-mutilation or (the frequent expedient of the rich) buying a replacement to die in the place of a beloved son.

For many young men such means of escape were simply not available. Marched off under the supervision of the police from useful and necessary jobs, they were often away for years at a time and perhaps some 45 per cent of them never returned, dying on blood-drenched fields as far apart as Corunna and Moscow, whether in the fury of battle or later from wounds. Many simply went missing. The decimation of family life and family businesses was dreadful. The Sub-Prefect of Sisteron who told Napoleon that he would probably be welcomed back into France if only he would forgo conscription and its horrors was speaking for the bulk of the nation. And yet, despite such bitterness, the army had a deep appeal for some. Propaganda played an important part in this. Those who could read could absorb the frequently mendacious glorifications of the bulletins, while literate and illiterate alike could enjoy the engravings of triumph Napoleon had been careful to circulate from his early days and which were eventually augmented by the cheap and cheerful *images d'Epinal*. These, bought for a couple of *sous*, made heroes out of the ordinary soldier and his generals, inspiring in a million cottages a faith quite as intense as the images of a morbid Catholicism that were often pinned up beside them. In the glory days at least army life was seen to offer prestige and adventure – the opportunity to escape the stifling round of *la France des petits villages* – as well as the lure of wealth and the altogether less tangible attractions of honour and *la gloire*. Even men as intelligent as Stendhal pined in later years for the excitements and camaraderie of army life.

Such a life had, of course, its own very strong values with which
to bind men together in ways both military and political. Toasts
were one minor but telling expression of this. As early as his first
Italian campaign Napoleon encouraged his men to drink 'To the
unity of French republicans! May they follow the Army of Italy's
example and, supported by it, regain that energy which is fitting for
the greatest nation on earth!' Army life and military virtues were
seen as the crucible of civic strength, and it was inspired by such
feelings as these that Napoleon sent Augereau swiftly back from the
first Italian campaign to restore what he considered proper order to
the failing Directory. It was such actions that seemed to prove that
the army was indeed the fount of national honour and it is
significant that Napoleon's most famous award – the *Légion
d'honneur* – was overwhelmingly a military distinction. By the time
the empire was collapsing in 1814 only 1,500 of the Legion's 32,000
members were civilians. Such people were quite simply unaware of
the moral discipline instilled by the physical rigour of army life. The
Council of State was told this in no uncertain terms. 'You do not
know our bivouacs, our forced marches, the privations which we
undergo or the sufferings we endure,' Napoleon told them. 'I do
know them and from time to time I share them.'

This personal identification with the *Grande Armée* was, along
with victory and booty, one of Napoleon's strongest suits in binding
his men to him. He was one of them and he made conspicuous
efforts to make this known. The army had made him and he in turn
would make the army. He understood it. It was in his blood. It was
his true home. He was not some aristocrat whose money and
heraldic distinctions had eased his way into the infantry or the
cavalry but an ordinary boy who had entered the artillery and risen
to the top with spectacular speed through ability, hard work and
ambition. He could present himself as embodying the
revolutionaries' ideal of the career open to talent. But he did far
more than this. Napoleon set out to woo the heart of his army with
all his highly developed gifts of self-presentation and detailed grip

on practicalities. He was acutely aware of the need to appeal not just to his officers but to the huge mass of ordinary soldiers.

He was eloquent in their praise when praise was due. 'Soldiers, I am pleased with you! You have fulfilled my every expectation! You have compensated for everything through your good will and your gallantry!' Such words, proclaimed after the Battle of Lützen to men who had lost perhaps 20,000 of their colleagues (the official estimate was 10,000) could still inspire devotion, even if there were too few cavalrymen to follow up the victory and so annihilate the enemy. Napoleon spoke his men's language and he cultivated approachability. 'Those soldiers who wanted to say something to him,' wrote one of their number in 1807, 'could approach him with confidence, sure that they would be warmly welcomed.' And, when they were old, they could be sure they would be looked after. Those who could still work might look forward to a job in customs and excise (their failing energies being harnessed to the blockade of British goods into the Empire) while those who could not work could live out their days in Les Invalides, to which they were admitted on the basis of need rather than of rank. But if Napoleon gave his men all these things he swept them up in others altogether more intoxicating. His sixty battles were nearly all astonishing feats of military genius and, at whatever terrible cost, bound men to him body and soul in the exaltation of *la patrie* and *la gloire*.

Such martial glory was in part balanced at court at least by Josephine's charm. She had, wrote the occasionally sycophantic Bourrienne, the rare talent of 'making each person feel that he had been singled out for the especial welcome'. Entering the reception rooms of the Tuileries on Talleyrand's arm, Josephine could overpower even his reptilian fascination by the charm with which she greeted the waiting members of the diplomatic corps. Napoleon, by contrast, would appear unannounced from a private staircase and was perfectly capable of marching up to an astonished diplomat such as Lord Whitworth and bellowing out so that all could hear: 'So you are determined to go to war! If you wish to rearm I will rearm too; if you wish to fight, I will fight also.' Having discharged his anger, Napoleon then strode out of the room. The incident was exceptional but not uncharacteristic. 'With Bonaparte's entrance,' Bourrienne recalled, 'a sudden change came over the room; every eye turned anxiously to read his mood in his expression – whether he was to be taciturn or talkative, gloomy or genial.' His manner was imposing rather than pleasing, inspiring awe rather than ease. 'He possessed all the attributes of being what society terms "an agreeable man",' Bourrienne continued, '– all save the desire to be one.'

Only Josephine could slightly moderate the effect, but below the surface of their public life there were still difficulties. Josephine spent money recklessly, and there were frequent explosions of anger from the naturally careful Napoleon when he learned that she had bought thirty-eight hats in a single month or yet more of her exquisitely tailored dresses by Leroy, dresses whose simplicity was only achieved by the most artful and expensive cutting. But there were more profound problems too. Napoleon's chauvinist attitude to women may have been encouraged by his Corsican origins, but his belief that women were 'mere machines to make children' hid a deeper and natural distaste, contempt and perhaps even fear.[9] He could not always easily or generously access his sexuality when he was with women – and, as he grew older, he was with many apart from Josephine. Stendhal, who was a connoisseur in such matters, etched with coldly horrified contempt a vignette of Napoleon the lover in his biography of him. He pictured the Emperor seated at a small table, his sword at his side, and working late into the night as he signed decrees. When a woman was announced he would tell her to go and wait in the bedroom without even looking up from his work. When she had served his purpose Napoleon would usher her out of the bedroom, candle in hand, and return to the little desk and the mound of papers. 'The essential part of the rendezvous,' Stendhal declared, 'had not lasted three minutes.'

Nor was it only women who seemingly stimulated Napoleon's often pitiful interest. Josephine and others were convinced that he was attracted to boys and young men. There was clearly a strong sexual element in Napoleon's attentions to the charming Tsar Alexander when he met him at Tilsit, an attraction stronger than to the women mentioned by Stendhal, even if it was unconsummated. A contemporary British cartoon which shows Napoleon embracing his fellow emperor with more than fraternal enthusiasm suggests that this was widely known. Napoleon's pulling the hair and tugging the ears of pretty-faced valets was, like his sudden promotion of handsome young soldiers, suggestive of his bisexual nature too, and Josephine (whose more attractive male servants he often purloined) was genuinely concerned. In moments of high stress she would tell her fascinated confidantes that her husband 'had no moral principles whatsoever, and he concealed his vicious inclinations only for fear that they would damage his reputation; if he were permitted, however, to follow his bent without restraint, he would gradually abandon himself to the most shameful excesses'. When Josephine directly confronted her husband with these accusations Napoleon's answer verged on megalomania. 'I am not like other men,' he thundered. 'The laws of morality and of society are not applicable to me.'

The sense of compensating for inadequacies in Napoleon's outburst is patent, but that is not to say he necessarily felt guilty about his being attracted to members of his own sex. Gossip invariably distorts the peccadilloes of the great, sometimes inventing before it distorts. It was rumoured, for example, that Napoleon committed incest with his sisters. There is, however, scientific evidence for what may well have been the underlying reason for his sense of inadequacy. Dr Henry, the man who conducted the autopsy on Napoleon's corpse, wrote discreetly in Latin that Napoleon's 'private parts were seen to be remarkably small, like a boy's'. Too much can (and has) been made of this, but if it is ridiculous to explain the size of Napoleon's empire on the inadequacy of his penis a genuine sense of inferiority may very well have been responsible for his delight in having his sexual adventures talked about and his own harping on about them. Caulaincort, of all Napoleon's followers the one who perhaps knew him most sympathetically, remarked on this latter trait. 'The Emperor was so eager to recount his amorous successes,' he wrote, 'that one might almost have imagined that he only engaged in them for the sake of talking about them.' It is a shrewd comment. Certainly, Napoleon's principal mistresses were well-known figures, some in their own right and all in relation to him. They included the actress Mademoiselle George, the contralto Giuseppina Grassini, and two women of his court: Madame Duchâtel and Madame Dénuelle. There was also, of course, the beautiful Polish countess Marie Walewska who he had met in Poland and who now, in the high summer of 1814, was making her way to Elba for a brief visit that is still shrouded in mystery.

## A Visitor

The Elban August was hot and dry. This gave Napoleon an excuse to say he wanted to move out of I Mulini and away from both the noise of the builders working on the place and the eyes of the growing number of tourists who were coming to the island – to stare at him, he complained, like some wild animal. The place he finally chose was the deserted and secluded chapel of the Madonna del Monte which, with its four empty cells, was situated on the west end of the island. He gave orders that a little money should be spent doing the place up and then, at the end of the month, moved there, attending to various business matters and beguiling the time with a little hunting while he waited for his countess.

Napoleon had been instantly attracted to Marie's generous figure, blonde hair and blue eyes. When she stepped forward from the crowd of other Polish patriots gathered in the Warsaw ballroom he declared: '*Ah, qu'il y a des jolies femmes a Varsovie.*' She was not to be won by a compliment. Marie Walewska was devout, modest and married. She was also a fervent nationalist and Napoleon, inflamed by her refusal of him, played on this with the full force of his cynicism. Poland was the bruised and battered plaything of the powers that surrounded her. Her people had a figurehead in Kościuszko, and all looked to Napoleon as their saviour. He now dangled before Marie the prospect of her country's freedom as a bauble in the game of seduction. 'Think how much dearer your country will be to me if you take pity on my poor heart,' he wrote and, when he was finally alone with her, took out his pocket watch, ground it under his heel and said he would do the same to Poland if she did not submit. By her own account it was only on their second night that, urged by her fellow nationalists and even her ancient husband, she lay back, thought of Poland and promptly fainted. Marie bore Napoleon a son and eventually moved to Paris where, living in a house by the Tuileries, she was known as the 'Polish wife'. All that Poland achieved from this was the factitious status of the Grand Duchy of Warsaw. Kościuszko's contempt for Napoleon was bitter in the extreme. 'He detests every great nation, and he detests even more the spirit of independence,' he declared. 'He is a tyrant.'

There were a number of reasons, aside from their personal relationship, that now urged Marie to Elba. For all that she had been obliged to spend the night of Napoleon's abdication weeping alone in an anteroom and he had left without so much as saying goodbye, she still had feelings for him. She also had the strong protective instincts of a mother, and Murat was threatening to confiscate the estate Napoleon had settled on their son. These reasons may have weighed somewhat with the father, but it is also possible that she was acting as a courier for him and was bringing information from mainland France. 'He considers his exile temporary,' Marie wrote later, adding cryptically: 'the information he demands is what he needs to choose the most propitious moment to bring it to an end.'

Now the brig carrying her and her entourage could be seen in the distance and, as it was diverted to San Giovanni to avoid prying eyes, the all-seeing Elbans, watching the signal fire lit on the beach, had a wiseacre's certainty that the smuggled visitors were none other than Prince Eugene, Napoleon's empress and the King of Rome.

Napoleon's valet gave the most incisive account of their brief rendezvous. 'Both evenings of Maria Walewska's visit,' St-Denis wrote, 'he came out of his tent wearing a dressing gown and went to her room where he stayed until daybreak. It was obvious to everyone what was going on,' he continued, adding that 'even the most humble of his subjects would have been more skilful at conducting a secret love affair than the Emperor.' The couple spent an afternoon with each other and their little boy wandering through the chestnut groves and listening to Marie's entourage singing national songs, but already Napoleon was tired of her. She had served her purpose and he only followed her halfway to the port before saying his farewells in the dark and leaving her to a dangerous seventeen-mile coach ride before she sailed away.

## Marie-Louise

Josephine had greeted the news of Napoleon's entanglement with his Polish mistress with the floods of tears that were her usual response to such occurrences but, in truth, she had far more troubling things to worry about than Countess Marie Walewska. The 'Polish bride' had borne Napoleon the son she had so conspicuously failed to provide. The price of her not producing an heir was divorce, but Napoleon was sure that Josephine's replacement could not be Marie Walewska. 'Yes, I am in love,' Napoleon dryly informed his brother Joseph while he was considering the matter of his new bride, 'and although I would like to crown my mistress I must look for other ways to further the interests of France.' He looked first to Russia. Tsar Alexander had a nubile sister and Napoleon made his overtures. The Dowager Empress would not hear of it. Napoleon, she insisted, was not as other men, and she despatched Prince Frederick Louis of Mecklenburg-Scherin to establish the fact. It did not take him long. A desperate Josephine was now loud in her claims of her husband's impotence. She said that Napoleon's semen was 'no use at all; that it's just like so much water'. He was apparently as dry as a castrato at the opera and it was true, in the words of the popular pun, that *Bon-a-parte est bon-a-rien*.

Metternich ordered things differently in Austria and made sure that, with Emperor Francis's daughter Marie-Louise, Napoleon had his new bride. 'That's just the kind of womb I want to marry,' Napoleon declared, and Marie-Louise, welcomed every mile of the way with flowers and letters, met her husband at Compiègne. He professed himself delighted. 'For two days we have not stopped exchanging proofs of the mutual feelings which unite us,' he told his bride's father. 'We suit each other perfectly.' By November he could confirm that Marie-Louise was five months' pregnant, and the difficult birth – 'Save the mother,' Napoleon had ordered when the anxious doctor presented him with the choice between her or the child – took place in the Tuileries on 20 March 1811. Outside, a hundred rounds of cannon fire summoned the citizens of Paris to celebrate the arrival of the King of Rome.

Napoleon seems to have adored the child with all the love of a father and the satisfied dynastic ambitions of an emperor. He sat him on his knee, pulled faces to make him laugh, turned the pages of a picture Bible for him and so filled the boy's bedroom with luxuries that even the chamber-pot was silver-gilt. His mother enjoyed the warmth awakened by her son. Marie-Louise was nervous, a hypochondriac, twenty-two years younger than Napoleon, sensuous and not particularly bright. She was however apparently loyal, honest and devoted. She assumed her wifely duties with what she hoped was becoming seriousness and wrote that she liked only one form of praise: 'that is when the Emperor or my friends say to me "I am pleased with you."' For his part Napoleon made sure Marie-Louise had only limited opportunities to stray. No man save two trusted secretaries were allowed into her apartments without a permit signed by him, and a lady-in-waiting was to be in constant attendance during her music and drawing lessons. No male would be able to boast that he had been alone with the Empress for even two seconds. Napoleon's letters to Marie-Louise when they were apart were invariably tender and courteous even if, during this period of Elban exile, they were increasingly anxious. Where was she? He had decorated the upstairs rooms of I Mulini for her and, on 18 August, wrote to her saying: 'your rooms are ready and I expect you in September for the grape-picking. No one has the right to oppose your coming. I have written to you about that. Come then. I am waiting impatiently for you.'

She did not arrive. Great pressure had been put on her not to join Napoleon, her health was understandably run down, and Marie-Louise was not at the best of times the sort of woman to stand up to the combined entreaties of the Tsar, the King of Prussia and her father. The latter had been very kind, she told Napoleon, but he had insisted that she was not to join her husband on Elba. 'I really feel that this will kill me,' Marie-Louise wrote to Napoleon, 'and I pray that you can be happy without me, though it is impossible for me to be happy without you.' She wanted to recuperate in Aix but this was equally out of the question (her presence in France might be a rallying point for remaining Bonapartists) and a return to Vienna was the only option. There Marie-Louise was closely supervised until the delegates arrived for the Congress when it was deemed better that she should be out of sight. Marie-Louise got her trip to Aix.

Her father, who had destroyed her marriage, now ensured that she should have every comfort. This last came in the form of Count Adam von Neipperg. One-eyed, suave and extraordinarily attractive to women, he was to accompany Marie-Louise to the curative waters of Aix. Her son, meanwhile, was to be left in Vienna as a pledge of her return. Long and close proximity to her escort soon had the effect that Metternich and Emperor Francis intended. Marie-Louise began to lose interest in Napoleon's entreaties. Instead, the delights of Switzerland seemed daily more appealing to both her and Neipperg and, by the time they reached the Bernese Oberland, they were lovers. Their relationship, which was to last for fifteen years, produced two children and was eventually crowned with marriage.

## The Uses of Adversity

Although he was without the comforts of a wife, two other members of Napoleon's family relived his Elban solitude. His mother arrived on the island at the end of July. '*Madame Mère*' was a small, formidable woman of sixty-four, deeply conscious of her Corsican origins and the dignities due to her position as the Emperor's mother. Napoleon, who regarded her with unfeigned respect and claimed she could govern a kingdom excellently, housed her in the Casa Vantini, which was close to his own house, and he seemed pleased by her presence there. His sister, Pauline Borghese, was an altogether different kettle of fish. Feckless, publicity-loving and self-obsessed though she was, Pauline was also warm, generous and undoubtedly fun. She could exasperate Napoleon when she twitted him for pomposity and rouse his ire by her openly sexual nature, her revealing dresses and her artfully languid reception of her numerous callers. Her pose was hypochondriacal, her love parties. Elban society speeded up in her presence. She beguiled her afternoons with a circle of the better-bred Elban women and at night danced with their menfolk, and threw dinner parties and musical soirées. It was partly due to Pauline's presence that Napoleon embarked on his plan to convert a disused Carmelite chapel into an opera house, calculating the costs very carefully as he did so while he pondered if travelling companies might be persuaded to mount a season. Other plans to modernise Elba also went ahead but some, like the project to revivify the little island of Pianosa, faltered and came to nothing. Despite the activity and despite the presence of Pauline there was a pervasive and growing sense of tedium to life on Elba. This Napoleon exploited shrewdly.

He was careful to convey his sense of being a burned-out exile to the increasing number of British tourists who came to the island. His appearance seemed to bear this out, and those who came to see a caged eagle found a paunchy man in middle age whose tired clothes were spattered with snuff and who shuffled round his domain wearing tarnished medals and shabby boots. Here, it seemed, was no ogre, and the fact that his conversation was genial and fulsome did much to relieve important visitors of their old vision of 'Boney' as the disturber of the world's peace. 'I want to dispel any illusions,' he was wont to say. 'I think of nothing outside my little island.' It was an often-repeated motif. 'I no longer exist for the world. I am a dead man. I only occupy myself with my family and my retreat, my cows and mules.' It was all very cleverly done, and in such ways the man who had claimed he would kiss another's arse to win him over ensured that an image of a harmless and even benign man went back to London and the rest of Europe.

It was, of course, a front but those who were taken in by it not only served Napoleon's purposes by believing a lie but were, in their turn, a source of valuable information on the state of mainland Europe. As he opened up to his listeners so did they to him and Napoleon was now avid for information. He developed a relatively sophisticated network for gathering it. Visitors supplemented what he could learn from books and newspapers, but in addition to these there were still the remains of his old system of informants, the efforts of his sympathisers, the news gleaned by his soldiers in their letters or on trips home and the information acquired by his family and friends. Much of what they had to tell him was encouraging to

Napoleon's secret ambitions. In November, for example, an old *grognard* turned up on Elba having made his way there via Lyons, Grenoble, Avignon and Toulon. A poor man, he had spent the nights where poor people stayed. He knew by heart their reiterated complaints and fears about prices, jobs and the possible reimposition of feudal dues. Even the once hostile Provençals now realised that the return of the Bourbons did not mean 'that the larks would tumble into their mouths ready roasted', and people everywhere were saying that the present regime couldn't last another six months. Napoleon opined that he had only one battalion of men and a single corvette. What could he do? He was told that no one would fire on him and that any assassin would be torn to shreds. Only the priests and aristocrats would jib at his return and they were 'a bunch of cowards who wouldn't dare show their faces'.

Those working for the new regime in France could confirm much of this. Bonapartists had infiltrated the highest levels of the Bourbons' secret service and were well placed to know that what the old *grognard* had told Napoleon was far from exaggerated.[10] Their spies told them that in Nancy the disaffected townsfolk were now speaking of Napoleon as a man betrayed. His misfortunes softened their harsher judgements and their confidence in his abilities was only a little dimmed. 'No one exactly conspires for him,' the informer continued, 'but this stupid infatuation is itself a kind of conspiracy which needs to be taken seriously since he can dream of using it to his own advantage.' And that is precisely what Napoleon was doing. As one very acute observer noted: 'the accounts which show him as indifferent, resigned and wanting peace and quiet don't seem to be sincere but are a political front on his part since, all the time the Congress is in session, he must keep up a pretence that doesn't upset the powers on whom his fate depends.'

Unfortunately for the powers, such reports received little attention. Indeed, they had been remarkably casual about their great enemy. Out of sight was out of mind. Royalist plots and suggestions that Napoleon be assassinated or moved to a place of greater safety came to nothing, and the system of surveillance exercised over him remained that improvised by Castlereagh. The matter had simply been allowed to drift with only Campbell – uninstructed, unofficial and unsupported as he was – to watch over it all. And now Campbell, although he was aware of the danger Napoleon's escape would pose, was getting restive. Napoleon was showing himself increasingly disagreeable and it was altogether more pleasant to spend the greater part of his time with his new Florentine mistress. Campbell was now often away and, in his absence, Napoleon could mature his plans. A cardinal point in these, a *causus belli* even, was Louis's refusal to pay him his pension. The stupidity of this was a measure of the man's political ability. It was perfectly obvious that if Napoleon were unable to support himself then he would take measures to rectify the position. Campbell was well aware of the danger. 'If pecuniary difficulties press upon him much longer, so as to prevent his vanity being satisfied by the ridiculous establishment of a court which he has hitherto supported in Elba, and if his doubts are not removed,' he declared, 'I think he is capable of crossing over to Piombino with his troops, or any other eccentricity.'

But the man who had rushed back from Egypt to save his country and single-handedly created an empire as massive as the Romans' was not going to be satisfied with a little coastal pillaging. In the deep and bitter isolation of Elba, beneath the trivial surface of his days, Napoleon was convincing himself that the French people desired his return and that, because he could do it, he must – for his own sake. The limits of the possible and the probable had never daunted him. His astonishing successes, his lightning speed, his absolute command of detail and the sheer force of his iron will had all, as a young man, convinced him he could sweep through the Middle East and humiliate the British in India. He had failed. The titanic scale of his ambition had driven him to raise an army of unprecedented vastness and invade Russia. He had failed there too. Now he believed that he could invade his homeland and, with the welcoming people behind him, sweep into Paris and regain his throne. This time he would succeed.

He made much of the humiliation of France and, never considering that he was responsible for it, vowed revenge. The idea of Wellington, currently British Ambassador in Paris, swaggering through his capital and returning to what had once been Pauline Borghese's palace there to sleep with two of Napoleon's erstwhile mistresses was an 'insult and injury to the feelings of the French people'. The sheer greed of the delegates gathered in Vienna was insupportable, and Napoleon harped on 'the state of humiliation to which France is now reduced by the cessions and aggrandisements, so unequal, of the other leading powers!' The chained eagle was desperate to fly. If in one great campaign he could sweep the Bourbons from their throne by the beat of his wings then the French people would rejoice in the restoration of *la patrie* and *la gloire* and he could go on to sink his talons into Britain and tear off the head of her prosperity.

## The Eagle Prepares to Fly

It would take careful planning. The rest would have to be left to chance, and there was a strong element of risk. What if Napoleon landed too early and the people were not yet ready for him? He would then face the appalling possibility of being destroyed by the Bourbon forces, the humiliation and worse of being defeated by no less a figure than the perfidious Marshal Ney. What if he arrived too late? He might very well find himself redundant, for those who loathed Louis XVIII would not necessarily welcome Napoleon and there had already been talk of replacing the 'Fat Pig' Bourbon with the altogether more svelte and attractive figure of Marshal Bernadotte, the man who had quitted Napoleon's side to become Crown Prince of Sweden. *Tant pis!* This was a time for care but not for irresolution.

Napoleon seems to have begun his preparations in early February with a view to making his break for freedom at the end of the month. Such a date suited him well for it would allow time for the *Inconstant* to be repaired after some recent accidental damage as well as just a sufficient number of days to ready stores and men without his plans becoming obvious. The end of February would also be a time of dark nights, the moon not rising much before nine. To distract attention from what he was doing Napoleon made sure that life on Elba continued in its usual round. A series of balls was held and a carnival parade heralded Ash Wednesday and the beginning of Lent. It was business as usual and, to further the suggestion that he and his soldiers were on the island for the duration, the middle of February saw Napoleon distributing parcels of land for his men to use as allotments and encouraging them to get on with their spring sowing. As they did so he himself worked with the maximum of secrecy for his weapons, as so often, were to be speed and surprise. The only other man certainly in the know at this stage was pudgy-faced and bespectacled Pons de l'Hérault, the director of the iron mines, and 'I confided in Pons only because his cooperation was essential in readying the necessary ships'.

Matters were made easier when, on the 16th of the month, Campbell decided he needed another 'short excursion to the Continent for my health'. He left on HMS *Partridge*, a matter deeply satisfying to Napoleon for, while the man might have observed what was going on, the ship could have prevented his own vessel from leaving port. Campbell, it seemed, was sailing out of harm's way, but if Campbell himself felt relieved and complacent about this he was in for an unpleasant shock. His rather too frequent visits to the mainland had been noted and were deemed 'improper'. A letter was sent to Castlereagh in Vienna advising him of the fact but, if Campbell knew of this, he could at least calm his anxieties and resentments with news fresh out of the Austrian capital. None of the representatives of the Great Powers was the slightest bit interested in Napoleon himself. '*Nobody thinks of him at all,*' Campbell wrote in his journal, underlining the sentences to express his relief. '*He is quite forgotten – as much as if he never existed!*'

All this time the forgotten man was busying himself with his familiar hyperactivity, for Napoleon had recently had another visitor who, disguised as a common seaman and going under the name of Pietro St-Ernest, had brought him important news. Fleury de Chaboulon was a self-important thirty-six-year-old bureaucrat who was currently out of work but had distinguished himself in the dying days of the Empire by the part he played in the defence of Rheims. He had recently had an interview with Maret, Napoleon's erstwhile Foreign Minister, and he had now come to Elba after a long and adventurous journey which had included crossing from Lerici with a band of smugglers. Some of what de Chaboulon had to say had staled with the length of his passage but other things were a spur to even greater action. In particular it seems highly probable that he told Napoleon of the plans laid by some of his former marshals to replace the Bourbon 'Pig' not with Bernadotte but with the King's brother the Duc d'Orléans. This would have been a catastrophe and would have rendered all Napoleon's efforts nugatory. As he himself later observed: 'the coronation of the Duc d'Orléans would have been for many persons, and especially for the foreign powers, a sort of compromise between the revolution and the restoration.' The threat to Napoleon lay in the fact that it just might make everyone happy. Now more than ever he needed to act with his customary speed.

His preparations continued apace. Napoleon planned for the newly repaired *Inconstant* to be painted to look like a British brig, loaded with sufficient victuals to feed 120 men for three months. She would then be kept ready at all times. By now the activity around the port was so great that everyone on Elba had come to realise that something was happening. Then, suddenly, the *Partridge* which had conveyed Campbell to his mistress arrived unexpectedly early. It could have been a disaster but, extraordinarily, her captain noticed nothing and Napoleon did his best to disguise what was happening. He ordered the *Inconstant* out to sea, suspended the loading of munitions and commanded his soldiers to work on their allotments. The captain of the *Partridge* disembarked with the English tourists he had brought over and, having satisfied himself that the *Inconstant* was sailing to Livorno for necessary repairs, walked up to I Mulini to establish that Napoleon was still on Elba and to watch his soldiers at work with their forks and spades.

Napoleon gave out that he was feeling unwell but in fact spent the day busily in his study drafting proclamations. These he then had rapidly printed so that they could be distributed immediately on his arriving in France. The proclamations show how intense his feelings were. They excoriated those who had betrayed him, derided the Bourbons and appealed to people's memories of the glory days of the Empire. Once there had been liberty and equality. Now all of that had been swept away. Napoleon declared that he knew very well how the people were suffering. 'Frenchmen, in my exile your complaints and your desires have reached me – you have asked for the government of your choice – the only legitimate one. I have crossed the sea and I am here to resume my rights, which are yours.' He addressed his soldiers with even deeper feeling. 'Victory,' he told them, 'swift, triumphant, lies before us. The eagle with the nation's colours will fly from village spire to village spire, even to the towers of Notre-Dame.' He would become once again the figure Ingres had painted.

Sunday, 26 February saw the Emperor at Mass, inspecting his troops and giving orders that they should be ready to embark at five that evening. Despite deciding that his cavalry would have to find horses once they had landed in France, space aboard Napoleon's ships was very limited and the chance arrival of the 194-ton *Saint-Esprit* appeared a godsend. Napoleon ordered that the vessel be seized, and although the captain dared not offer any resistance he protested in the most vehement terms when his captors began throwing his cargo into the sea. Napoleon sent his treasurer, Peyrusse, over to deal with the matter, instructing him to pay in hard cash. Ever the accountant, Peyrusse insisted on seeing every bill and haggling over the total. Napoleon grew impatient at the delay and had himself taken over to the *Saint-Esprit* where, sweeping all the bits of paper onto the floor, he told Peyrusse that he was nothing more than a bundle of red tape and ordered him to pay the amazed captain at once and in full.

That matter was no sooner dealt with than fall-in sounded from the barracks and Napoleon's troops were seen marching down to the port. A crowd of onlookers had gathered and little boats flecked the waters. Up at I Mulini, Napoleon remained calm and collected although there was deep emotion all around. Even the iron features of *Madame Mère* were wet with tears. It was now seven o'clock. Two hours later Napoleon, dressed in his green field uniform and his familiar grey coat, kissed his mother and sister for a last time, got into his little carriage and drove slowly down to the harbour. A crowd of dignitaries followed him on foot. As they approached the swelling crowd the cries of '*Vive l'imperatore!*' grew thunderous. Napoleon himself was then rowed across to the *Inconstant* from where a single gun shot rang out to welcome him aboard. Everything else was still and silent. Napoleon turned round to look his last on Elba. The mountains, houses and fields of his island of exile were clear in the moonlight that fell, too, on the sea in a thousand dancing pieces. A little after midnight a gentle breeze finally got up. The sails of the *Inconstant* filled and the Emperor was slowly carried across to France.

# 3

# THE FLIGHT OF THE EAGLE

## 27 FEBRUARY–20 MARCH 1815

## The Crossing

Despite the calmness of the seas there was slow, stealthy danger all around. Three or more French ships were cruising between Elba and Corsica, and who could guess what the loyalties of their crews might be. Vessels from the Royal Navy were also on patrol, while the *Partridge*, with no less a passenger than the unfortunate Campbell on board, was making slow progress off Leghorn. It was ironic indeed that the *Partridge* and the *Inconstant*, respectively carrying the watcher and the watched, should have passed each other unseen in the night, but any of these alien vessels, glimpsing the half-dozen ships carrying Napoleon and his men to France, could have raised the alarm. Napoleon himself gave orders that his little flotilla should fan out and each captain make his own way to the Golfe Jouan.

This was sensible enough, but it took all the returning Emperor's luck and leadership to get the better of other near disasters. By Monday morning the light breeze had dwindled almost to nothing. Progress towards the French coast was becoming painfully slow and the captain of the *Inconstant* was suggesting a return to Portoferraio. That was entirely out of the question. Napoleon ordered the raising of more sail and the cutting free of the *Inconstant*'s towed boat. She made a little faster progress, but a while later the lookout spied a warship bearing down on them. Napoleon once again gave his orders. The potentially hostile vessel was to be allowed alongside the *Inconstant* and, if she attacked, his men were to prepare to board her. In readiness for this, the *Inconstant*'s guns were primed and her ports opened. The two vessels meanwhile drew nearer and nearer until the oncoming ship was at last recognisable as the *Zephyr*, a familiar cruiser in these waters and one regularly captained by a friend of Napoleon's commander of marines. Aggression now gave way to deceit. Napoleon ordered his grenadiers to remove their bearskins and lie down flat on the deck. With any luck they would not be seen. The anxious minutes slowly passed as the two ships drew closer still. The captain of the *Zephyr*, used to seeing the *Inconstant*, had no reason to be suspicious of Napoleon's Elban flag with its red stripe on a white ground and three golden bees fluttering in the light wind. Napoleon summoned his commander of 'marins' to his side and ordered him to hail his friend the captain of the *Zephyr* through a speaking trumpet.

'Where are you bound for?'

'For Leghorn,' came the reply. 'And you?'

Prompted by Napoleon the man called back: 'For Genoa. Any commissions?'

'No. How is the great man?'

'Absolutely fine.'

And with that the two ships went their respective ways, their encounter seemingly of no significance.

Dawn the following day saw yet another potentially hostile ship appear only to disappear over the horizon in the direction of Sardinia. A delighted Napoleon was now convinced that fortune was favouring the brave. 'It's one of my lucky days,' he declared. 'An Austerlitz day.' He was feeling bonhominous and he clasped his seasick treasurer by the shoulder and told him to cheer up. A little good water from the Seine would soon put him to rights. Napoleon then began to expatiate on the brilliance of his plan. 'There is no precedent for what I am attempting,' he began, 'but I am counting on several favourable factors: the astonishment of the people, the state of public opinion, the general discontent, the love of my soldiers and the imperialist sentiments still running under the surface in France.' Surprise and speed were again his greatest weapons. 'I look to the stupefaction of the government, the lack of time for reflection, the infectious enthusiasm which so bold and unexpected a stroke may rouse,' he continued. 'Amid a hundred rushed plans, none of them properly thought out, I shall arrive and find no organised resistance.' The whole essence of Napoleon the strategist was here: the daring, the iron-willed certainty of quick success, the absolute refusal to think about the limits of the possible. He had fashioned a vast empire and lost it. Now he was gong to recapture it with little more than a thousand men.

Some of those men were less than confident, thought him utterly reckless and followed him as much from dogged loyalty and habits of obedience as anything else. When, back on Elba, Napoleon had breezily informed Drouot, his devout, Bible-studying military governor there, that the whole of France wanted him back he had seen Drouot's face cloud with thoughts of impending calamity. Cambronne who had also loyally followed him into exile had been barely more enthusiastic. Asked where he thought they were going after orders had been issued to ready the troops to embark, Cambronne merely said: 'I have never attempted to penetrate my master's secrets,' and then added that Napoleon could count on his devotion. These men were no more enthusiastic now and, completely loyal as they were, their emperor considered it necessary to inspire them with a lie. He told them that Paris was in arms, that a provisional government had been appointed and that several regiments had already sent him loyal addresses. 'I shall arrive in Paris without firing a shot,' Napoleon declared as he turned to go to his cabin. In that respect at least he was foretelling the truth, but he could hardly have known it for sure.

## The Landing

As the last moon of February rose, the lookout on the *Inconstant* glimpsed the lights of the other vessels in Napoleon's flotilla making towards them, and dawn of the following day saw them all off the Cap d'Antibes. Napoleon himself appeared on deck, ordered his Elban flag to be struck and the tricolour to be hoisted in its place. The men were also commanded to wear the tricolour cockade in their bearskins. The imperial invasion of France was about to begin. To prepare for it, two parties of men were sent ashore. Captain Lamouret and twenty soldiers were despatched to take a little coastal fort. Finding it to have been dismantled they stationed themselves on the Cannes–Antibes road. In the meantime a certain Captain Bertrand was sent to Antibes in mufti in order to distribute the proclamations and get a supply of passports. He was arrested almost immediately and brought before the local military commander. While he was being interrogated the commander was informed that a detachment of Elban soldiers was waiting to enter the town. They were led by an overexcited Lamouret who had decided to quit his observation post and take the garrison in Antibes. The local commander parlayed with him just long enough for his own men to spread through the fort and then raise the drawbridge once Lamouret and his men were inside. It was hardly a glorious beginning.

The main part of Napoleon's expedition had now anchored in the Golfe Jouan. So enthusiastic were some of the men to disembark that they waded ashore, waist deep in the water. By the middle of the afternoon men, guns, baggage horses and treasure were all on French soil and the army was preparing to bivouac in an olive grove. Cambronne, in the meantime, was despatched to Cannes with strict orders that whatever happened he was not to fire a single shot. 'Remember,' Napoleon told him, 'I wish to win back my crown without shedding one drop of blood.' His invasion was to be presented not as an act of larceny but his rightful return to power at the behest of the people of France. To ensure that this came about, Cambronne and his men were to put a stop on mail leaving Cannes (secrecy was of the utmost importance) and requisition horses and mules. These last were urgently required. It was perfectly clear to Napoleon that his route to Paris must be the most arduous one. His bitter journey to Elba had shown him how virulent was royalist feeling in Provence and, in order to avoid conflict, he had decided that his own route to his capital must be a hard and circuitous one to be made quickly across the precipitous footpaths of the Alps. He now realised that he would have to do this with less than his full complement of men. Efforts to free the soldiers under arrest in Antibes having proved nugatory, they would have to be left where they were, the victims of their over-enthusiasm and bad luck.

Their arrest nonetheless meant that speed was now of the utmost importance. Napoleon's army would have to travel faster than the news of his early reverses. He ordered a forced midnight march to Cannes. Here Cambronne had been busy requisitioning necessary supplies from a reluctant mayor when the Prince of Monaco passed through in his carriage. Napoleon summoned him to his tent on the outskirts of the town and asked the Prince if he would go along with him. The adroit aristocrat said he was going home and an amused Napoleon answered: 'So am I.' The people of Cannes in the meantime ventured out through the bitterly cold night to stare anxiously at the force that had so suddenly arrived. Were they pirates sent by the Bey of Algiers? But if the citizens were curious they were also harmless and Napoleon, adamant in his belief that he should be accused of no violence towards his once and future subjects, ordered his soldiers to show them no roughness as he warmed his feet by the vine-wood fire.

The citizens of Grasse were equally disturbed, but talk of armed resistance came to nothing when the authorities discovered they possessed no more than five serviceable muskets and no ammunition. The following day Cambronne entered the town alone and was once again assured by the Mayor that his citizens were loyal to the Bourbons. Cambronne put him in his place with all the firm courtesy he could muster. 'Monsieur le Maire, I am not here to talk politics with you but to ask for rations for my men who will be here shortly.' The Mayor, faced by a single Napoleonic officer, complied. Napoleon himself, however, considered it tempting providence to enter Grasse with his men and, bypassing the city, halted for the night on the level fields of Roccavignon. There loyalists brought him and his men flowers and wine along with a blinded old *grognard* who, led up to his erstwhile general by his wife, cried, '*Vive l'Empereur!*' and was promptly embraced by him. It was the first time for many months that Napoleon had heard the old, familiar acclamation on French soil. It was a stirring moment.

The next sixty miles of the journey would be altogether more arduous. The path to Digne was mountainous. The guns would have to be left behind and the treasure mounted on mules. Precisely how demanding this stretch of the journey would be soon became apparent. The men were obliged to proceed in single file along precipitous tracks covered ever more deeply in treacherous snow. Those who had horses were forced to lead them by the reins, the lancers were borne down by the weight of the saddles they were obliged to carry and their every step was made the more difficult by the rest of their equipment and their heavy leather breeches. Napoleon himself toiled on foot along with them, slipping sometimes, and trying to balance himself with his walking stick. It was the sort of action that won the love of his men and was a testament to the iron force of his will. He was now forty-six, but by eight o'clock in the evening he and his soldiers had ascended to 4,500 feet and covered over thirty miles in twenty hours. A force so determined was not to be resisted and the people of Castellane thought it best to comply with Napoleon's demand for 5,000 rations of bread, meat and wine along with his requisitioning of transport. And still the army pressed on through the cold, the snow, and along the treacherous roads where men could slip and even the sure-footed mules were at risk. At some point during this agonising twenty-nine mile march one of the mules lost its footing and fell over a cliff with 300,000 francs in gold.

By now the news of Napoleon's landing was loud in the south of France. Action against him, however, was dilatory and circumspect. The combined elements of surprise and incompetence that he had banked on seemed to be working. The local authorities eventually ordered all the brigades of the gendarmerie and the National Guard to concentrate on Digne, where they were also determined to arm the citizens. The citizens themselves were less than enthusiastic, however. While being far from resolutely Bonapartist in their sympathies they had a strong local loyalty to their own comfort and security, and they feared that hostility to their erstwhile Emperor would result in him sacking their town. The regional authorities were minded to see their point, hid the public funds and retreated to a safe distance while Napoleon himself marched on Digne. On his arrival, the citizens were not impressed, despite a speech and the issuing of newly reprinted versions of the proclamations. Napoleon had encountered no opposition, but so far only four recruits had rallied to his flag – two deserting soldiers, a gendarme and a shoemaker. Was this the real temper of public opinion?

Perhaps not. The arduous mountain march had been through a relatively backward and sparsely populated region. The first test would be a major city, and now the main highway to Grenoble now lay open before him. Napoleon divided his men into three columns, sending Cambronne nearly twenty-five miles forward to secure Sisteron and its all-important bridge before the royalist troops, reluctant to take on Napoleon though they were, should blow it up. Cambronne found that the town was not occupied by the enemy while its mayor not only refused payment for the rations he was required to provide, but actually came out to greet Napoleon on his arrival. He was nonetheless loyally wearing a Bourbon lily on his breast which Napoleon quietly told him to remove to ensure that his men did not attack him. Then, stopping at the Bras d'Or,

Napoleon set about gauging the public mood. How did the people feel about his return? The Sub-Prefect replied that they were more surprised than anything else. Would they welcome him back on his throne? The man spoke with becoming honesty. He thought the people would welcome Napoleon provided they didn't have to see the return of the conscription that had so decimated their families, threatened their livelihoods and led to appalling loss of life. Napoleon put on an appearance of being suitably impressed by this. He had made mistakes, he confessed. Now he was here to put them right. There were cries of '*Vive l'Empereur!*' as he left the town. A woman ran up to him with a hastily made tricolour and Napoleon's army was swollen by the addition of a few officers on half-pay, an old drummer and a military engineer and his boy. It was a start.

The villagers on the route to Gap were distinctly more enthusiastic as he passed through, and the windows of Gap itself were illuminated as he entered the town. Here was real enthusiasm. The drums of the National Guard beat a welcoming tattoo and the men of the city danced all night and sang songs round their bonfires. The joy of the ordinary people was obvious but what of Napoleon's erstwhile officers? Unbeknown to him, Colonel Louis-Florimond Fantin des Odoards (he who had so enthused over the prospect of the Russian expedition) was staying in Gap when Napoleon marched into the town. Now the acclamations of the people threw him into an agony of conscience. Honour and duty told him to stay loyal to the Bourbon government which he disliked, while memory tugged him back to Napoleon. He debated with himself all through the night and was often 'on the point of emerging from my hiding-place and throwing myself into the arms of old comrades of the Guard whose voices I recognised, and saying to them: "Take me to Napoleon."' Only the thought that he had promised to accompany a young travelling companion gave him his reason – or his excuse – not to show his hand. Such was the personal turmoil Napoleon's presence could cause, and such feelings would soon be growing stronger and more widespread. In the meantime, when Napoleon marched out of Gap the next morning, the crowd accompanied him for six miles. It was an auspicious start for his advance to Grenoble.

## Paris

The regional Bourbon loyalists had so far proved themselves reluctant at best to face Napoleon's force but they had, of course, sent messages to Paris. The first of these arrived as Napoleon was leaving Gap. The fat and breathless Director of Telegraphs begged the Secretary of the King's Cabinet to deliver the paper in person to the King. The gout had recently moved into Louis's plump hands and opening the envelope was a painful business. He read the missive and was silent for several minutes before declaring: 'It is revolution once more. Bonaparte has landed on the coast of Provence. Have this letter taken instantly to the Minister of War, so that he can come and speak to me at once and decide what steps are to be taken.' Soult, the vain and incompetent minister whose opinion was being sought, thought there was little enough danger and suggested that the King's two nephews, the Duc d'Angoulême and the Duc de Berry, should raise forces in Nîmes and Franche-Comté respectively. Their father, the Comte d'Artois, was supposedly to raise troops in Lyons. Despite the fact that the troops in Lyons were apathetic and the Duc de Berry never reached Franche-Comté, the Bourbon family would sort out their family difficulty with the loyal help of such turncoats as Marshal Ney. To observe the constitutional niceties, the prorogued Chambers were summoned to meet and ordinances were signed declaring Napoleon a traitor whom it was every soldier's duty to kill. A feeling of complacent confidence reigned. Napoleon's bid for power was simply idiotic. 'There is no cause for alarm,' wrote the Comte de Sesmaisons. 'The man's folly is inconceivable. The situation is being well handled. Everything ought to be over in a week.'

*'I am your Emperor. Know me!'*

As Napoleon pressed on towards Grenoble the nature of France's divided loyalties was becoming clearer to him. While hatred of the Bourbons was almost universal among the citizens of Grenoble, the city itself and the surrounding region were in the hands of two men who, for all they owed their careers to Napoleon, had rapidly disowned him after his abdication. The commander of the troops in Grenoble was General Marchand, a lawyer turned soldier who had risen to be a count of the Empire and a wealthy man. His hasty defection to the royalist cause had saved his fortune but ruined his reputation. A similar fate had occurred to the prefect of the region, the famous mathematician Fourier, who had once been one of Napoleon's protégés. Both men now decided that in honour they could not turn their coats again, and while Fourier drafted a proclamation denouncing his former patron, Marchand summoned a meeting of his leading officers. All swore loyalty to the Bourbons and all eventually agreed that it was best to march out against Napoleon and his little army the following day when the soldiers had been given the opportunity to swear once again an oath of fealty to the restored monarchy. The officers also suggested that it might be best if Marchand himself did not review his troops since their respect for him was slight.

Such a mood of contempt among the ordinary soldiers coincided with that of the civilians of Grenoble and, when Fourier posted his proclamation denouncing Napoleon, it was greeted with a cry of *'Vive l'Empereur!'* Marchand's printed statements were defaced as soon as they were stuck up, while the following day the waking citizens discovered to their joy that a secret agent had pasted across the city Napoleon's proclamations inviting them to join him. The fury of this paper war suggested to Marchand and his officers that it was wiser not to march out against the usurper after all. Neither the troops nor the citizens could be relied on, and while the city itself was put on the defensive a company of engineers was sent out to delay Napoleon's progress by blowing up the bridge at La Mure. In this they failed. Some of the disorderly and disgruntled soldiers had already shown their temper by tearing the white cockades from their hats and they again made their feelings known when the Mayor of La Mure declared that blowing up the bridge would do nothing to stop Napoleon crossing the nearby ford and would, besides, do serious damage to local trade. The engineers prepared to settle in at La Mure and wait for reinforcements but the commanding officer of these, believing that it was Napoleon's forces who were ensconced at La Mure, drew back to Laffray where he summoned the engineers to join him.

It was now Cambronne's turn to march into La Mure with the advance guard of Napoleon's army. He was warmly received, and when Napoleon himself arrived shortly afterwards he was cheered to the echo. He asked the Mayor questions designed to deepen the man's loyalty and watched as the enthusiastic inhabitants brought out wine for his troops. The sun rose, it grew hot, and Napoleon himself took an empty glass from one of his *grognards* and won the love of all by drinking from it. With that he and his advanced guard pushed on through the long narrow pass to Laffray, Napoleon himself riding in a carriage at the rear of his troops. After a while he was suddenly surprised to see his Polish lancers riding back towards him. He got out of his carriage, mounted his horse and rode towards them. It appeared that the officer commanding the engineers from Grenoble and their reinforcements had decided to hold Laffray in an effort to prevent or at least slow down Napoleon's progress. The officer had now been joined by a fiery young royalist from the city called Delassart and together they were watching Napoleon through their telescopes. The Emperor was clearly perturbed and eventually sent out a messenger to the men holding Laffray. 'The Emperor is on the point of advancing towards you. If you fire he will be the first to fall and you will answer for it to the whole of France!'

There was utter silence and not a man stirred until the Polish lancers and the men of Napoleon's Old Guard began to move forward. The last, veterans of scores of battles, were utterly fearless, proud and wholly devoted to the Emperor. The men in Laffray began to tremble. It was impossible to lead them forward but they might at least be made to turn in the hope that they would not desert. The Poles drew closer. The hot breathing of their horses could be heard. The men in Laffray were then ordered to turn once again and to advance. As they did so, the Polish lancers wheeled about and exposed them to the Old Guard. Napoleon ordered these choicest of his men to advance with their muskets reversed under their left arms. It was still his iron determination not to fire a shot and to regain Paris without a drop of blood. And now, in a supreme gesture, he led his men forward in person, daring the enemy troops to fire on him. This they were ordered to do. The abject men clutched their weapons but still Napoleon came on. He was within easy range when he began to speak.

'Soldiers of the Fifth,' he said with a steady voice of command. 'I am your Emperor. Know me!'

He marched a few paces further forward and threw open his famous grey coat to enhance his vulnerability.

'If there is one among you who would kill his Emperor, here I am.'

It was all too much. The men from Laffray broke ranks. Cries of '*Vive l'Empereur! Vive l'Empereur!*' rent the air and echoed from the hills. White cockades suddenly littered the ground, torn from shakos now waving from the points of bayonets. The men knew that their leader was among them once again and their hearts were bursting with joy. Relief ran down their faces in tears. They pressed about him, stretched towards him, touched him, and were tumultuous in their ecstasy. Even their commanding officer was stirred and as he, the man who had ordered them to shoot Napoleon, stepped forward to hand Napoleon his sword, he felt the Emperor's arms fold round him in a gesture of consolation. There would be no more Bourbons, no more feudalism, but freedom and the will of the people. 'I am counting on the people.' Napoleon knew at last that he could. All the way to Grenoble cries of '*Vive l'Empereur!*' echoed and re-echoed from the fields. 'We first dared to claim the rights of man. Here liberty is reborn and France recovers her honour.'

## Grenoble and Lyons

Inside Grenoble, now restless and angry with excitement, General Marchand pinned his hopes on the arrival of a squadron of the 4th Hussars and, in particular, the line regiment commanded by the brilliant young Comte Charles de Labedoyère. At twenty-eight years old, he was one of the most promising young officers in the army and one who had enthusiastically thrown in his lot with the Bourbons. Their ineptitude soon tarnished his loyalty and now, as he listened to the rumblings of civilian discontent in Grenoble, to the muttering of the troops stationed in the town and to the murmurings of his own men, his previous convictions blackened completely. Labedoyère realised that the defence of Grenoble was something worse than a fool's errand and, drawing his sword, he ordered his excited men to the Porte de Bonne crying, 'Who loves me, follow!' His regiment loved him to a man and, cheering the Emperor ever more vociferously, they marched out of the city and towards Napoleon, their shining military eagle carried high on a willow branch. The speeches of those senior officers who went in pursuit were drowned with cries of '*Vive l'Empereur!*' and they returned despondently to Grenoble as Labedoyère himself marched towards what he thought was the future.

Marchand ordered the closing of the city gates. He sent the soldiers on the ramparts meat and wine, but neither defensive measures nor bribery were to any avail and he finally resolved to evacuate the city. He thought he could wait until early morning, foolishly forgetting that Napoleon's greatest tactics were speed and surprise. Napoleon was already approaching Grenoble and, as evening fell, Marchand was aware of tumult in the fields outside the city and looked across to see the imperial column marching towards him, their pathway lit by the flaring torches of two thousand peasants armed with pitchforks. The locked and massive gates barred their way but their cries of '*Vive l'Empereur!*' became a terrible and contagious tattoo that was soon taken up by the men on the ramparts and the citizens in the streets. The imperial forces demanded entry, the royalists thought of grapeshot. Grenoble was well supplied with munitions, the would-be invaders could easily have been decimated, but the hypnotic cry of '*Vive l'Empereur!*' drowned any orders, shattered any discipline and Marchand was obliged to confess that he had lost his men. What about his officers? Could they not fire on Napoleon? Marchand turned to the loyalist of his commanders but was told that they would be hacked to pieces if they so much as raised a musket.

But now the waiting besiegers were growing impatient. They began to hammer at the mighty gates, the soldiers with their musket ends, the peasants with iron bars. The forces in Grenoble offered no resistance and instead began to batter at the gates as well. The repeated thuds echoed round the city as the men sang at their work:

> *Bon! Bon!*
> *Napoleon*
> *Va rentrer dans sa maison!*

But still the great gates stood firm. The wheelwrights of the Faubourg Saint-Joseph disappeared to their wood stores and returned with a massive improvised battering ram. Ten of their strongest men groaned as one as, lifting their burden between them, they began rhythmically to launch it at the gates, back and forth, back and forth, until the wood started to splinter and the tie-beams to wrench apart. Marchand made his escape, the gates fell open and, in a pandemonium of ecstatic loyalty, Napoleon entered Grenoble. As he was being borne through the streets a group of sweating workmen elbowed their way through the frenetic crowd and laid a gift at his feet. 'Instead of the keys of your good town of Grenoble,' they declared, 'we bring you its gates!'

It was deeply satisfying and Napoleon now knew he could at last afford briefly to rest. He and his men had covered two hundred miles in six days, faced danger, hostility and, in the last days, increasing loyalty. Now a great city was his, five regiments had swarmed to his side and Napoleon was no longer an adventurer but a real force in France and a real challenge to the Bourbon throne. He received the officials of the city like a conquering prince and reviewed the men of the garrison, every one of them wearing his tricolour cockade and ardent to follow his would-be Emperor as the band struck up the *Marseillaise* – '*allons, enfants de la patrie*'. It seemed that the day of glory was indeed not far off.

Certainly it seemed so to Colonel Girod de l'Ain, newly married and living in Gex, just north of Geneva.[1] He was busy planting his garden when the news of Napoleon's entry into Grenoble reached him. Ignoring Voltaire's advice that such an activity was a sure means of happiness in a life where all is not for the best in the best possible of all worlds, he threw down his spade and in a little over a week was making his way to Paris and his old regiment and his old general. The journey was arduous. The heavy snow was thawing, the mountain passes were like rivers, the horses were chest-deep in water. Nothing would deter the excited Colonel, however, not even the machinations of his fellow citizens. He found the whole country to be in turmoil. He travelled in uniform but wisely took the precaution of providing himself with both a white and a tricolour cockade, exchanging them according to the colour of the flags flying on the local belfries. The authorities of both persuasions questioned him zealously but his answers were convincing, and at Troyes he caught the diligence that would whisk him to Paris and glory. His story is a model of the loyalties of thousands like him – an image of the effect Napoleon's personal presence had.

Thirty-six hours after entering Grenoble, Napoleon himself set off for his next conquest: Lyons. It was imperative that the second city of France fall to him and it seemed that the people were willing him to succeed. Crowds of peasants lined the roads, relay after relay of them as Napoleon proceeded from one village to the next, his newest recruits leading his swelling force, their ardour burnished by the honour and reflecting confidence on the admiring onlookers. Then came the news that the Comte d'Artois was determined to defend Lyons and, as his first move, was planning to blow up two bridges leading into the city. Napoleon heard the news with anger and incredulity. His was to be a bloodless coup. It was vital that it should be so. But inside Lyons the determination of the Bourbon Prince was merely sound and fury. He had been betrayed by incompetence and was soon to be defeated by enthusiasm. He was virtually alone and all but powerless. The 30,000 men promised by Soult had not arrived and the handful of troops at his disposal were in no mood to fight for him. The National Guard was little more than a paper force, and the Count had nothing more than two exhausted guns for his defence. There was not even sufficient powder to blow up the bridges. He was determined to defend Lyons all the same. This was a Bourbon matter, a family affair. He begged men of goodwill to come to his side. A very few signed their names. He handed out money and was greeted with a meagre cheer. These meant nothing. As the Count reviewed his troops his dragoons were scowling at him.

The following day he was joined by the Duc d'Orléans. His fresher eyes had a truer view of the situation. It was clear that the game was up and that the only thing to do was withdraw. The Count was indignant. They could not just surrender Lyons. He needed other advice, better advice. He would await the arrival of Macdonald, one of the three of Napoleon's erstwhile closest followers who had officially witnessed his unconditional abdication of all his rights to the throne of France and who was now a loyal Bourbon supporter. Macdonald eventually came and the council of war stretched on to midnight. The commanders said they could no longer rely on the loyalty of their men. Lyons should be evacuated. An atmosphere of sullen humiliation hung over the council until Macdonald finally spoke up. He would make one last appeal to the men. He would speak to them in their own language. He was all for imitating Napoleon and in this he was bound to fail. The men supposedly guarding the Duc d'Orléans had already thrown away their white cockades and, the following day, did not even bother to turn out. Those troops that did marshal refused to be reviewed by the Comte d'Artois and their officers were at one with the men.

It was humiliatingly embarrassing for Macdonald and he suggested that he review the troops on his own. The Bourbon princes could join him when he had worked up the men's enthusiasm. This last proved impossible. Macdonald's royalist oration fell on the stony ground of the Place Bellecour as the troops listened in irritated silence. Macdonald had done his best, however, and he was determined that his masters should know it. He asked the Comte d'Artois to attend him. The Prince's presence deepened the irritation. Every face was scowling. Not a man cried, '*Vive le Roi!*' The furious Bourbon ordered the men to dismiss and, passing unsaluted through the great crowd gathered to greet Napoleon, got into his coach and drove away. The Duc d'Orléans had already gone and Macdonald was on his own. Surely he only needed twenty loyal men, he argued. If they were fired on by Napoleon then surely they would fire back. Not one prepared to do so could be found. Very well then, Macdonald would fire the first shot himself. But his position was hopeless. The crowd was now rising in a crescendo of enthusiasm as Napoleon's hussars entered the city to the rapturous greetings of peasants and silk workers crying, '*Vive l'Empereur!*' Macdonald fled in ignominy as Napoleon himself now struggled to make his way through the crowds towards the palace of the Archbishop. There he installed himself in the apartments so recently vacated by the Bourbons. In the streets the tumult continued all night as the crowds in their fury wrecked the homes of known royalists and screamed for the Bourbons' heads.

The fall of Lyons was a synecdoche of the last quarter-century of France's history. While the people showed themselves bloodthirsty with the Jacobin enthusiasms of the Terror, Napoleon himself resumed his position as Emperor. He undid the feeble work of the Bourbons with his habitual speed. Arcane feudal orders tying the royal family and its adherents to the Catholic Church were suppressed. Feudal titles were suppressed. The use of the white cockade was suppressed. Royalist names were scrubbed from the roll of the Legion of Honour. Electoral rights were reformed. The tricolour and the national cockade became mandatory. The Chamber of Peers was abolished. And still Napoleon moved on towards Paris. Sixty thousand gathered to greet him in Villefranche and showed their loyalty by painting the houses red, white and blue, and decorating them with eagles cut from metallic paper. Even the chicken bones Napoleon left on his dinner plate became relics. Officials in Mâcon called him a miracle worker. In Châlons he gave medals to the loyal and at Autun, on 15 March, he rested for the night.

When news of Napoleon's approach reached nearby Auxerre one Captain Coignet, a Napoleon loyalist, was both exhilarated and wary.[2] A line regiment of the 14th had arrived in the town. They were wearing white cockades. The Commissioner of Police announced the news of Napoleon's arrival and let it be known that the government had ordered his arrest. There were shouts of '*A bas Bonaparte!*' and '*Vive le Roi!*' Coignet was in agony. Then, suddenly, he saw the soldiers take off their shakos and place them on their bayonets with loud cries of '*Vive l'Empereur!*'. Their advanced guard returned to the town hall that evening with tricolour cockades proudly on show. Inside the town hall itself the Commissioner of Police was going through the same agony of conscience that now afflicted the greater part of the nation. Outside the troops were waiting with flaming torches. Eventually the Commissioner emerged with a new proclamation and shouted '*Vive l'Empereur!*' at the top of his voice. The following day everybody poured out to greet the great man himself. Napoleon was surrounded by what Coignet reckoned was a band of 700 of his old officers. Troops were flocking to him from every direction. Coignet was desperate to be one of them. He watched the Emperor review his men in the Place Saint-Étienne and, to his utter delight, was spotted by Napoleon himself. He was called into the presence of the man who never forgot a face.

'So here you are, *vieux grogneur*.'

'Yes, sir.'

'What rank did you hold on my staff?'

'Baggage Master of General Headquarters.'

'Very well, I appoint you Quartermaster of my Palace and Baggage-master-general of Headquarters. Have you a horse?'

'Yes, sir.'

'Then follow me.'

Thus were large parts of the nation won over to Napoleon's cause.

## Marshal Ney

Thursday, 16 March was a wet morning in Paris. A gloomy ministerial meeting took place in the Tuileries at which the King and his advisors discussed the very real possibility of civil war if Napoleon was not immediately halted in his tracks. Everything the ministers had already done had worked against them when it had not collapsed of its own accord. They had despatched troops to fight Napoleon and those troops had become Napoleon's army. The call to raise three million of the National Guard was a gesture as grandiose as it was impractical and was treated with the contempt it deserved. Merely a few thousand old soldiers and out-of-work labourers of uncertain loyalty and dubious ability rallied to the cause. Regulars on leave ignored the summons to return. Only embittered officers on half-pay showed any enthusiasm, and that was as much for their purses as their King. The regular army was sullen, the mass of the people resentful, the bourgeoisie offered nothing more than sentimental pledges and the Deputies had their own agendas. The little group in the Tuileries decided their best ploy was to show that the King was really a constitutionalist after all and ordered a royal sitting of the Chambers. At three o'clock in the afternoon, accompanied by the newly humiliated Comte d'Artois and the Ducs of Berry and Orléans, the King, with some difficulty, mounted his carriage and, wearing the star of the Legion of Honour round his neck like a halter, drove through the rain to the Palais du Corps Législatif. Louis XVIII had tried to learn his speech by heart and, all though the journey, said it over and over to himself like an anxious schoolboy. The effort made him oblivious to the tepid acclamations of the crowd and the utter silence of the troops.

When he arrived at his destination two of his courtiers helped support his enormous, gout-ridden weight towards his throne. His features were drawn with the painful effort but he could perhaps derive some comfort from the medieval panoply of the occasion. A great crowd of the aristocracy had gathered, its members being, in the words of one of them, 'distinguished by the magnificence of their clothes, the richness of their appearance and even more noticeably by the near universal feeling of love, concern and anxiety'. Shouts and formal greetings echoed through the chamber. Trumpets sounded, and the noblewomen in the crowd waved so many white handkerchiefs and so many banners embroidered with Bourbon lilies that their efforts were like a snowstorm. Louis eased himself onto his throne, the highest aristocracy formed a crescent round him and he signalled to his chancellor to bid first the Peers and then the Deputies be seated. A hush appropriate to a great moment of national jeopardy fell on the assembled company. The King greeted them and then in what one of his loyalists described as 'a strong, sonorous voice', addressed his subjects.

The speech, so quickly learned, was deeply felt. The words were reassuring. The King had come among his people to draw close those ties that bound them together. There was much to be confident about. The *patrie* was reconciled with all its erstwhile foreign enemies and the alliances formed would not be broken. The King's own efforts, he claimed, had done much to create national unity. In phrases spoiled only by their lack of truth he told how 'I have laboured for the happiness of my people, and I have received, and indeed daily receive, marks of their love for me'. It was time to make the supreme, the clinching promise. 'Now, at the age of sixty, could I end my career in a nobler way, than by dying in the defence of my country?' Louis's vaunted courage made him the supreme patriot. 'I fear nothing as regards my self,' he intoned, 'but I do fear for France.' He enumerated the very genuine perils she faced and touched on matters of altogether more substance than his own factitious heroism. 'Those who come among you lighting the torches of civil war bring with them too the plague of foreign war.' The recent past would be revived in all its ghastliness. Napoleon, who the King would not name, was coming to destroy the constitution and place the country under his iron yoke once more. The charter of the constitution, which Louis had done his best to ignore, was now 'our sacred standard'. The two Chambers should give it the required authority and consent to war. 'This war will then truly prove to be a national war and show what can be achieved by a great people united by their love for their King and their deep love of the nation.' Louis could afford to feel confident for at the back of his mind was his assurance that Marshal Ney, 'the bravest of the brave' and a man more outspoken than most in his denunciations of his erstwhile patron, would achieve all that had to be done on the battlefield.

Ney had already vowed to bring Napoleon back to Paris alive in an iron cage. The vehemence of the image was the measure of the man. Redheaded, tobacco-chewing and uncouth, Ney had had a career that was a paradigm of the possibilities open to a man who showed astonishing courage on the Napoleonic battlefield. He had been born in the same year as the Emperor, the son of a cooper from Saarlouis. Such little education he possessed he had acquired for himself. He was quarrelsome and volatile, and believed that under a carapace of loyalty he was entirely devoted to his own ends. His astonishing, reckless courage had earned him his sobriquet and his promotion. The list of battles he had fought in was a Napoleonic roll call. Conspicuous gallantry both in the Peninsula (where he quarrelled violently with his commanding officer) and a host of battles on the eastern front including Jena, Eylau, Friedland, Bussaco, Smolensk and Borodino, had secured his appointment as a marshal, his elevation first to the Dukedom of Elchingen then to the Princedom of Moskowa, and an income which Napoleon himself reckoned at 300 million francs. It was Ney who had seen that the pitiful fragments of the *Grande Armée* completed the retreat from Moscow, Ney who fought with heroic determination during the campaigns of 1814 and Ney whose voice as much as any other had convinced Napoleon that unconditional abdication was his only possible action when those campaigns collapsed. Ney then threw in his lot with the Bourbons with unseemly enthusiasm only to find himself treated with what he considered slighting hauteur, an insult made all the more bitter when his wife all too often returned from the Tuileries in tears, a victim of the refined bitchiness of the ladies of the old regime.

Now Ney had been despatched to Franche-Comté but had received no specific orders as to what he was to do there.[3] He seemed to be at the whim first of the Duc de Berry who had never left Paris and then of the Comte d'Artois who had retreated ignominiously back there. It was worse than galling. It seemed to epitomise the entire patronising and incompetent attitude of his Bourbon masters. Left to his own devices, Ney did what, as a soldier, he thought best. He moved his army of some 7,000 to Lons-le-Saunier, conscripted more men, hastened his artillery support and resolved to move on Mâcon. Then, on the evening of 12 March, he

learned from a messenger the disastrous news that Lyons had fallen
to Napoleon and that his old master was confident of making his
way to Paris without a shot being fired. Rumours passed on by the
messenger that Napoleon had Austrian support Ney put down to
Napoleon's usual lying and boasting. Ney's own confidence was
boosted when his informant told him that Ney himself had already
saved France once by forcing Napoleon to abdicate. Now he would
save her for a second time. It was all very gratifying. 'If I can secure
the triumph of the King then I shall be the liberator of my country,'
he said.

But Ney preened himself on a service to which he could not give
his heart. Phrases from Napoleon's proclamation began to haunt his
mind. The proclamation had been written by a soldier for soldiers
and its resonances were very deep. Ney thought of the eagle flying
across France from church spire to church spire and coming to rest
on the towers of Notre-Dame. That was what he knew best. That
was the language of the glory days. What had the Bourbons to
compare to it? They left him without troops. They left him without
orders. They, who knew nothing of battle, were too high and
mighty to let a war hero like him ride in their carriages. Resentment
began to fester, but Ney was also aware that he had betrayed his true
master. For the moment, however, it seemed better to stick with the
devils he barely knew than run to the devil he did and he ordered up
a hundred thousand cartridges from Besançon.

But report after report of Napoleon's triumphant progress
blighted the Marshal's false hopes. As a soldier he knew very well
what it meant to face a force now twice the size of his. As an
erstwhile commander in Napoleon's army he knew very well what
it meant to face the man. In these moments of growing doubt two
letters arrived from Napoleon himself, brought by sometime
colleagues. The first of these letters, signed by Bertrand but
probably inspired and perhaps even dictated by Napoleon, put the
Emperor's case. Napoleon's was no fool's errand. Success was
certain and all was prepared. The people were for him. The army

was for him. If Ney dared to oppose then his hands would be red with the blood of civil war and he would stand accused before the whole of France.

The second letter was from Napoleon himself. 'You are to carry out Bertrand's orders and join me at Châlons. I will receive you as I did on the morrow of the Battle of Moskova.' Ney looked across at the men who had brought the letters. Their jubilant enthusiasm measured the depth of his plight. The tricolour was streaming across France and the lilies were wilting on their stems. Royalist agents confirmed as much. Night fell, and the storm that was troubling the whole of France raged with concentrated vehemence in Ney's own hot and volatile head. Ney was a man of action and deep instinctual feelings. He was a soldier who knew that resistance was in vain and he realised that its results would be catastrophic. The winds were rising. Out across the fields the eagle was riding the storm with imperious confidence, blithe in his true element. Ney realised he was caught in the whirlwind and he let its forces blow him where they would.

The following morning he summoned his two senior officers and, inspired by his own wild-eyed desperation, lied to them. Patching together fantasy and old shreds of rumour, he resolved to appear a decided man. 'The whole matter is settled,' he said. It had been for the past three months. The King was a promise-breaker and would be removed from his throne. Who would replace him? At first it seemed that the Duc d'Orléans was the most suitable candidate but opinion had veered more and more towards Napoleon. The listening officers, loyalists both, were appalled. 'How do you expect me to serve that bastard?' one of them broke out. 'He's done me nothing but harm, while the King's only done me good. Besides, I'm in the King's service and frankly, Monsieur le Maréchal, I at least am a man of honour.' Ney, incandescent with guilt and anger, fired back. 'And so am I! That's why I'm not going to go on being humiliated like this. I'm tired of seeing my wife come home in tears because of the snubs she's received. It's pretty clear the King doesn't want the likes of us! Only a soldier like Bonaparte will treat the army at its true worth.' He snatched up the order Napoleon had issued to the troops, saying: 'This is what I'm going to read to the men.'

The two officers bowed to his fury and ordered the men out on parade. The sullenness of the troops evaporated in the Marshal's new-found enthusiasm, and cries of '*Vive l'Empereur!*' tore the air. 'Only the Emperor Napoleon is fit to rule our beautiful country,' Ney told them. 'Soldiers,' he continued, 'I have many times led you to victory, now I shall lead you in that immortal phalanx that follows the Emperor to Paris!' The shouting was tumultuous. That night there was a party in the mess. Glass after glass was raised to Napoleon's success. Amid the high spirits only Ney himself sat silent and moodily self-absorbed. Deep inside him something essential had fractured.

## The King Flees Paris

In the midst of his triumph Napoleon himself was isolated and increasingly secretive for in truth he trusted none of those who acclaimed him. He sought to protect himself with impregnable suspiciousness. He alone was the man of destiny. The fate of nations turned on him and no one else. This was one of his most rooted beliefs. As early as his Egyptian campaign Napoleon had asked the people of that country: 'Is there a man blind enough not to see that destiny directs all my operations?' The idea was with him still. His hands only grasped the lever that would move the world. His ambition alone would shape its future. As Napoleon progressed towards Paris the great mass of the ordinary people who were so loud in his support – the peasants in the fields and the workers in the cities – were, as always, 'the rabble of the country' who existed only to be led. He needed their acclamations but their very vociferousness reminded him of the danger they posed. Napoleon was still the man who, as a youth, had wanted to fire on the mob in the Tuileries and had repressed a popular rising with 'a whiff of grapeshot'. Silent at the heart of his loudly triumphant progress towards Paris, Napoleon let the people will him towards a success that was to exist for him alone.

The army on which Napoleon relied was to be surveyed with a critical eye similar to that with which he looked upon the people. Just as he viewed the enthusiasm of the civilians with wariness, trying to gauge their mood before entering large cities especially and then often doing so like a thief in the night, so Napoleon made efforts to gauge the mood in the local barracks. What concerned him here was over-enthusiasm. There were rumours of plots against his life but revenge and bloodshed would have been a disaster. Napoleon wrote to the general of his advance guard saying: 'I forbid you to fire a single shot. You are to allay the excitement and contradict the rumours which are exasperating the men. Tell them that I do not wish to re-enter my capital at their head if their arms are stained with French blood.' Such hot-headedness was a real danger, but it was not for the sake of the army that he was moving on Paris. The army was his means, not his ends.

Nor was it just the ordinary civilians and soldiers that Napoleon distrusted. He knew that the bourgeoisie would look first to their purses and those he had as yet to fill. As to men of greater standing, figures like Ney had revealed their natures by turning their coats for a second time. Ney himself had professed the fierce morality of his purpose, writing to tell Napoleon that 'if you continue to govern tyrannically, then I am your prisoner rather than your supporter'. He ended his letter with sermonising. 'The Emperor must from now on govern with one purpose only, the happiness of the French people and the undoing of the evil which his ambition has brought on *la patrie*.' Napoleon quickly read the letter through, tore it into bits, told Ney he was off his head and ordered him to collect regiments to take to Paris. Nor could Napoleon trust his own wife, although at this stage he was unaware of the fact. 'The people are running to me in droves,' he wrote to tell her. 'Entire regiments are quitting and joining me,' he went on, adding: 'I shall be in Paris by the time you receive this letter.' He concluded with a last appeal: 'Come and rejoin me with my son. I hope to embrace you before the month is out.' Napoleon was unaware of the fact that Marie-Louise, happy in the arms of Count Neipperg, had recently written a public letter to her father renouncing both her husband and the French crown while also refusing to return the King of Rome to his father. Napoleon quite simply did not know that the brightest jewels had been prised from his crown whose repossession was his one true aim, his sole purpose. Ignorant as yet of his loss, Napoleon travelled on in his lumbering coach, his face dark and his features set in silent, wary mistrustfulness.

Indeed, there was suspicion everywhere. Among the leading figures in Paris, M. Fouché, of course, could be trusted by no one, especially when he was more than normally busy which, indeed, he had been of late. It was a prosperous time for plotting. His own favourite scheme was to set up Marie-Louise as regent for the King of Rome, something which would have given him the immense political power of an éminence grise to a woman and a child. Never a man to follow a single line, Fouché was also in contact with Bonapartists, royalists and constitutionalists. He had opened a secret correspondence with Metternich, and was well aware of the machinations of that group of marshals who wanted to put the Duc d'Orléans on the throne. Now, with Napoleon loose in the country once more, Fouché found that he was being openly courted by those close to the King who needed him quite as much as they feared and loathed him. They offered him back the Ministry of Police and Fouché, not wanting to be openly associated with what was clearly the losing side, turned it down saying with Delphic subtlety that if his would-be benefactors would save the King then he would save the monarchy. The bemused, suspicious courtiers were not minded to believe him and decided to have him arrested. The man they despatched was not up to the job. Fouché stared at him, asked to read his warrant, declared it 'irregular' and, vowing to protest in writing, went into his study. A secret staircase let him down into the garden. A convenient ladder allowed him to scale the wall, and Fouché scuttled round to the apartment of one of his cronies where, for the time being, he decided to lie low. He had a clear-eyed view of what was about to happen. He knew that Napoleon would take Paris 'and in three months' time either he or I will not be there'. M. Fouché was very determined about which of them would survive.

Other plans hatched by the courtiers were no more successful or, indeed, credible. Now, as Napoleon drew ever closer to Paris, it was a question of what to do with the King. It was suggested that he withdraw to La Rochelle where, in time, he could foment a civil war that would return him to his throne. The absurdity of this was obvious even to the royal advisors. Others suggested that Louis drive out in his carriage and meet Napoleon head to head. The sheer majesty of his presence would oblige the usurper to withdraw. That idea evaporated with the breath that spoke it. It was then mooted that the Tuileries should be fortified. The King did not like the thought of a siege and, in his heart of hearts, was already meditating flight. Others had shown him the way. The fashionable ladies of the Faubourg Saint-Germain had snatched up their diamonds and made for their coaches. The crown jewels and a vast amount of money were on their way to Britain, and others were now withdrawing their savings as stocks tumbled and the clerks in the passport office worked their fingers numb. The proprietors of the stagecoach companies were running a thriving trade. Hard news was difficult to get but rumour made plain that the army was still deserting in droves and, when their general tried to win over the remains of the Old Guard with promises of money, promotion and titles of nobility, he was told it was too late. 'We regret that we cannot obey you. We have received the Emperor's orders and we are resolved to obey them.'

By the evening of 17 March, Napoleon had reached Auxerre and the following day the King made plain his decision to flee Paris. He was advised to do so at night. 'There is no need,' one of his courtiers whispered acidly, 'to let the sun shine on the disgrace.' Most of his closest advisers were kept in ignorance of the King's plan, for secrecy was essential if Louis were to avoid the fate of his royal brother who had been ignominiously captured as he fled his capital during the revolution. It was only at 11.30 p.m. that the King informed his circle that he would leave in half an hour. Some few minutes later a dozen carriages rattled across the flagstones of the Tuileries from where they would take their passenger first to Lille and eventually to Ghent. Louis's own coach drew to a halt under the awning of the Pavilon de Flore. A crowd of palace loyalists gathered in tense and emotional silence to watch their monarch desert them. Eventually a door opened and he appeared leaning heavily on the arms of two of his nobility. He had been his usual placid self all day and was reluctant now to ruffle his equability. Public displays of emotion were unbecoming to a king, even a disgraced one. The crowd however could not contain its feelings. The sight of their ageing, fat, defeated ruler had for them all an almost unbearable pathos. They fell to their knees. They cried out '*Vive le Roi!*' They wept. From somewhere in the throng of people a hysterical voice cried out: 'He wears a crown of thorns!'

It was all most distasteful and Louis whispered to his aids that he should have been spared the ordeal. He nonetheless rose to the occasion as best he could. 'My children, your devotion touches me. But I must have strength. Spare me, for pity's sake. Return to your families. I shall see you all again soon.' With that he heaved his bulk into his waiting coach and drove away. Only a little later did he discover that his things had not been properly packed or had been mislaid. It was very irksome not to have enough shirts but it was even worse not to have one's favourite slippers. Turning to Macdonald, who had joined him at Abbeville, he said with petulant sincerity: 'You'll know one day, my dear Marshal, what it is to lose slippers that have taken on the shape of one's foot.' The following day the King passed – slipperless – from his realm and, once in the relative safety of Ghent, settled down to his real avocation. The street urchins of the city climbed onto the windowsills to watch him at it. Staring in goggle-eyed they counted the number of glasses of exquisite wine that helped the French King gourmandise his way through dish after dish of exquisitely prepared food. They kept a tally and shouted it to the passers-by. They noticed that sometimes the effort was so great that the royal face perspired. To the solid burghers of Ghent their guest, 'Louis dix-huit', became *Louis di zweet* – 'Sweating Louis'.

## Napoleon Takes Paris

Napoleon spent the night of 19 March at Pont-sur-Yonne. The following morning he set out for Fontainebleau. Nearly a hundred heavily armed cavalrymen surrounded his coach, so great was his fear of assassination. Darkness was falling as he entered the vast courtyard, once the scene of his tearful departure. Now there were cries of excitement but these failed to make much impression. Napoleon was exhausted. He leaned on Bertrand's arm as he mounted the horseshoe staircase and went to his old room. A log fire was burning and an old servant greeted him in tears. He asked to have his boots pulled off and lay down on the bed, desperate to snatch what sleep he could before his troops assembled at the palace. He was still tired when he woke at eight the following morning to the sound of the pandemonium created by his arriving soldiers. None of his staff, it seemed, could reduce the 20,000 men to order. Napoleon was alone, tired and had decisions of the utmost consequence to make. He did not yet know that the King had fled and he was trying to make up his mind if he should move on Paris directly or stay at Fontainebleau for a little while longer. He decided to stay for a few hours more and proposed spending the night in Essonnes. The following day would be his son's fourth birthday. It seemed that the boy would not be in Paris for it. But at midday

Napoleon's gloom lightened when he learned of the flight of the King. His face brightened with delight. 'Good,' he said, 'I shall be in the Tuileries tonight.' A little while later he heard of the defection of the greater part of the remains of Louis's army.

Action was now imperative but the crowds thronging the road to Paris ensured that Napoleon's progress was slow. The city itself was remarkably quiet. Earlier in the day the mob had been on the streets crying for their Emperor but they had been dispersed by the National Guard. It was clear that there would be no disorder. There was little traffic in the streets, many of the shops were shut and tiny booths did a roaring trade in fried potatoes and brioches. In the cafés waiters drank with their customers and toasted Napoleon's return as people began to make their way to the Tuileries where the tricolour was already streaming in the sharp wind. Gradually the old staff of the imperial palace returned to their posts, bright in their old liveries. The great reception rooms were crowded with men in brilliant uniforms loudly greeting each other and hailing the bloodless victory. Then someone saw that the carpet in the Throne Room was powdered with Bourbon lilies. This was unfortunate, but closer inspection showed the lilies to have been merely sewn over the imperial bees that originally decorated it. A score of court ladies, careless of their dresses (amaranth was the colour of the season), fell to their knees and began pulling at the hateful threads. They unravelled as easily as the monarchy itself and very soon the carpet was ready for imperial feet.

But they did not come. Agonising minutes turned into hours and there was no Napoleon. Still the crowds were delaying him. Then, at nine o'clock, he finally appeared, borne on a roaring tide of carriages, horses and officers, jubilant peasants, suddenly contented bourgeoises, children and innumerable soldiers. The door of his carriage was flung open and the Emperor could be seen dressed in the green coat of a colonel of chasseurs of the Imperial Guard. His face was deadly pale, his anxiously chewing lips were narrow, his jaws were overhung. Thin, dusky brown hair was scattered over his temples but he made no attempt to hide his balding pate. His pot belly now protruded so considerably that his underwear rode up over the top of his trousers. He was forty-six, he was reclaiming his empire and the ecstatic crowd surged forward, grabbed hold of him and passed him from hand to hand until he was eventually rescued by his soldiers who carried him shoulder-high into his palace. There, in his old study, he had the litter of missals left by his predecessor swept away and replaced by maps. Looking at the image of *la patrie* reduced to its old borders he whispered, 'Poor France!' He would recover her glory, his glory. The ecstatic crowds were willing him to. He still mistrusted them, despised them even, but he knew what he owed them. Over and over again he said: 'It was really those who had nothing to gain who brought me back to Paris. It was the second lieutenants and the privates who did it all – it is to the people and the army that I owe everything.' Their cries had been the storm the eagle rode and now, finally, the king of birds was in his eyrie and alone.

# 4

## PARIS

### 21 MARCH–12 JUNE 1815

## Remastering France

The amount of work to be done was prodigious and would have daunted anyone but Napoleon whose immense reserves of energy and heroic resolve were, for the moment, undimmed. He laboured constantly, sleeping for intervals of perhaps three hours at a time and then returning to his desk. When his doctor asked him to rest or at least take some exercise he snapped back that he hadn't the time. Those around him were amazed by his clarity of insight, his mastery of detail, the daring of his enterprise. He dictated a vast correspondence which touched on every important matter. The vigour of his conversation – his harangues and political observations – his daily orders and future plans, all witnessed to a great mind working at the top of its bent. 'The Emperor,' wrote one observer, 'studied everything with that insight and high intelligence that were always so remarkable in him and talked about where he stood with a penetration denied even to his enemies.' There were, of course, moments of lassitude, doubt and despair. Carnot once found him staring at a portrait of his still-absent son with tears pouring down his face. There were times when Napoleon thought that Destiny, once his handmaiden, had deserted him. He shrugged such thoughts off and returned to his desk. He believed that he alone could defend France from the gathering enemies which his own presence had summoned, keep the slackening human machinery around him running, hold together increasing disunity of opinion and crush it where he could not. The impossible, after all, was a phantom to frighten the timid and a refuge for fools.

The first thing Napoleon needed to do was to try and bind the country together, to make sure not only that he kept die-hard followers happy but that liberal opinion was mollified, defiant royalism emasculated and – perhaps his most worrying problem – that the strong Jacobin elements inspiring the crowd that had willed him towards his throne did not explode into anarchy and bloodshed. His old, deep-seated soldier's fear and loathing of undisciplined crowds remained very strong. Action against the royalists, by contrast, at first seemed relatively easy. Those in Paris were ordered to leave the capital and not venture within ninety miles of it. Warrants were issued for the arrest of leading royalist figures such as Talleyrand, who had shrewdly followed his King into exile. Their wealth was then sequestrated to fill the imperial coffers. So much was straightforward. It was far more difficult to deal with extreme opinions among the people at large, especially the Jacobin tendency who believed that its time might have come round again. During the glory days they had been skilfully sidelined and emasculated. France had been very largely depoliticised and the threat the Jacobins posed became increasingly a memory. Now those memories were awake. Such powerfully disruptive forces had to be dealt with or at least contained, and it was in Lyons that Napoleon had made his first painful gesture of appeasement.

Throughout his forced march from the Golfe Jouan Napoleon had been careful to present himself less as a returning Charlemagne than the returning First Consul, the revolutionary soldier, the man of the people. His proclamations began with the electrifying word 'Citizens'. He told the people of Grenoble: 'I want less to be sovereign of France than the first of her citizens.' Throughout, his conversation was carefully salted with the phrases of a tribune. Napoleon was the child of the Revolution. He had now come to deliver France from her aristocratic oppressors. He had come 'to free the people from the slavery that the priests and the nobility wanted to reduce them to'. It was a very dangerous tactic to say such things but a necessary one and it rose to a first climax in Lyons. 'I am coming back,' Napoleon told the shouting crowds of the welcoming city, 'to protect and defend the interests that our Revolution has given us.' Such phrases served to bring anti-Bourbon feeling to head. The raising of the tricolour across the land symbolised a return to the old values. The abolishment of the Bourbon aristocracy and feudal obligations were necessary and promising auguries of things to come. The next matter was altogether more difficult, however. 'I want to give you,' Napoleon went on, 'an inviolable constitution, one prepared by the people and me together.' It was a promise that had somehow to be honoured.

The temper of the country made the prospect increasingly frightening. In provincial cities across the land – in Bourg, Nantes, Rouen, Brest, Bourges and Dijon – priests and aristocrats were repeatedly harassed.[1] The *Marseillaise* was heard all too often in the streets of Paris. There were red bonnets among the crowds. When Napoleon himself saw some of these surging towards the Faubourg Saint-Germain he knew that a single careless word or look from him would fully wake the monster of anarchy and re-erect the guillotine. The press was already pouring out dangerously inflammatory phrases. 'Since this is the war of the nobles against the people, it's necessary for the people to rise up as they did in '92 and exterminate their enemies once and for all.' There was deep concern in the Tuileries. As one of Napoleon's aides told him: 'I find the hatred for priests and nobles as widespread and violent today as it was at the outset of the Revolution. It is whipped to a fury!' Napoleon was perfectly well aware of the fact that a legitimate empire could not be re-established on the basis of mob rule and he 'had no intention of becoming a king of the *jacquerie*'. But virulent hatred on the left was matched by the indignation of the liberals. 'He has reappeared,' wrote one of them in a venomous article for the *Journal des Débats*, 'this madman dyed with our blood! He is another Attila, another Genghis Khan, but more terrible and more hateful because he has at his disposal the resources of civilisation.' The author, terrified by his own outspokenness, fled to Nantes, vowing that he was a man of honour. 'I am no turncoat. I shall not drag myself from one government to the next, cloak shame in sophistry or stammer lies to save a life stained with dishonour.' He was summoned to the Tuileries and he came.[2]

The man who now stood before Napoleon was a curious sight indeed. He was tall and his red hair clashed with the vivid if bedraggled yellow of his suit. His shoulders stooped and, from time to time, he nervously pushed his glasses up his nose when they had been disturbed by his tic. His name was Benjamin Constant and he was newly and hopelessly in love with one of the most beautiful women in Paris – that Madame Récamier who gave her name to the sofa on which David painted her reclining without her shoes. Her royalist hand had guided his pen but here was the unlikely figure who could yet save Napoleon. The matter was now an urgent one. Napoleon had earlier promised that he would summon the electoral colleges to Paris in May to reshape the constitution. Thirty thousand delegates would gather in the Champ-de-Mars where a sort of Arcadian parliament would prove once and for all that Napoleon was no longer a military dictator ruling by fiat but the benign leader of a so-called Liberal Empire. The prospect had once seemed rather pleasing. 'What a spectacle!' Napoleon beamed. Certainly it would have enormous propaganda value in uniting the nation under his eye. Now that eye was increasingly jaundiced. The promise seemed rash and the man in the yellow suit would have to sort the problem out. Napoleon worked on him with his practised charm until it was his hand that guided Constant's pen. The bewildered man moved from hatred and fear to admiration and willing service with a speed so great that any thoughts that he might be turning his coat were forgotten. Constant returned to *la divine* Récamier as elated as a schoolboy and with much homework to do. 'What an amazing man he is,' he told his disbelieving mistress. 'Tomorrow I am to bring him an outline for a new constitution.'

True to his quickly changed word, an exhausted Constant returned to the Tuileries the following day. Nervously, he read the sixty-seven draft articles of a constitution which would considerably curtail the Emperor's erstwhile powers. All press censorship was to be abolished. There was also to be complete freedom of religious belief and the state itself was to be tied to no Church. Next to the law. No civilian was to be tried before a military court and verdicts in those where they did appear were to be given by a jury rather than a judge sitting alone. An imperial pardon could be granted to any criminal or anyone who abused his office. Ministers were to act within strict legal definitions. Both Chambers were to have the right to amend legislation and propose new laws in certain areas. The proceedings of the Chamber of Peers (the hereditary life members of which were to be Napoleon's appointees) were to be published but their sessions, like those of the Representatives, could be prorogued by the judges. Perhaps most gallingly of all, conscription – that bane of the people of the Empire – was to be subject to an annual authorisation by both Chambers.

Napoleon smiled to hide his fury and suggest assent. The Additional Act, as it was properly known, or the 'Benjamine' as it was slightingly referred to by some, had apparently appeared altogether more acceptable than Constant dared hope and he soon found himself possessed of a State Counsellorship and a comfortable salary. Not so Napoleon's redoubtable opponent Gilbert de La Fayette. An intransigent egalitarian, he had turned down all of the bribes the Emperor had offered him including the Legion of Honour, an award which he described as 'ridiculous'. Now he called the 'Benjamine' 'a weird combination of imperial, liberal and terrorist measures'. He would use them to his own advantage, however, and would soon emerge from his life of rural retirement to become an implacable public critic of the Emperor and a deadly enemy.

Napoleon himself in the meantime, refusing to let the Constitution Committee discuss the new legislation and announcing in the newspapers that he himself had accepted the terms of the Act, called for a plebiscite to ratify the document as a whole. There would be no analysis of its individual clauses but the results of the election would be announced at a great public ceremony known as the Champs de Mai. Privately, of course, Napoleon was furious. 'They are trying to weaken me,' he exclaimed, 'tying my hands.' He felt as if the whole of France was pushing him into the background as if determined not to see him. This was ridiculous and, in his mounting fury, Napoleon let slip the true direction of his thoughts. 'They ask me what has become of the Emperor's famous firm hand, which France needs now to master Europe.' That was still his aim. That was still his purpose. And the laws that drove it were not the fiddling terms of a 'Benjamine' but the iron laws of fate. 'They can talk to me all they want of their ideas of "goodness", "abstract justice" and the "natural laws"! The first real law is "necessity" while the most essential form of "justice" is national safety.' How could the nation be safe if he could not even conscript soldiers readily? For the moment there were only a very few who saw through to his true motivation, a very few who realised that if Napoleon had learned nothing he had forgotten nothing either. 'Do not rely on this liberal constitution which he appears willing enough to give us today,' they muttered. 'Once he's at the head of a victorious army again he will soon forget all about it.'

Many people contended themselves with merely feeling alienated but others were more active. The Bonapartists resented the curtailing of the Emperor's powers and some among them joined the proliferating groups of *fédérés*, armed bands of petit-bourgeois and artisans dedicated to preventing the country from swinging to the right.[3] They mushroomed across the western region particularly but their influence was felt across the whole of France and, eventually, in Paris. In particular they found support in the working-class suburbs of Saint-Marceau and Saint-Antoine from where, in the middle of May, some 15,000 of the *fédérés* suddenly emerged fully armed and made for the Tuileries. It was horrifying and politically very difficult, for the object of their fervour was Napoleon himself. He had listened to their cries of how they had hated to have a king imposed on them by their enemies. He heard their acclamations of his achievements. 'We have welcomed you back enthusiastically because you are the representative of *la patrie*, her defender and the protector of the rights of the people!' Then they demanded that they be given arms. They swore to fight only for the sake of France and Napoleon himself. He came out to greet them, unarmed and alone. A whiff of grapeshot would have ruined him and a lie seemed altogether more advisable. He had counted on the army and the people, he said, and the army and the people were now amply rewarding his trust. 'I shall give you arms! . . . I have faith in you!' He had, of course, no such thing. Their intense excitement, dangerous as it was, nonetheless demanded a gesture and, after they had marched once again and shown their feelings by burning the Bourbon flag, Napoleon instituted twenty-four battalions of *fédéré* infantrymen. They were to be trained by regular officers and issued with 3,500 disabled muskets for drilling purposes only. Better the loyalty of toy soldiers than the fury of the mob.

Would-be Jacobins on the other hand derided Napoleon's so-called Liberal Empire as a useless compromise. 'Abandon your unsettling moderation,' they cried, working themselves up into an anti-aristocratic fury. 'How can you have peace and quiet when you protect the enemy within? These people must be cut from our breast like a cancer!' The old cry of 'Lynch the aristocrats!' was heard again. It was not raised without some justification for the aristocracy themselves were also in arms. There had been incidents led by such figures as the Duc de Bourbon and the redoubtable Duchesse d'Angoulême, 'the only man in her family', as Napoleon described her. These were relatively minor if sometimes unpleasant affairs, but altogether more serious was the royalist resistance in the west that eventually focused on a local magnate, the Marquis de la Rochejacquelin.[4] The western region was traditionally loyal to the Bourbons and was muttering with discontent. Early in April there was a spate of well-coordinated royalist terrorist attacks on the gendarmerie and military headquarters in nearly a dozen towns. The authorities sent desperate messages to Paris begging for help. 'The revolt here will explode out of all control if any more troops are withdrawn. Then we will need a whole army in Brittany.' Napoleon himself did not see the matter as a priority, but success encouraged insurrection and the widening of plans. La Rochejacquelin was in contact with King Louis in Ghent, met with him and then set off for London. There he asked for military aid and was to some degree successful. He returned from his mission on the British frigate the *Astrea* with 2,000 of the promised 14,000 muskets. During his absence his cause had grown widely popular and somewhere between 15,000 and 30,000 men in the departments stretching between Brittany and the Vendée were ready to follow him even if armed only with old farm shotguns, clubs and pitchforks.

The men were sufficiently confident to march on another seven towns, and the desperate despatches sent to Paris now suggested that civil war was about to break out, if it hadn't already erupted. Even government ministers began to take the situation seriously. Napoleon at last decided to act. He readied a force of nearly 3,000 gendarmes, two regiments of Guards, twenty-five battalions of infantry, eight squadrons of cavalry and three batteries of artillery. This was a sledgehammer to crack a nut and there was one man in the government who urged that the matter could be dealt with in an altogether cheaper and more dextrous manner. M. Fouché suggested that one of his innumerable contacts, a disgraced royalist officer called Malartic, be sent to the west where he could use his influence with his fellow aristocrats to persuade them to postpone their activities at least for the time being. Fouché was in deadly, cunning earnest.

*Fouché*

Once the return of Napoleon was an established fact, M. Fouché had left his hiding place and come to the Tuileries at the request of the Emperor.[5] It was a late invitation and a fateful one. No other candidate had been willing to take over the police department and so Fouché was the only choice for what was his natural role. The courtiers made way for him as he entered and stood before his erstwhile master, a thin, tall, slightly stooping man whose greying, reddish-blonde hair suggested his fifty-six years. Napoleon, who detested, admired and needed him, looked across at the immobile face of one of the very few men who would never cower before him and knew all too many of his most distressing secrets. This was a dangerous ally summoned at midnight and in desperation. Even now Fouché's tight and pallid features suggested the constantly working energies of his frigid fanaticism. Dressed in plain black clothes amid all the brilliant decor and brighter uniforms of the palace and its courtiers, Fouché gave the uncomfortable impression of being a monk disguised in evening dress, of being something other than he seemed. And indeed it was as a monastic schoolmaster he had started out on a career which had fallen like a shadow across every aspect of French history for the past twenty-five tumultuous years.

Teaching physics to little boys from rich homes failed to satisfy Fouché's ambitions, which burst forth at the Revolution with terrifying ferocity. He denounced God, he denounced wealth, he denounced nobility and voted for the execution of the King. Teased by Emperor Napoleon over this last move Fouché, who now rejoiced in the title of the Duc d'Otrante and an income of fabulous extent, replied that it was 'the first service I was able to render Your Majesty'. The imperturbable quickness of wit, the unblinking cynicism, were deeply attractive to Napoleon – a mask over the merciless depths they hid. The extent of Fouché's sadism had been written in blood across Lyons during the Reign of Terror. Sent to France's second city to instil the virtues of liberty, fraternity and equality, Fouché set about his task by committing wholesale and 'salutary' atrocities. Humiliation and looting were merely the tributaries that fed the rivers of blood. The smell of these last was so terrible as aristocrat after aristocrat made his final obeisance to the guillotine that the killing fields had eventually to be moved out of the city in order to avoid the risk of disease. One thousand, nine hundred and five men and women died. Always the efficient bureaucrat, Fouché wrote back to his masters in Paris saying: 'We are causing much corrupt blood to flow, but that is our duty since it is for the sake of humanity.'

Fouché had been bitterly opposed to Napoleon's taking on the role of First Consul, and Napoleon had retorted by closing down the Ministry of Police. Finding that he needed Fouché back when he himself assumed the imperial crown, Napoleon began to discover (if he did not know it before) the extent of his police chief's compulsive duplicity. The erstwhile Jacobin who was now a servant of the Empire was alleged by some to have been involved with the royalist assassins whose unsuccessful attempt on Napoleon's life had led directly to his coronation. Nothing was proved and Fouché set up for Napoleon the most efficient secret policing system in Europe. 'I must be the complete master when I'm in charge,' he declared, and he secured his position by putting spies on the little fish while he himself set about knowing everybody important: the dissident intellectuals gathered around the author and popularist Madame de Staël, erstwhile Jacobins, erstwhile religious leaders and those flowers of the nobility who had not left Paris. It was quite something to see M. Fouché riding in the Bois de Boulogne every morning with the ineffably aristocratic Adrien de Montmorency. Even Talleyrand was impressed. And when Fouché was not out on horseback with the great he was reading their letters. Even Napoleon's correspondence passed briefly across his desk before being sent on to its intended recipients.

Fouché's knowledge of everybody else's business was prodigious (he had a very exact list of the number of Pauline Borghese's lovers) and his need to plot remained as compulsive as his view of events was clear. Fouché had as sound an insight as Talleyrand into the disasters of Napoleon's utter refusal to accept the limits of the possible – he advised against involvement in Spain and Russia, and urged making a peace with Britain – and it was with Talleyrand that he briefly allied himself in 1807 to topple Napoleon from his throne. Even that incident left Fouché largely unscathed, and it was only three years later, in 1810, when it was discovered that Fouché was sending letters to Britain about removing Napoleon once again that he was sacked and exiled to rule a distant province. Now he was back, promising the Bourbons that he would restore the monarchy while willingly accepting office under Napoleon. In tune with the times as always, Fouché publicly at least reconstituted the imperial police as a body only too willing to uphold the values of the so-called Liberal Empire. Meanwhile, there was the large question of the Allies gathering their armies to the north of France and the altogether smaller matter of the royalist insurgents in the west.

With an elegance that surely brought a smile to even Fouché's bloodless face he set about arranging matters in a way that would please all the parties and secure his own position regardless of the outcome. The useful Malartic, the disgraced royalist officer with influential contacts in the west, was summoned to Fouché's office. Fouché sat him down and patiently explained why a revolt in the Vendée was not such a good idea. Indeed, he said, it was very harmful to the cause it was designed to serve. Not only would the Vendée itself be reduced to rubble with terrible loss of life, such a civil war would give Napoleon a vast army to prolong indefinitely his struggle against the Allied forces now gathering to the north. That was where the fate of France would be decided and it should be decided quickly. Fouché looked across at his bewildered interlocutor with as much of a pleading expression as was possible to him. 'Help me to stop this useless spilling of French blood,' he said of the rising in the Vendée. 'It's the only way left.' Malartic, armed with a safe conduct, at once went about his new master's bidding and was successful in convincing a couple of royalist leaders of the wisdom of Fouché's insight before appealing to La Rochejacquelin to disband his troops. The embittered, cornered aristocrat was furious despite his recent crushing military reverses. To back down was the merest treason. The mayors of every town and village in the Vendée were ordered to conscript their available menfolk. Even when his lieutenants deserted him La Rochejacquelin still determined to fight on, firing angry letters from his desperate corner to those who had gone over to the *tyran dévastateur* of France. He was now alone, weakened and exposed. Fouché had made his forces evaporate and La Rochejacquelin died in a futile little skirmish, his hope of restoring the Bourbons crushed.

M. Fouché could allow himself a considerable measure of self-congratulation. Napoleon was pleased with him even while a great reserve of royalists had been spared a pointless death. The little matter of the Vendée had been admirably solved without a civil war and now there remained the altogether greater matter of the Allies massing to the north. Their presence had been Fouché's means of persuading the royalists to disarm and now their growing numbers would be his means of securing his own power. Chatting to a colleague he observed how Napoleon would soon be obliged to move north to deal with the forces there. 'Once he is out of the way,' he went on, 'we shall be in charge of the situation here.' That was agreeable, but the likely outcome was even more so. 'Let him win one or two battles, he will finally lose the big one and that is when we shall really have our work cut out.'

With that, M. Fouché hurried away. There was much for him to do. He wanted to smother Paris in posters depicting 'Louis the Pig' as a robber carrying off his swag from the Banque de France. Hatred of the King had to be maintained. He had to write to Metternich too. It was surely altogether more advisable that the Bourbons should be returned in the form of the Duc d'Orléans rather than his ridiculous brother. And he needed to secure his own position as well, just in case the worse should happen. He needed to draft a letter to the Duke of Wellington arranging for a safe place of exile in Britain should things turn really nasty. Fouché had thought out every contingency and even Napoleon (who was now having his police chief trailed by none other than the less than subtle Fleury de Chaboulon who had once brought him important news to Elba) was dumbfounded. 'He is simply a born intriguer,' he sighed, 'and no one can stop him doing it' – not even Napoleon. It was a sinister confession.

## Reactions

In the meantime Napoleon himself, the master Fouché followed with such an adroit lack of scruple, was pursuing his own diplomatic charade. Needing peace as a time in which to prepare for inevitable war, Napoleon was loud both at home and abroad about the modesty of his intentions now he had returned to Paris. He wrote a private letter to his father-in-law, the Emperor of Austria, saying that his efforts were directed solely to consolidating his throne so that, one day, he might leave it strongly secured to his son – 'the child Your Majesty has enveloped in paternal kindness'. A circular letter was then addressed to the other monarchs of Europe. Napoleon tried to explain to them that the Bourbon dynasty had been forced on the French people and was no longer to their taste. The Bourbons, for their part, had distanced themselves from the people's needs and customs. Napoleon, on the other hand, had been 'carried to the heart of my capital by their love'. He now wanted peace with honour to reign across Europe. The years of battle were behind them. A new era had dawned in which the chief concern would be the 'sacred' struggle for the happiness of the people. 'Jealous of her independence,' Napoleon declared, 'the unwavering principle of France's policy will be an absolute respect for others' independence.' Nobody believed him, of course. 'So,' declared Talleyrand with a raised, ironic eyebrow, 'the wolf's become the shepherd, has he.' The copy of the letter sent to London remained unopened on the Prince Regent's desk in Carlton House. The shuffling, alcoholic and disreputable aesthete who was the heir to the British throne would not have appreciated being addressed as '*Monsieur mon frère*'.

Napoleon tried a similar tactic on his immediate circle. During the evening of his return to the Tuileries he spoke confidentially to two of them. 'My concern is to live a quiet life and spend the rest of my days repairing the damage that twenty years of war culminating in an invasion have done to France,' he said. The breathtaking hypocrisy of the remark was backed up by sound political arguments. Given that the French people had summoned him home with one voice and the Bourbons had put up not a shred of resistance, the Great Powers gathered in Vienna would have to think very carefully before they acted against him. They would come to regret a hasty response. Kings, of course, would understand such things, but there were others in the Austrian capital who were altogether more dangerous. Men like Castlereagh and Wellington were capable of turning crowned heads against *la patrie* and even Napoleon himself. They were warmongers and it was best that France should be prepared for them. The deviousness of this was patent. France was going to be remobilised under the veil of national self-defence.

The more intelligent men gathered about Napoleon were appalled by the predicament he had placed them in. It was perfectly clear to Fouché from the start that the Emperor's promises of peace were tosh and his hopes for European love and friendship were as vacuous as they were insincere. The Allies would never tolerate what had happened and Europe would once again be convulsed by war. 'There is nothing any of us can do to stem the inevitable tide for the whole thing will be settled within four months,' Fouché declared. His cold analysis was unerring, but those who had followed Napoleon with greater love and more naive admiration were hurt and baffled. The devoted Caulaincourt who had wrapped his cloak around Napoleon to protect him from the cold as they hurried back from the horrors of the Russian campaign felt bound to confess that the Emperor was now off his head – that he was *'fou'*.

Put in charge of the Ministry of Foreign Affairs, Caulaincourt could only foresee disaster. Napoleon quite simply refused to listen to reason, he said. The Emperor was surely aware that the situation in France had changed completely since his Elban exile. In their determination to get rid of the Bourbons the people may well have shouted *'Vive l'Empereur!'* but their expectations had risen as sharply as their hopes, and it was daily becoming more and more obvious that they no longer wanted the iron hand of old-style imperial government. Such brutal ways were intolerable to a people whose deepest desire was the freedom Napoleon's proclamations and early actions after his return had seemed to imply. The people had very much wanted to shape their own destiny on the Champs de Mai rather than having a 'Benjamine' thrust on them wholesale and with no opportunity to discuss its individual clauses. But that was impossible. Caulaincourt saw very clearly that Napoleon 'simply cannot dare to grant the wide-ranging liberties everybody wants. He has promised them, yes, but only as a sop until he is on his feet and returns to his old ways.' It was awful, a blundering towards violence amid deepening darkness. 'He is heading in the wrong direction,' Caulaincourt sighed, 'his step is faltering. He is completely out of his depth. And why is he purblind to the fact that the only real feeling he inspires in the people is fear itself?' Many of them could foresee what would happen – see war and defeat followed by the rape and dismemberment of France herself.

## The Allies

The Allies, regrouping themselves as the Seventh Coalition against Napoleon, made their own position perfectly clear. On 13 March they signed a declaration that admitted no diplomatic obliqueness, no whisper of a compromise. By fleeing from Elba and breaking the terms of the treaty that had sent him there Napoleon had destroyed 'the sole legal title to which his existence is attached'. As a consequence of this he had deprived himself of the protection of the laws, and 'manifested in the face of the universe' that there could be neither peace nor truce with him. Napoleon was, in their grave and terrible opinion: 'outside civil and social relations, and . . . as an enemy and disturber of the peace of the world, he has delivered himself over to public prosecution.' The would-be Emperor was a pariah, and steps were very rapidly taken to isolate France and quarantine her as the source of a contagion that could easily blight the rest of the Continent.

Tiny incidents showed the massive hatred in which the French were held. When two of their soldiers accidentally strayed across the frontier close to Maubeuge, British squaddies beat them up, then tore the eagles off their uniforms and ground them into the mud. Three days later thirty-two prisoners of war at last making their desperate way out of Russia were interned in Breda. The Austrians banned the export of anything that might help Napoleon's war effort. Orders went out to round up his family. Private French ships sailing the Atlantic and the Channel were seized. Diplomatic couriers from France were forbidden the freedom of the roads. Newspapers across the Continent from the Rhine to the Oder took up the cry. So the French thought they weren't beaten, they declared. Very well then, they would have to learn that they were. The whole lot of them should be exterminated, declared the German-speaking press. The world could never be at peace all the time there was a French people. They should be shot like the mad dogs they were.

The British press was by and large more subtle and reckoned its readership could distinguish between the cause of France and the cause of Napoleon.[6] The first was truly a sad plight, and how could the British sit idly by while the house of their neighbour was burned to the ground? Napoleon, on the other hand, was all but universally demonised in the pages of the *Times*, the *Observer* and the *Morning Post*. The news of his return had galvanised soldiers especially. When the orderly entered the mess room of the 51st Foot in Portsmouth and put down the newspaper that proclaimed it there was a sudden ecstasy of excitement among the officers. 'Glorious news!' went up the cry. 'Nap's landed in France! Hurrah!' The news spread like wildfire through the barracks. That night, as dining ended, the President rose to drink a bumper toast to 'old Nap' and none if any of the officers went sober to bed that night.

There was much for them to do all the same. Thirty-two-year-old Captain Cavalié Mercer of 'G' Troop the Royal Horse Artillery busied himself in Colchester barracks.[7] One of the other troops stationed there was broken up, the best horses of both were amalgamated and, within three days, the men were ready to march at a moment's warning. The town itself was an image of much of England. Couriers passed through incessantly as the nation woke to the reality of impending war. Continental émigrés bustled about in breathless haste as if they feared that even there they might find the hand of one of Napoleon's secret police clapped suddenly on their shoulder. The news they spread was hectic, desperate, unreliable. Louis XVIII had been arrested. No, he had taken refuge in the Pays-Bas. No, he was in Ostend. Then came real, hard news. Mercer and his men were to march forthwith to Harwich in order to embark for the Continent. The order was 'received with unfeigned joy by officers and men, all eager to plunge into danger and bloodshed, all hoping to obtain glory and distinction'. Men and equipment were in perfect order and the banks of the beautiful Stour basked in the sunshine as the company moved off.

Youths who were not with them and their like ached to join them. Rees Howell Gronow, just eighteen and three years out of Eton, was an ensign in the 1st Regiment of Foot Guards.[8] He had seen a little service in Spain but was now on duty in London. He was cut to the quick at the thought of missing the action. To be there was the height of his ambition. What could he do? He used his contacts. Sir

Thomas Picton of the 5th Division saw how desperate the boy was and realised he must do what he could. Yes, Gronow might accompany him to replace one of his aides if they were killed 'which is not at all unlikely'. Gronow would have to secure leave, however. That was out of the question and the boy was out of pocket. It took him little time to think what to do. He went to Cox and Greenwood's, the army agents, where many another like him had raised a loan and obtained £200. He then went to a casino in St James's Square, put the whole lot on the turn of a card, won £600 and promptly left to accoutre himself. Tattersall's had two excellent if expensive horses for sale and he bought them. A new uniform and shining equipment ate up the rest of his winnings and then, along with his groom, Gronow set off for the Continent. He could surely see the battle and be back in time for guard duty.

Boys even younger were similarly stirred. William Leeke had left school at sixteen and had no wish to follow his father's advice and while away his days as a parson among the gentle rivers of Hampshire.[9] He toyed with the idea of the law but, meeting a young officer at a ball and hearing his stories of action in Spain, he suddenly decided exactly what he wanted to be. His wealthy father bought him a commission and letters to influential friends resulted in the choice of a posting either to America or India. The first did not appeal, particularly when he read in the paper that a peace had been ratified there. India it would have to be. He spent some hours imagining his future life among the temples and bazaars. He then happened to pick up a later edition of the paper that had seemed to decide his fate. It proclaimed that Napoleon had escaped from Elba. He wrote at once to his cousin in the 52nd Foot, was promptly accepted and rushed to London where, with the help of a kindly colonel, he kitted himself out with every conceivable item: a uniform, a sword and pistol, a canteen which thoughtfully included unbreakable wineglasses, a soup tureen and two empty three-pint bottles which he filled with the best brandy money could buy. Thus the power of the press over a life that had barely begun.

Among the British newspapers only the *Morning Chronicle* spoke up in Napoleon's defence. In fifteen days, it declared, Napoleon had seized back a throne from which the whole of Europe had been unable to dislodge him in so many years. History had never seen anything like it. The attention of Parliament, the writer went on, should be drawn to the reprehensible Allied policy which would surely lead to the reopening of war. Here was the voice of the liberal intelligentsia, those 'Napoleonised' Whigs whose more aristocratic members gathered in Holland House and found their literary spokesman in the glamorous, dangerous figure of Byron. Having only very recently woken to find himself famous, the notoriety of the poet of *Childe Harold's Pilgrimage* and the deliciously shocking *Corsair* was heightened by his open support for Napoleon. Byron, who owned a fine gilt-framed print of the Emperor in his robes, had been heartbroken by his abdication and dashed off in a day ninety lines of his 'Ode to Napoleon', which he then rather shamefacedly gave to his publisher to issue pseudo-anonymously:

> *'Tis done – but yesterday a king!*
> *And armed with kings to strive –*
> *And now thou art a nameless thing*
> *So abject – yet alive!*

The Whigs persisted in their defence of Napoleon right up to the time the cannons roared and they carried their protests into the Commons. Francis Burdett lambasted Castlereagh for calling Napoleon's return an invasion. How could three million people be invaded by a single man? The people of France hated the old order and the Bourbons had lost their throne through their own shortcomings. It would be outrageous to wage war on a nation to reimpose a monarchy it didn't want. A petition against the war circulated through the City of London. Castlereagh rejected it after a long and acrimonious debate. The Ministry was nonetheless obliged to clarify its thinking. An important principle was at stake, and eventually an ambiguous compromise was reached whereby it was agreed that the war about to be waged was not a dynastic struggle for the House of Bourbon but a vital matter of European security. The divine-right monarchs of Europe lifted their hands in bewilderment at the curious ways of democracy. They had, after all, long experience of mistrusting the British.

The British had entered the war against Revolutionary France in 1793 when Napoleon himself was an all but unknown junior officer penning Jacobin pamphlets in Provence.[10] Strongly though many of them disapproved of the ideals of the Revolution, the struggle was not then and was not to become a principally ideological one. The Prime Minister, Pitt, declared that he had no 'intention to wage war against opinion', however rebarbative that opinion might be. His motives were altogether more practical and mundane. The steam power of the Industrial Revolution required that British goods be exported to the mainland of Europe through the great ports of Flushing and Antwerp. The revolutionaries were equally determined to have these as their own, and the British waged war in order to prevent this happening and to preserve stability and the balance of power in Europe as a whole. Their concern, in other words, was the profit on the cotton barons of Manchester rather than the political well-being of the silk weavers of Lyons, which interested them only in so far as the latter were a possible market for the former. Garnished with propaganda though these aims were, they remained constant throughout the long struggle. It was this consistency, affected as it was by circumstances, that ensured that the British at one time or another had hostile relations with most states on the Continental mainland.

The principal circumstance to affect British relations with the other states facing France was Napoleon's imposition of the ever-widening Continental System and the steps taken in Westminster to use the navy to retaliate. In particular, the Orders in Council which tried to force all neutral countries' trade with France and its Empire to pass through British harbours had a devastating effect on those obliged to endure it. Nonetheless, alienating allies and undermining peace efforts were altogether less important than strangling French prosperity and ensuring that foreign fleets did not become part of the Emperor's navy. At various times during the conflict Britain found herself declaring or even waging war with Denmark (the victim of two fierce pre-emptive strikes) and Spain (whose treasure fleet was seized in 1804), along with Sweden, Prussia, Russia and Holland. Nor was it just countries on the Continental mainland that were attacked. French colonies too were grabbed along with any others that might serve a useful purpose. The list was long: Malta (secured to keep the French out), Sicily (secured to keep Malta fed), the Cape of Good Hope (secured from the Dutch in 1795 and temporarily restored in 1802). There were, in addition, such exotic and far-flung locations as Tobago and Pondicherry (secured in 1793), Martinique, St Lucia and Guadeloupe (1794), Ceylon (1796), Trinidad (1797), Surinam (1799).

It was a mighty haul for less than a decade's work, and the combination of what appeared as high-handedness and naked colonial ambition bred suspicion among those allies of Britain – Austria, Russia and Prussia especially – who felt expected to sacrifice themselves down to the last peasant in order to keep Napoleon at bay and Britain contented. They grumbled, they turned their coats, they asked for subsidies. These last were often grudgingly forthcoming. Was Britain, declared its Secretary of State for War, 'to be merely the great bank of Europe, on which the different nations of Europe should be empowered to draw on in defence of their own existence?' The answer to Mr Windham's question all too often seemed yes. It was worth it nonetheless even if the banker did sometimes come up with less than promised. British trade had to be secured, and if money had to be shelled out to keep Europe unsettled and Napoleon tied up in endless conflict then it was money well spent. And the British got better at spending it. Castlereagh in particular became adept at handing out 'British gold' and so keeping the later coalitions against France reasonably united.

What had been achieved by handouts, diplomacy and the Royal Navy had to be secured in the end by the army. Napoleon would only be finally defeated on land. By the closing stages of the Napoleonic Wars the British army was a highly efficient and disciplined machine. It also made huge demands on the country which was now fully committed to the ghastly novelty of Clausewitz's view of the nation in arms. A sixth of the population was available for service and by 1812 Britain had to hand nearly a quarter of a million soldiers and over 100,000 sailors. It was the most extensive mobilisation the country had ever known. The agonising question facing the British at Vienna was whether the others would join together to ensure that Napoleon was 'put absolutely outside the possibility of exciting troubles'. The Prussians and the Russians were urgently encouraged to see further than their own territorial ambitions for what Castlereagh called 'the salvation of Europe'. Eventually they did indeed see their advantage in the larger plan and, on 25 March, signed another treaty – an open one this time that included them all. The war would be vast and terrible. 'It must be done on the largest scale,' Castlereagh told Wellington. 'You must inundate France with a force in all directions. If Bonaparte could turn the tide, there is no calculating upon his plan.' This was to be a war to the death and it was even now beginning. 'I have the honour to inform you,' wrote Lord Clancarty to a colleague on 29 March, 'that his Grace the Duke of Wellington set out this morning from Vienna, to take command of the army in the Low Countries.'

Young men like Mercer, Gronow, Leeke and hundreds of others were already making their way towards him. Leeke was in Dover and plucked up the courage to go into a billiard hall where his fellow officers were passing their time. He joined their game, won some money and then, determined to show himself at least that he was a gentleman, contrived to lose it all on the last game. He was so sick as he made the passage to Ostend that there were moments when he wanted to die but, revived by some men loading cannonballs, he bought a packhorse and took a barge to Ghent, his spirits raised by a kindly major general who offered him one of the two ginger biscuits he had in a paper bag. Thus someone little more than a schoolboy going to the wars. But life was hardly easier for the youthful Gronow. The minute his ship reached Ostend a British naval officer and his men boarded and began unceremoniously hoisting the horses ashore. Gronow protested. The scramble and confusion, the frightened and dripping horses and the anxious, sea-soaked men, were a nightmare to a discipled soldier. The naval captain was blunt in his riposte. 'I can't help it, sir; the Duke's orders are positive that no delay is to take place in landing the troops as they arrive, and the ships be sent back again; so you must be out of her before dark.' So that was that. Napoleon was inflicting another Continental war and there was no time for niceties.

## The Emperor's Family

Over in Paris, the arduous labour of preparing for a war which he now knew would take place sooner rather than later occupied Napoleon's uncountable waking hours. He allowed himself little respite. A public figure must be seen, however, and there were brilliant lunches where Napoleon mingled with many of the great actors, scientists and literary figures of the day, showing them his enthusiasm and the considerable extent of his knowledge. He also had many of his family around him most of whom, as always, were proving themselves difficult. *Madame Mère* remained her imperious self. Joseph acted where he could as the family ambassador. Pauline was kept away by illness, but Jérôme was furious that he was not allowed to parade himself as King of Westphalia and so refused to appear at all. The row between him and Napoleon festered for weeks, but Joseph was able to broker some measure of agreement between the Emperor and the truculent Lucien, who was given a medal and rooms in the Palais Royal where, by and large, he did very little. Napoleon's brother-in-law, the hot-headed Joseph Murat, and his wife Caroline were an altogether different matter, however. Determined to hold onto their Neapolitan throne at any price, they betrayed Napoleon who had given it to them, signed up with the Allies and then, deserted by their new friends, declared Italian independence and were soundly beaten by the Austrians when they presumed to attack them. Having retreated to Naples and been thrown out by the British they arrived in Cannes where they were allowed to remain having been forbidden Paris.

The silence from Napoleon's immediate family was as pitiable as the preparations he made to receive them. So convinced was he still that Marie-Louise would return to him that he sent ambassadors to Austria (they seem not to have reached their destination) and announced to the world her imminent return to Paris. Marie-Louise was finding the charms of her count altogether more agreeable than those of the Emperor, but perhaps of even greater importance to Napoleon than his wife was his son. He had entered Paris on the boy's fourth birthday and a triumphal return, marked by so significant an anniversary, was intended to proclaim the revival of his dynasty. The boy, of course, was nowhere to be seen. His grandfather and his advisors had decided that he should be kept under heavy guard in the Schönbrunn. There was no telling what lengths Napoleon might go to in order to have possession of his son. He had already proved himself capable of ordering an international kidnapping when he had brought the Duc d'Enghien to Paris simply to have him shot. The child's presence in the Tuileries would be a symbol altogether too potent for the Allies but, to make ready for it, Napoleon had the nursery redecorated and a staff employed. The rooms remained as empty as his hopes of ever seeing his son again.

Yet the boy was the pledge, the guarantee that the immense efforts Napoleon was making would allow his dynasty to flourish long into the future. And it was this above all that mattered to him. It was for his own glory that *la patrie* was being thrown into turmoil. The glory of France herself was but the train of Napoleon's imperial robe. He had learned nothing, as Fouché acidly declared, and had returned from Elba as despotic as ever. The ceaseless midnight labouring in the Tuileries was the monumental egoism of a man who had refashioned the destiny of Europe in his own image and could not see himself apart from it. He had, quite simply, nowhere else to go. His herculean ambition, energy and intellect had drawn the mighty forces of the time into his hands and he had redirected them with terrible ability. Napoleon had reshaped a chaotic republic into an empire. He had reinvented war, on a scale the nations of Europe had never seen before. And still he was the young general at the Bridge of Lodi who had felt the world flee before him as if he were being carried in the air. It was the eagle's view and nothing could dim it – nothing, not an empty treasury, a ravaged homeland, an ever more loudly grumbling people. War was his element and war would put everything to rights. Napoleon needed one last mighty and victorious campaign. The Allies swarming on his northern frontier were offering him exactly that. Another Austerlitz and the world would be his again.

## Reactions in France

The people of France protested with increasing vehemence. The thought of more wars appalled them and the statistics from the recent years told their own dreadful story. Fifty thousand men a year were lost in Spain. Twenty-five thousand had been slaughtered at Eylau, 73,000 at Leipzig. Somewhere in the region of a quarter of a million men had failed to return from the ghastliness of the Russian campaign. Upwards of 900,000 had been lost in the wars as a whole. There was hardly a chateau, a townhouse or a cottage across the land where there wasn't an empty chair or the frail memorabilia of a dead relative or loved one. Now it was going to happen all over again.

Detailed information about the level of discontent arrived daily on the desk of the Interior Minister, Lazare Carnot.[11] He was an ugly, boorish man of sixty-one, cold and caustic, with a grief-creased face (his wife, who he adored, had died a couple of years before) and inflexible rectitude. Carnot's early life had been a classic example of the career that was not open to talent under the Bourbon monarchy. He had entered the army and risen as far as his very considerable energy and talents allowed him before finding that all further promotion was barred because his prosperous middle-class family did not possess the required number of heraldic quarterings to guarantee his status. Carnot embraced the Revolution with the cold fervour of a frustrated man. He voted for the execution of the King, and became part of the infamous Committee of Public Safety where he advocated the ruthless suppression of all dissent and the use of absolute power in times of national crisis. He was made President of the Convention and became one of the five senior members of the Directory. Falling foul of that regime, Carnot fled to Germany when his arrest and deportation to French Guiana were proposed. Napoleon recognised his austere talents, however, and, realising that he needed them to ensure discipline in the army, appointed Carnot his War Minister during the First Consulship. Carnot proved himself dedicated, austere and blunt, telling Napoleon to his face that he thoroughly disapproved of the Consulship becoming an appointment for life. The people of France, he said, had not gone through the Revolution only to have kings return under another name. Having spoken his mind, Carnot retired from public life and, like one of the Roman heroes so admired by men of his stamp, lived modestly on his farm and devoted his time to studying fortification and the abstruser reaches of infinitesimal calculus. Now he re-emerged to reduce his country to order once again.

The scale of the task was daunting. With the efficiency that was second nature to him Carnot despatched commissioners across the length and breadth of the country. Within a fortnight the enormity of the situation was apparent. Napoleonic France and, with it, Napoleon's ambitions relied on the efficiency of a heavily centralised bureaucracy. Now it appeared that the majority of state servants were either sullenly resentful or actively hostile to the new regime. The majority of them were men retained by Louis XVIII from imperial times but Napoleon's return had not refired their enthusiasm. A correspondent from Bonanay confessed frankly to Carnot that the civil administration was gangrenous. 'All the Emperor's merits, the enthusiasm of the citizens, his glorious return to the capital after rapidly covering 220 leagues during which he was cheered to the echo by the crowds would achieve nothing whatsoever unless the prefects, general secretaries, sub-prefects, mayors . . . and employees of every sort were changed.'

Carnot recognised that this could only be successfully achieved piecemeal but difficult times required harsh measures and wholesale sackings were ordered. The replacements were, for the most part, calculatingly diffident in their approach to their unenviable tasks and often downright obstructive. Some refused to raise the tricolour, others posted up proclamations from the late King, yet others frequented with royalists and many were royalists themselves. Prefects from ancient families refused to sack recalcitrant mayors even when ordered to do so by the ministry, and it became clear in Paris that they were all a danger to Napoleon's enterprise. Eventually all the small-town mayors were fired and, in an effort to suggest the Emperor's supposed democratic intentions, elections were called. The people returned two-thirds of the old candidates. This was the clearest possible statement of public opinion, for the mayors were the workhorses of provincial administration. It was they who collected taxes, organised conscription, billeted recruits, called up the National Guard, supervised elections and supposedly put new legislation into effect. Without their cooperation Napoleon's ambitions would be very difficult to realise.

Nor was it just the mayors who were proving hostile. Every section of society showed its bitterness towards Napoleon, whether it was the schoolboys in the state-funded *lycées* who jibed at praising the man who would soon be sending them to the battlefield, the Catholic Church that had long hated the servile position to which it had been reduced or the judiciary who quite simply refused to swear their loyalty to the regime. The army, too, was widely hated. The great power for *la patrie* and *la gloire* was no longer the object of automatic awe. The eagles were irreparably tarnished. The names of battles emblazoned on the regimental flags were no longer an index of victory but rather a roll call of the hundreds of thousands of the dead who had given their lives for no lasting purpose. Now the army found itself subject to verbal and even physical abuse. Officers were insulted in the streets. Cries of 'Death to the Bonapartists!' echoed round Marseilles as the jeering citizens threw rocks at soldiers sitting in a café. At the other end of the country the Bourbon flag waved over the cliffs at Boulogne. And in every town, city and village in between incidents proliferated. The mayors were complicit in such demonstrations and it became obvious to Carnot that he had blundered by being too absolute and that wholesale sedition was now a very real menace. Underlying it all was the nationwide fear and loathing of inevitable war.

The propaganda machine, always subject to Napoleon's heavy-handed use, was thrown into action. 'There's no need to fear war any longer,' cooed the *Journal de l'Empire*. All the official newspapers did the same. The pro-Bonapartist sympathies of the *Morning Chronicle* were translated for the benefit of French readers who it was hoped could be persuaded that Britain was not a hostile power. Napoleon himself, as was his wont, kept himself up to date with the whole range of the British press and knew that the *Morning Chronicle* was far from representative in its views. And where real sources were lacking, lies were invented. False correspondence supposedly from Augsburg and Brussels talked of peace but this was so patently untrue as to be treated with contempt. Satirical posters appeared everywhere offering a two-million-franc reward to anyone finding the lost peace. Bitter travesties of imperial decrees were pasted up alongside them claiming to be issued by 'Napoleon by the grace of the devil and the laws of hell, Emperor of the French' and demanding the sacrifice of 300,000 men a year – or three million if the circumstances required it. With conscription now a certainty the national slaughterhouse was open for business.

The greatest insult was Napoleon's high-handed management of the 'Benjamine'. It was the clearest proof of his utter contempt for the aspirations of the French people. They had groaned under the Bourbons. Many had believed that the day of liberty might well be returning with Napoleon from Elba. He had said all the right things and done all the right things. He seemed indeed to embody a mature form of the Revolution. Some sort of genuinely representative government was surely in the offing. It was not. The 'Benjamine', drafted overnight by a man as volatile in his loyalties as he was brilliant and hyperemotional, was not a document open to discussion. No committee was allowed to examine it and the people were allowed to vote on it only as a fait accompli. Their opinion was of no importance and anyway a military victory – an overwhelming military victory – would soon make it redundant. And, in the meantime, election results could be rigged. 'If a nation wants happiness,' Napoleon declared, 'it must obey orders and shut up. Bigwigs, priests, citizens, every one of them must be levelled to the same obedience. That is the way to ensure public order and a steady throne.'

He could not have been more wrong. The promulgation of the Acte Additionale lost Napoleon the love of many of his most fervent admirers. Fleury de Chaboulon recognised this and wrote how Napoleon's actions paralysed and put an end to any previous goodwill felt towards him. Loyal Bonapartists were muttering bitterly and Carnot was appalled. As usual, he spoke his mind. 'Sire, I implore you not to fight public opinion. Your "Acte Additionale" has upset the nation. Promise the people you will modify it to meet their wishes.' His words were received with contempt and he tried again. 'I am not deceiving you,' he said, 'when I tell you that your own well-being, and ours too, depends on your taking heed of the country's wishes.' Napoleon would do no such thing. Lying was so much more effective. The people had had their vote and now the votes were being counted. Only 4,802 people in a nation of twenty-six million had rejected the 'Benjamine'. This was breathtaking and recklessly stupid manipulation made all the more insulting by the fact that the armed forces – most of whom were illiterate – had voted overwhelmingly in favour of the Act. But the opinion of the army mattered no more than that of the people, and the votes of fourteen regiments were thrown into the litter bin because they arrived 'too late'.

If the people were frightened, humiliated and angry they were also poor. The latter years of war especially had devastated the economy. French industry was relatively undeveloped, and while Carnot realised France could not readily challenge the British Industrial Revolution, encouragement to initiative had to be given. A *Conseil d'Industrie Nationale* was set up to discuss improvements. The use of steam power was encouraged and a generous annual prize established for the most innovative piece of new machinery. None of this would show immediate effects but the worst aspects of national poverty could be partly alleviated by the setting up of national workshops and, in Paris especially, the issuing of orders for large-scale public works. It was better having people laying cobbles than throwing them. The state finances were, nonetheless, wholly inadequate to Napoleon's ambitions and tax revenue would inevitably be paltry in a ravaged nation however abundant its natural resources.

The Finance and Treasury ministers were summoned to report. Questions were fired at them and answers demanded. What had been King Louis's budget? A little under three hundred million francs. How much did Napoleon need? At least that amount for the army alone, and probably more. Taxes would have to be hiked. The people would groan but that was unimportant. Even then the sums were paltry compared to the vast revenues Napoleon had been used to; 1812 had seen him able to spend – or squander – nearly three times the sum available to him now. Much of that had been raised outside of *la patrie* for it was the conquered nations that were to contribute booty to her *gloire*. Over 153 million francs had been demanded from the Low Countries while ravaged lands from Spain to the eastern limits of the Empire had contributed too, harassed peasants in Andalusía paying for men dying on the return from Moscow. Those resources were no longer available, of course, and other means would have to be found to get the War Ministry the 70 million francs a month it needed.

It was an alarming situation and extraordinary measures would be needed to face it. Fantasy began to creep into the projections as Napoleon put pressure on his ministers. An 'extraordinary revenue' might be raised if the state were to sell off its assets, its properties and forests especially. The move had been tried before and had never been satisfactory. There were frequent and acrimonious problems with title to properties sequestrated from the aristocracy, while the laws of the market place ensured that a sudden glut of estates for sale would force down prices. Nonetheless, it was reckoned that over 400 million francs might be raised. The problem was that this vast sum was already owed by the state for the expenses incurred in earlier wars. Suppliers had not been paid, cities and individuals were entitled to large returns on the loans they had offered and the devastation they had suffered as a result of Napoleon's wars. Many government officials had not received their salaries. To renege on such matters would destroy whatever confidence remained in the would-be imperial government.

Economies could be made, of course, and the French navy was all but decommissioned since the nation was facing a land war. Patriotic offerings were also encouraged. The results of this last move were touching if pitiful. Boys donated their pocket-money. The pupils at the *lycée* in Grenoble were encouraged to send 400 francs, those in Nancy 500. A woman from the slums of Paris sold her trinkets and sent in 100 francs. Old soldiers offered their pensions and government officials donated sums from their pay-packets. Other professional bodies rallied to the cause, but significant sums were not forthcoming. Here was yet more evidence that the people of France no longer willingly associated Napoleon's ambition with national glory. They had had enough. They were frightened, they were resentful and yet somehow they had to be mobilised for war.

## The War Machine

That onerous task fell to Marshal Davout, who only accepted it with considerable reluctance.[12] A brilliant soldier in the field, Davout was not an experienced bureaucrat. He had, however, an immense if far from popular reputation. As a cavalry officer in Napoleon's Egyptian campaign, he had shown exceptional courage and a cool head, qualities which he was to reveal throughout his career even while his mood darkened as his two marriages collapsed and he became obsessively dedicated to his profession. His only other interest was spending the vast sums of money he earned with a prodigal's delight. Austerlitz and Jena had seen him at his most glorious for it was on those fields that Davout had single-handedly beaten a Prussian army twice the size of his own. The fact that he threatened to horsewhip the altogether more cautious Bernadotte (one of the most invariably critical of Napoleon's generals) who had refused to come to his aid suggests Davout's natural harshness of manner that went along with his exceptional single-mindedness, his penchant for detail and faultfinding and his unswerving dedication to the army and to Napoleon himself, for all that their relations were far from cordial and were now to deteriorate even further. Davout was, however, the only one of Napoleon's twenty-five marshals not to have deserted him after 1814 and his presence in the War Ministry was of fundamental importance.

There Davout often laboured for twenty hours a day, his great domed head buzzing with ten thousand anxious details, until he snatched a few brief hours of rest on the camp bed set up in his office. The range of matters he had to attend to was prodigious. It was his responsibility as War Minister to house and feed all the nation's soldiers, find them arms and uniforms and arrange for horses, transport and supply depots. The fact that this had to be done in record time and on a precarious budget added to the sheer difficulty imposed by the scale of the operation, the poor state of the army after its defeat and the increasing savagery of a critical and harassed Napoleon. Like his master, Davout wanted everything done at once and precisely. Traits in Davout's own character expanded to meet the needs of the hour, and his office in the Rue Saint-Dominique was loud with barked orders and chaotic with ever-growing piles of paper.

In accordance with his publicly declared aim of wanting peace, Napoleon initially ordered the setting up of eight *corps d'observation* which were to guard the frontiers of a country now menaced by the Allies. It took only a month for four of these supposedly defensive armies to be refashioned into mighty war machines. The chief of them was the *Armée du Nord*, which was to be augmented by the Armies of the Rhine, the Moselle and the Alps. The observation corps of the Jura, the Pyrenees and, a little later, the Var could also be called on, as could reserve corps in Bordeaux, Toulouse, Lyons and Paris. Men were urgently needed and, in addition to calling up the tens of thousands of men scattered across the country's twenty-three military districts, it was also decided to call up large parts of the National Guard. Since some of these men were in their fifties it was clearly inadvisable to send them to the front line and so a distinction was made between mobile and sedentary units. Napoleon ordered the former to be spread along the northern frontiers of France by 10 May, a typically impossible demand which necessarily lagged far behind its deadline. In the meantime, the sedentary units were put on alert to defend their home regions should this be needed.

If calling these men up proved difficult (many members of the National Guard showed themselves dangerously refractory), equipping and feeding them proved a nightmare for Davout. He now had a third of a million men to provide for. Supply depots had to be organised but his original hopes of provisioning 100,000 men and 40,000 horses were dashed when Napoleon, realising that to make up the deficit by requisitioning would further embitter an already volatile country, demanded provisions sufficient for six months for 250,000 men and twice the original number of horses. This was intolerable and Davout's plight was only saved when he unearthed the dishonesty of others and turned it to his own advantage. A highly placed Treasury official had used a front man to sign a provisioning agreement with Louis XVIII. With Napoleon's arrival from Elba the business had mysteriously ceased to function. Corruption could be countered by blackmail, and Davout issued orders to the nation's prefects telling them to raise supplies locally and send their bills in to the proprietor of the now defunct business. He, realising he was cornered, hurriedly agreed to sign a fresh government contract and to supply Napoleon's army in the north with four million francs' worth of victuals in a month. At least the army would be able to march on its stomach.

It remained to be seen if it would have uniforms and arms. Erstwhile suppliers, their old bills still unpaid, were reluctant to risk their capital again or would do so only at extortionate rates. Very well then, Napoleon (or, rather, the already overworked Davout) would set up national workshops to manufacture what was needed. Inevitably, the sudden creation of vast factories was a dream that soon turned into yet another nightmare. Napoleon gauged the failure of enterprise from his police reports. These told him how numerous men reporting for work at the new factories had been turned away. Davout was questioned as to why. There were insufficient materials, he opined. There was insufficient space, too. In that case the men should be made to work at home. Surely it was perfectly possible to equip an army with munitions made piecemeal in craftsmen's cottages? Two hundred and forty thousand muskets were needed. Davout must produce them. They were essential to the defence of the country.

Davout laboured incessantly, a bitterly angry and often savage Napoleon haunting his days and nights like an incubus always ready to criticise, to demand the impossible and to spit forth his spleen when the impossible did not materialise. Two weeks, and still the new armaments factories were not operating! Surely Davout realised that Paris was full of unemployed workers only too keen to earn a few sous. He was to set up a committee of officers to hurry these men into work. It was to be done now. Napoleon didn't want to hear any more about it, but he still deluged forth a torrent of advice. The idea that there was insufficient factory space was absurd. Davout was to take over barracks, slaughterhouses, music halls, churches – anywhere large quantities of people habitually congregated. And while he was about it he was to extend armaments production into the provinces. The matter should have been seen to three weeks ago! It was a matter of overwhelming national importance that musket manufacture proceed at 200 – no, 300 or 400 – a day. Nothing else would do. And what about all the broken muskets scattered around France? They could be repaired, surely. Davout knew nothing about these, but the Emperor's grip on facts remained remarkable. There were 350 repairable muskets in Montreuil, nearly 6,000 at Douai and almost twice that number in Lille. Davout was to get hold of them at once. 'War could break out at any moment and still . . . nothing has been done!' And the situation regarding uniforms was just as bad. An army without uniforms could not be led. The fate of France boiled down to that. Incredibly, money was found – some fourteen million francs in all – and upwards of 1,250 uniforms a day were turned out from scores of workshops in Paris, Lyons, Toulouse and Bordeaux.

But now relations between Napoleon and Davout worsened by the day. Both men were furiously overworking and their rows were in proportion to the frayed state of their nerves. There was a terrible scene over the Observation Corps of the Var. Napoleon had authorised the establishment of this, but when Davout asked for the necessary forty million francs he was given a monumental and wholly unjustified dressing-down. How could he entangle Napoleon into spending so much money? There was no decree affirming it. Permission had been given in principle only. Given the parlous state of the country's finances this was the short road to ruin. In fact the written orders had been drawn up and even the general of the corps appointed. The sheer scale of what he was involved in, the combined pressures of time, money and continuous anxiety, were wearing Napoleon down. His usual grip on fact, his imperious sense of order, his unthinking reliance on his own unfathomable reserves of energy were all being tested beyond their limit. The general at the Bridge of Lodi had been a youth but Napoleon was now a man in middle age. He had the deep-seated and dangerous furies of the middle-aged too rather than the flashing anger of the young. He muttered ominously that if things went on like this then Davout would be sacked, there would be 'a parting of the ways'. Only a man of Davout's resilience, selfless loyalty and unquestioning patriotism could have stood up to this and even he took measures to avoid the humiliating tempests of abuse that drenched him every time he visited the Emperor. He began issuing orders without Napoleon's approval so that his wishes could be fulfilled and another burst of anger be delayed for a day or two. It was the only way.

But still the great war machine Davout was trying to organise was behind-hand and ill-equipped. Lack of money and lack of time made everything impossible, and problems proliferated like hydra's heads. Musket production fell into arrears because the workers had not been paid for six weeks. And how were the cavalry to ride into battle without saddles and reins? Napoleon asked. There weren't even enough horses for them. Only about a third of the necessary 8,000 had been procured. Still there were food shortages too and sloth – sloth and dithering incompetence everywhere. Everybody's reports were vague. Nobody seemed to know their job. No one knew the real importance of money, especially when it was so scarce. No one had an eye for detail. Why were the artillery battalions Napoleon had just reviewed at the Tuileries without the little boxes of grease essential to the maintenance of their equipment? Davout's position became more and more impossible, his master more and more vindictively demanding. They continued to row, then fell into bitter mutual silences as they laboured on, barking at their subordinates when they could not snap at each other. And still the great war machine lumbered and groaned its way towards some form of readiness for the fulfilling of Napoleon's titanic and increasingly desperate ambitions.

An army raised, equipped, trained and ready to smash the mighty combined forces of the Allies massing to the north was to be ready by the last day of April – just six weeks after Napoleon's return to Paris. On that day it would be divided into its constituent parts. The great spearhead that was the *Armée du Nord* comprised the 1st, 2nd, 3rd and 6th Corps and three divisions of cavalry. The *Armée de la Moselle* was made up of the 4th Corps. The 5th constituted the *Armée du Rhin*, the 7th the *Armée des Alpes*. The frontiers with Switzerland and the border with Spain were to be protected by the rest. In addition, divisions of the National Guard were to man forts and protect the great inland cities in order to counter the terror and depredations seen in the last days of the campaign of 1814. The coasts would be defended by professional gunners. It was an extraordinary demand but the amazing reality, achieved with such difficulty, was still less than Napoleon's desires. He had dreamed of 300,000 men in arms. He fantasised about a reserve of 232,000 more, half of them former soldiers who had either deserted or retired, half of them raw recruits from the newest conscription lists. The more than half a million men in fact turned out to be under 300,000, and a third of those were required for the defence of *la patrie* and the suppression of dissidents. All of them grumbled and many of them (often encouraged by the local authorities) failed to turn up. When numbers fell below expectations the terrible 'mobile columns' of the press gangs – each 125 men strong – were sent out to quicken the enthusiasm for war. 'Do what has to be done,' Napoleon demanded. 'Music and drums . . . arouse the enthusiasm of the young!'

It did not happen. The country was sullen, obstinate and angry. Trouble and sedition shook the provinces.[13] The armed uprisings of the royalists, dangerous as they seemed, were but one expression of this. In Poitiers the people smashed a bust of Napoleon. In Toulouse, Rouen, La Rochelle, Versailles and Bayonne the inhabitants stole out in the dark, pulled down the imperial proclamations pasted to the walls and replaced them with those issued by the Bourbons. In Amiens and Marseilles they did the same in broad daylight. The people of Provence enlivened their traditional dances with cries of '*Vive le Roi!*'. In Lille they even cried out: '*Vivent les Anglais!*' When a young conscript in Saint-Omer seized a flag at a review and trampled it in the mud his commander was so terrified of the crowd running amok that he sentenced the youth merely to twelve hours in the police cells. Trouble flared so violently and bloodily in Agde, and the cries of 'Down with the Eagles!' were so loud in the streets, that it took two battalions of soldiers to restore order. And the soldiers themselves were all but universally hated. Feeling against them in Orléans was so vehement they wanted to quit the city. Marseilles, in the meantime, was virtually out of control for all that 2,000 soldiers were garrisoned there to keep down the 96,000 inhabitants. The bourgeoisie of the city were defiantly royalist and the poor, inflamed by the closure of the port and the consequent loss of work, were behind them. The police were reluctant to act and the National Guard were on the side of the citizens. An army officer was murdered. Such incidents sapped what little enthusiasm there was among the conscripts. It was the saying in Lille that desertion was the proof of loyalty. Things were so bad in Rouen and Beauvais that the battalions of the National Guard had to be made up entirely from replacements. Thus the loathing inspired by the six terrible weeks of Napoleon's iron-willed rearmament of the nation that increasingly loathed him for the fear and death and carnage, the expense and dreadful suffering, that hovered always about his eagle's wings.

But still the preparations went on. Four thousand labourers were despatched to ready the defences of Lyons. Five thousand were instructed to fortify Paris and build redoubts on the heights of Montmartre. Napoleon was particularly urgent in his orders that his capital should be protected against the humiliating defeat inflicted on it in 1814, though the surrender had, in truth, been the will of the people. 'Do everything in your power,' he wrote to Davout, 'to organise and speed up the defensive measures now in hand.' He wanted more than three hundred cannon. Barges laboured up the Seine with 136 cannon made available by the decommissioning of the navy. Hundreds more came from elsewhere around the country. They were placed strategically across the city, thirty-eight of them on Montmartre, others by the Saint-Denis canal and in the suburbs. Two hundred were eventually drawn up on the lawns in front of Les Invalides. Six thousand artillery men were found to man them.

The most beautiful capital city in Europe had become a fortress, but still one insufficiently defended by an army, a third of which consisted of untrained citizens. And still there were not enough gunners and so teenagers from the *École Polytechnique* and the Military Academy at Saint-Cyr were drafted in to train on the guns outside Les Invalides. The dreadful noise brought no comfort for it suggested far less protection and safety than the apocalyptic horrors that would surely descend on Paris once the war was lost. Far closer to the true thought of the anxious many were the satirical posters pasted up and claiming to be a proclamation from the Tsar. 'People of Paris, we will deliver you from this cannibal dead or alive, otherwise your city will be razed to the ground. People will say: "Here once stood Paris."'

## The Champs de Mai

Such wit probed to the deep heart of the people's fears, but Napoleon's Paris was to have one more gaudy spectacle. He had promised that the Acte Additionale would be ratified at the Champs de Mai ceremony. The date of this, like everything else, had slipped and the ceremony was actually called for 1 June – exactly three months after Napoleon's landing on the coast of France. What had once been promised as an open democratic forum, however, was now stage-managed as what was hoped would be an imperial triumph. Thus the changes wrought by a hundred days. The preparations for the event were elaborate and the spectacle was intended to be magnificent. An enormous ceremonial stand had been erected, its two wings opening out as if to embrace the solemn stone facade of the *École Militaire* which was, for the moment, largely obscured by a great wooden structure complete with seating for dignitaries. In the middle of this was a raised and lavishly draped pavilion that contained the Emperor's throne.[14]

The guests started to arrive at nine o'clock on what was evidently going to be a fine, sunny day. Among their number were the 500 delegates of the electoral college, earnest men, determined in their independence, resolved not to be overawed by what they were about to witness and already resolved to nominate as their President one Lanjouinais, who had long been a stern critic of imperial policy. Among their number as well was Dubois d'Angers, who was to read their address to the Emperor. This unenviable task was made all the more bitter for the speech having been earlier censored and altered under Napoleon's orders. Unfortunate phrases were cut out. Sentences such as 'we have rallied to you because we hope that you have brought back to us from your retirement the full repentance becoming a great man' were removed. A deal of threadbare imperial rhetoric was added. Nothing could be allowed to tarnish Napoleon's glory, which was vouched for by the 45,000 troops from every part of the army arrayed to either side of the stand. By ten o'clock the grandees were arriving. The gorgeously bedecked high officers of the Legion of Honour, the courts and the universities took their places around the throne. All waited. Then, at eleven o'clock, the roar of a hundred cannon from the Tuileries, their thunder redoubled by the guns protecting a Paris prepared for siege, announced the departure of the imperial procession.

It was astonishingly impressive and so immense that it took more than an hour for the marvellously uniformed Red Lancers of the Imperial Guard to appear, their magnificence even now suggesting the glories of the past. Hundreds more cannon were fired as they hoved into view. The beating of drums quickened the blood. The Governor of Paris appeared on his splendid charger surrounded by his staff, his soldiers and a bevy of heralds bedecked with medieval magnificence and showing off the imperial bees. Charlemagne had indeed returned. The best things were worth waiting for and it was a while before Napoleon himself appeared, the crowd in the meantime being beguiled by a cortege of nineteen state coaches each drawn by six perfectly matched horses. Then, at last, the Emperor's own state carriage appeared, the fabulous gold confection first used at his coronation and resplendent still with the iconography of his imperial power. It was perhaps difficult to see the small, exhausted man couched inside but around him the dignified magnificence of his remaining marshals dressed in blue and gold and surrounded by their servants in brilliant liveries created a fabulous impression as they passed by and gave way to the cavalry units bringing up the rear.

It was all exhilarating as it was meant to be, but the cries of '*Vive l'Empereur!*' that greeted it had a different timbre from the old days. Something was lacking, and a sort of nervous forced conviction had taken its place. This was, after all, a glory underpinned by the state police. Only four days earlier Napoleon had written a letter to Fouché saying it was high time that his men suppressed dissent more rigorously. His regime was surrounded by insurrectionists and while the army could put them down it was time to stop those who encouraged them with words. Indeed, it was more than time. As the terrifying press gangs roved the country looking for recruits, laws allowing the death penalty for deserters and those enciting them were prosecuted with vigour. The day following the great procession in Paris the first of a hundred spies, agitators and deserters would be rounded up in Lille alone. All the other big cities would follow suit. It seemed to work for a while. A week after he had set about his task of repression the Prefect of Lille was writing to say: 'for the first time I've heard cries of "*Vive l'Empereur!*"' They were no doubt as forced as those now echoing round Paris. They were certainly nothing like those shouted as Napoleon had progressed to his capital after the escape from Elba. Those few weeks had seen revolt and civil disobedience on the part of the people and an iron-willed ambition to rally them for a war none wanted on the part of the Emperor. No wonder the joy was tinged with doubt.

There was far worse to come. The imperial coach eventually arrived on the Champ-de-Mars and the Emperor descended. He could hardly have looked more ridiculous if he had tried. He had been very careful at his coronation to make sure that his white robes had been covered by a massive cloak and been mostly exposed in the crepuscular gloom of Notre-Dame. Now he appeared in daylight and before the vast crowd in what his younger and wiser self had kept largely hidden: white silk shirt, breeches and stockings along with a great black velvet toque decorated with waving white ostrich feathers. Small, paunchy and middle-aged as Napoleon was, the effect was grotesque. The little Spanish cloaks he had insisted his reluctant brothers wear only made the whole arrival of the imperial family more ridiculous. The triumph had suddenly become the masquerade it truly was, but the Emperor was in no mood to appreciate the fact.

He was exhausted by his labours and embittered by his success. What he had forced on France in the past weeks was remarkable but it was not enough and there was hostility and danger everywhere. The Great Powers of Europe had leagued against him and resolved on his extermination. Large sections of his own people were in revolt and many more were muttering. The army was short of men, the arsenals short of weapons, the treasury short of funds. For this

Napoleon had laboured sixteen hours a day and been denounced by an ungrateful people while, at the same time, being hampered as he thought by a lax administration, a faithless police force and incompetent men at the top. The old energy and enthusiasm of those around him had waned. The manic activity of which he was the focus was demoralised as sometimes Napoleon himself was. He shrugged his shoulders and said with cold bitterness: 'Now we'll find out if France will look after me any better than she did the Bourbons.' It was a grim, exhausted man who sat himself down on his throne and looked at the crowd which was, he could not but help notice, sadly depleted of many of the great men from the glory days.

Now there was the ceremony to endure: first a mass and then the speech from the elected delegates. Dubois d'Angers stepped forward to deliver the pert hypocrisy forced on him. A 'new contract' had been forged between the people and His Majesty, he began, and the delegates had gathered from every part of the Empire to acknowledge the new laws. These were troubled times, however. There were enemies everywhere. 'What do all these Allied kings want with us?' d'Angers asked. What had France done to provoke their vengeance and aggression? Because she wanted to be herself did she 'deserve to be degraded, torn apart, dismembered'? No, she would fight. 'Sire, nothing is impossible' – a phrase which surely warmed Napoleon's heart since it was his own – and 'no effort will be spared.' The embarrassing speech eventually came to its conclusion. 'Every Frenchman is a soldier,' d'Angers averred in words that were again Napoleon's own. 'Victory will follow our eagles, and our enemies who have counted on divisions within our ranks will soon regret provoking us.' It was all a horrible, hollow sham and was greeted with the faint praise of the civilians and the acclamations of the soldiers who were carefully watched by their officers to see that they shouted as they were told.

It was now for Napoleon to give his first public speech since returning to his capital. It was a work of studied deceit and a rehashing of old ideas that had once galvanised the nation. 'As Emperor, Consul, Soldier, I owe everything to the people,' he began. Today they did not seem unduly impressed. 'In prosperity, adversity, on the battlefield, before the council, on the throne, in exile, France has been the one constant object of my thoughts and actions.' After his defeats of 1814 he had 'sacrificed' himself for the sake of the people, hoping that the Allies would maintain 'France's natural frontiers, her honour and her laws'. They had done none of this. *La gloire* and *la patrie* had both been sullied and he had returned now to reburnish them honour bright. He had wanted to do so in peace but he had been obliged to war. Now, armed with the new constitution he had given them, the electoral delegates should return to the departments, tell the people how serious the situation was and work for victory. The foreigner was not to be trusted. The Allies pretended they wanted only him – Napoleon. What they in fact wanted was France. This was a breathtaking denial of all the available evidence, but the Great Powers would be rendered harmless and Napoleon and the people would be as one. 'My rights are theirs, my honour, my glory, my happiness are in fact the honour, glory and happiness of France itself.'

The tepid applause from the civilians showed that few believed this anymore and the acclamations of the soldiers rang hollow in many ears. It was nonetheless time for Napoleon to swear his oath to follow the constitution and for the rest of the crowd to follow him. A solemn, hollow rumble rose up from the great press of people: *Nous le jurons!* It was brief. It was ghastly. It was over. The undebated Benjamine was France's law until Napoleon should choose to tear it to shreds. Then, with the *Te Deum* sung, it was the moment to distribute medals. Napoleon handed out three before his disgust and disappointment at the evident failure of the great occasion – its grating, manifest hypocrisy – got the better of him and he turned away and hurried down the steps from his throne. There was only one place where he could go. There was only one place where he could be sure of a welcome. Like a man desperate to breathe he hurried away from all the factitious pomp and mounted a ceremonial platform in the wide space of the Champ-de-Mars. Suddenly he was surrounded by people waving tricolours and then by his soldiers – thousands upon thousands of them. He handed down metal eagles for the flags into their feverish hands. Did the men swear to defend their country? *Nous le jurons!* Would they swear to die in the defence of France? *Nous le jurons!* Would they swear never to let foreigners defile Paris again? They swore it with deafening enthusiasm. Here were the true French people, for 'every Frenchman is a soldier', and Napoleon was in ecstasy.

He returned to the Tuileries and, just before dawn on Monday, 12 June, was ready to depart for war. He gave his last orders, convened his council of ministers and told them that the country would be in the hands of his brother Joseph during his absence. Then he attended to personal matters. Napoleon secreted over a million francs' worth of diamonds into his coach, just in case. He asked that large chests of arms be sent to two of his mistresses. Then, by three o'clock, he was ready. Imperial pomp was forgotten. Napoleon got into his carriage wearing the blue infantry coat with red epaulettes of a grenadier. He was surrounded by aides de camp, ordnance officers and four hundred Imperial Guardsmen. He was a soldier once again and, as he ordered the driver to make for Soissons, he dreamed that it would be as a soldier on the sodden fields of Belgium that he would regain his throne with one final, mighty victory.

# 5

## WATERLOO

### 12–21 JUNE 1815

## Allied Preparations

The glittering leaders of European high society saw no reason why the great forthcoming war against Napoleon should not be a great social occasion too. The diamonds and brocaded uniforms that had sparkled in Vienna were packed up in leather boxes and trunks and taken to Brussels. The capital was *en fête*. Russians, Austrians, Prussians, Dutch, Belgians and Germans danced and dined with the large number of the British upper crust who had made the short crossing to the Continent and were now installed in elegant if temporary splendour there. Among the last were Mr and Mrs Thomas Creevey and their family. One day, while they were out walking in the park, they chanced upon the Duke of Wellington. For all that the two men had wrangled with each other in the House of Commons a decade earlier, the fiercely radical Creevey and the high Tory peer addressed each other with the wary courtesy that became them both as gentlemen. Pleasantries were exchanged and then Creevey said: 'Will you let me ask you, Duke, what you think you will make of it?' Wellington stopped and said in the most natural manner: 'By God, I think Blücher and myself can do the thing.'

Creevey wondered if there would be any French desertions. Wellington, who had given much thought to his great opponent's way of doing things, reckoned that the ordinary French soldiers and officers would be loyal to Napoleon to a man. 'We may pick up a marshal or two, perhaps; but not worth a damn.' Their fickleness was all too well known. 'No: I think Blücher and I can do the business.' Wellington's determined eyes then looked across the park and fell on a private soldier gaping at the statues. 'There,' he said, pointing at the soldier, 'it all depends upon that article there whether we do the business or not. Give me enough of it, and I am sure.'

Getting enough of the 'article' was not an easy matter. The Allies had resolved in Vienna that they would mount an immense joint force consisting of over 200,000 Austrians, Bavarians and Hessians, 117,000 of Blücher's Prussians, 150,000 Russians and 93,000 British. The Austrians, however, were not expected until July and it was far from certain when the Russians would arrive. For all that the Tsar had clapped Wellington on the shoulder in Vienna and said, 'It is for you to save the world again,' he had subsequently found out about the secret treaty Talleyrand had brokered between France, Austria and Britain to oppose hostility from Russia and Prussia and he was sulking at the implied insult to his territorial ambitions. Now he was dragging his feet, but even a tsar had his price. If the British would pay hefty reparations for their underhand ways then Russia would play its part in saving the world. After all, the British were notoriously rich 'and another two million pounds sterling will not kill them'. Thus it came about that out of the Allies only the British and the Prussians were actually in place. Hence Wellington's studied insistence that he and Blücher together could indeed do what had to be done. It was nonetheless a situation that required the coolest nerve and Wellington, haughty and reserved as he often felt the need to be, spent much time on his horse while his officers played cricket and waited for battle. Those who knew Wellington well and were familiar with his bronzed complexion and great beaked nose knew what such riding could mean. 'It was time to look out.'

It was not only the Great Powers that were proving refractory, however. Wellington's own government was hampering his efforts. He had arrived in Brussels to find he had 14,000 of his own troops. He needed, he said, at least 40,000 more. By the time of his conversation with Creevey the British had merely doubled their original contingent. It was gravely worrying, and the situation was made worse by the acrimony of the politics involved. Many of the great Whigs were hostile to the idea of a war and most of the royal family were hostile to Wellington. The Duke of York in particular, Commander-in-Chief of the British army, loathed him with a deep-seated professional jealousy and declined to send Wellington the officers he really wanted – the veterans of his Peninsular campaigns. It was exasperating. 'I am overloaded with people I have never seen before,' Wellington wrote, 'and it appears to be purposely intended to keep those out of my way whom I wish to have.' Some of the unfamiliar faces were also distinctly unwelcome. The quality that Wellington principally required in an officer was 'cool, discriminating judgement' but Lowe, doyen of the Horse Guards and now Wellington's quartermaster-general, was 'a damned fool' who harped on so persistently about the Prussians being better soldiers than the British that Wellington sent him home. Fortunately he was replaced by just the sort of man Wellington wanted, Colonel Sir William de Lancey, who was indeed a Peninsular veteran and his erstwhile Deputy Quartermaster-General.

Nor were all the ordinary soldiers necessarily the force that Wellington himself would have chosen. A considerable number of them had not fought with him on the Peninsula and an alarming quantity had never fought at all. Only five out of the sixteen cavalry regiments had seen action in Spain, although a further three had been involved in Portugal. The greater part of the twenty-five battalions of infantry had indeed served under Wellington in Spain or seen action in Holland, but the 3/14th Regiment was perilously young, fourteen of its officers and more than 300 of its men being under twenty. Nor was callowness the only problem. Wellington's army was to be an Allied, polyglot one, British soldiers fighting alongside men from the King's German Legion, 16,000 Hanoverians, 29,000 Dutch and Belgian soldiers, nearly 7,000 Brunswickers and 3,000 troops from Nassau.

Wellington solved what could have easily proved an appalling problem with an adroit efficiency born of nature and experience. As he said later: 'I had discovered the secret of mixing them up together.' Veterans were to be put beside raw recruits to stiffen their resolve. Those known to be reliable were drawn up in ranks beside those who might not be. And there was an alarming number of the last. The labyrinthine complexity of alliances made and broken over recent years meant that some of Wellington's men had actually fought alongside the French they were ranged against now. It was only in later years that Wellington himself confessed how uneasy this made him. The combined army he finally sent into the field might have numbered 92,309 soldiers but 'I had only about 35,000 men on whom I could thoroughly rely; the remainder were but too likely to run away'. Here was yet another worry to be shouldered with unflappable, iron determination – something else for Wellington to think about as he rode up and down.

Matters were made no easier for him at the top. The fact that the Allied army was deployed in what was briefly known as the United Netherlands meant that due consideration had to be given to King William of Belgium, widely ridiculed as the 'Old Frog' and, even more annoyingly, to his son the 'Young Frog'. The Prince of Orange as the latter was properly called was the titular head of a princedom far to the south and close to Avignon which had ceased to exist 150 years before. He himself had been born in Holland but left when he was merely three to live as an exile in London and Berlin, and then as an undergraduate at Oxford. He was not very bright, he was twenty-two, he was the Crown Prince of a country he did not know and now chance and status required him to be placed at the head of 40,000 men and fight against Napoleon and a French army bent on ravishing Europe.

The young man's new uniform so glittered with promised glory that it blinded what little sense he had. Resolved to make the House of Orange famous once again in the annals of war, he set about removing from his army all those German officers that Wellington described as the 'men on whom most reliance could be placed' and substituting for them French 'officers who had risen under Bonaparte' and who were 'admirers of his system and government'. There was worse to come. Training was inadequate, discipline was slack and, behind the scenes or sometimes even in public, the Belgian Minister of War nurtured a hatred for the British bred of long and bitter years fighting them unsuccessfully in South Africa and Java. It was some relief that a command structure so fatuous was also inefficient, and it became clear that nothing would get done until Wellington himself pulled rank on the princeling and got himself appointed Field Marshal and Commander-in-Chief of the whole Anglo-Dutch-Belgian force. 'I've got an infamous army,' he opined, 'very weak and ill-equipped, and a very inexperienced staff.' With this he had been asked to save the world.

It would not do, however, to let the burden of the responsibility show. Maintaining morale was of the utmost importance in these difficult circumstances and it was vital that the seriousness of the situation did not become oppressive. The advice Wellington gave to one of his aides was that he followed himself. 'Pray keep the English quiet if you can. Let them all prepare to move, but neither be in a hurry nor a fright, as all will turn out well.' He discreetly suggested that the flamboyant and heavily pregnant Lady Frances Weddurburn Webster (with whom he was very close) make arrangements for her departure. He suggested King Louis move from Ghent to Antwerp. When the Duchess of Richmond said she wanted to throw a picnic close by the frontier Wellington advised against it. 'You'd better not go. Say nothing about it, but let the project drop.' The Duchess had approached him earlier, however, and with greater success.

'Duke,' she had said, 'I do not wish to pry into your secrets . . . I wish to give a ball, and all I ask is, may I give my ball? If you say, "Duchess, don't give your ball," it is quite sufficient, I ask no reason.'

'Duchess,' he replied, 'you may give your ball with the greatest safety, without fear of interruption.'

There were other delights to look forward to as well, occasions on which Wellington could appear with all the imperturbable self-possession of a Tory grandee. For example, he took pretty little sixteen-year-old Lady Jane Lennox to one of the numerous cricket matches his men were playing. Women, indeed, filled much of his spare time. Unhappily married to the reclusive, ageing and ailing Kitty Pakenham, Wellington took his sexual pleasures with all the untroubled gusto of a Regency man of fashion. Not for nothing did his men nickname him the Beau. Those of Napoleon's mistresses he had slept with in Paris compared his performance favourably with their erstwhile protector's and Wellington's magisterial indifference to gossip about his private life ensured that it was widespread. 'He amuses himself by humbugging the ladies,' wrote one of them. 'The Duke of W——,' wrote another and primmer correspondent, 'has not improved the *morality* of our society.' Wellington loved parties, threw several when he was in Brussels, 'and makes a point of asking all the ladies of loose character'. Among these was Lady Weddurburn Webster, who had recently been associated with Byron as well. In addition there were also more mundane personal matters to attend to. Hoby of St James's Street had sent him some Wellington boots that didn't fit properly. They were too tight and too short. Two more pairs about an inch and a half longer in the leg were requested. The smug little lay Methodist preacher set to work. After all, he declared: 'if Lord Wellington had any other boot maker than myself, he would never have had his great and constant successes; for my boots and prayers bring his Lordship out of all his difficulties.' Perhaps they would again.

Wellington was fully aware of the skill of the enemy he faced. Tsar Alexander's grandiloquent phrase about him saving the world might have been appropriate to such a great occasion as Wellington's departure for the front, but altogether more useful was the conversation he had enjoyed in Vienna with somebody less flamboyant: Field Marshal Prince Karl Philipp Wrede. The Prince was one of the great soldiers of his day, having learned his craft by fighting with Napoleon himself at Marengo, Eylau, Friedland and during the Russian campaign. Wrede had seen Napoleonic triumph and disaster close to. He knew Napoleon personally and was sufficiently an intimate to ask him about his theories of war. 'I don't have any,' he was told bluntly. 'I absolutely do not have a campaign plan.' Both Wrede and Wellington were men of sufficient insight to realise that this was not professional circumspection but the simple truth. As Wrede himself declared of Napoleon: 'All he required was that his troops should be assembled and posted as he directed, and then he marched and struck a great blow, defeated the enemy and acted afterwards as circumstances would allow.' Speed, massive force, boundless ambition and improvisation based on an absolute grip of the logistical facts were Napoleon's means, power his end. If Wellington despised utterly Napoleon's unprincipled grasp of the latter he had a profound respect for his grip on the former. The past was no certain guide to what his great, sinister enemy might do now, however, and Wellington's preparedness, watchfulness and quick-wittedness were everything.

He had one other force on which he knew he could rely – Blücher and his Prussians. The two commanders had met the previous year and, very different though they were, they had soon formed a close and respectful professional relationship. Where Wellington was detached and haughtily aristocratic, scornful of fools, analytical and, when necessary, politically adroit, Blücher, the fierce-eyed, formidable old warrior of seventy-two, was a resolutely unintellectual man: bluff, jolly, disarmingly modest, more than a little boorish and completely ruthless. By and large his men adored him but if 'Old Forward March' as they called him loved his men as 'my children', his punishments could be terrible. Only recently, on

2 May, a couple of his recently arrived Saxon regiments threatened to mutiny and Blücher had ordered the entire division to disarm and disband, and then seen to the burning of its flags and the execution of seven of its officers. Disloyalty and reneging on one's word were anathema to Blücher and he had given his word to Wellington. He would cooperate with him come what might.

Wellington now had as an ally a man whose hatred of the French was almost pathological. Moreover, the core of Blücher's army had been trained with the new Prussian discipline that had emerged after their nation's humiliating defeat at Jena. Blücher could inspire them and, where his naivety might betray the virtues of his courage, he had a general staff of exceptional expertise. Its chief, von Gneisenau, was a man of dour mechanical efficiency and a restlessly suspicious mind. The two made an odd, ideal combination even if von Gneisenau was wary of Wellington and believed that the Englishman did not always tell the whole truth. In this he was correct although the matter can be overstated. It was absolutely essential that Wellington preserve Blücher's trust and confidence. Wellington knew only too well that the situation he found himself in was riddled with difficulties and grave potential dangers. Throughout these days of preparation he was concerned constantly about the possibility of catastrophic defeat and the loss of his army. He had no intention of retreating. His explicit aim was the defeat of Napoleon and advance on the French capital. He needed to be ready for the worse all the same, and if he was diffident about the efforts he was making to secure his lines of retreat to Antwerp and Ostend that was in order to keep morale high. He could afford no wavering in his own army or in Blücher's troops.

Recent history helped Wellington here. For all the mutiny threatened by his Saxon contingents, a powerful hatred of Napoleon and his works surged through the majority of Blücher's troops. The defeat at Jena had been humiliating and, just as youths in Britain felt impelled to enlist, so boys in Prussia burned to revenge their nation's wrongs. Among them was one Franz Lieber, the son of a businessman in Berlin and later a professor of political science in New York.[1] His two older brothers had already fought against Napoleon in the campaigns of 1814, and the sixteen-year-old Franz was jealous of their wounds and glory. Now, when his father announced that Napoleon had escaped from Elba and was on the loose again, Franz was in ecstasy as the venerable old man told him to clean his gun and go off to fight in a war he was too young to join and too excited to resist. Lieber signed up with the Colberg Regiment, which, he said, was 'composed of brave and sturdy Pomeranians, a short, broad-shouldered, healthy race'. He then kissed goodbye to his sobbing mother and made his way into the centre of Berlin. There the hatred of Napoleon could be measured by the length of the queue of the other young men waiting to enlist. The women in the meantime vowed to follow those of Vienna and wear no silk or jewels, waiting in sombre colours until their husbands, brothers and sons returned triumphant. It took Franz Lieber three hours to reach the head of the queue and sign his name. Then, marshalled by bugles and singing patriotic songs, he turned his back on the Brandenburg Gate and marched off to the Waterloo campaign.

## The French Advance

By 14 June, Napoleon had reached Beaumont. It was an auspicious date, the anniversary of the great victories at Marengo and Friedland. The Emperor reminded his troops of the fact when he addressed them. Looking across at the men – a mixture of veterans and raw recruits, loyal Bonapartists and embittered royalists – he then told them that 'the time has come to conquer or die'. For all his confidence, however, Napoleon's position was unenviable since his force of 122,652 men was facing two armies whose combined strength was 222,555. He nonetheless had a strategy for such a situation, a strategy he had applied early in his career at Rivoli and far more recently at Leipzig. He called it 'an attack on the central position'. It was a very dangerous manoeuvre but it could be devastating. In this case it consisted of launching one entire army at the vulnerable junction point between Blücher's forces and Wellington's. That junction point was Charleroi. With Charleroi seized Napoleon could then pin down one of the opposing armies with his wing while destroying the other with his main force. As each enemy army retreated towards its home base – Wellington in the direction of Antwerp and Ostend, Blücher towards Liège and Coblenz – so they would be driven ever further apart, thereby destroying what they had hoped would be their combined strength. It was a brilliant if daring strategy but a tried and tested one. Wellington and Blücher had, of course, foreseen the possibility of Napoleon's employing it and had made contingency plans. These, however, required time before they could be put into effect. For Napoleon to succeed, speed and surprise were, as always, essential.

Marching orders for the advance of Charleroi were then given to his Chief-of-Staff, Marshal Soult, and here the problems began. A difficult and argumentative man, Soult was generally disliked and there was bitter, ancient animosity between him and General Vandamme whose III Army Corps would launch the offensive at half-past two the following morning. Part of Grouchy's cavalry would already have been sent on in advance to act as a screen. Reinforcements for Vandamme would then be sent out at four o'clock, by which time the two other prongs of the attacking force would also have been despatched, one column marching towards Charleroi along the west bank of the Sambre, the other advancing from Phillipeville. These forces would combine, overwhelm Charleroi itself and give Napoleon the road to Brussels. The whole massive but intricate movement was carefully planned and, just as importantly, very carefully timed to make sure that the roads would not be clogged with masses of men.

Human error and human weakness began to wreak their damage almost immediately. First the commander of the Imperial Guard, the

17. Napoleon at Fontainebleau

18. The Congress of Vienna

19. Adieu at Fontainebleau

20. Departure of Napoleon for Elba

21. The return from Elba

22. Napoleon returning in triumph

23. Return of Napoleon to the Tuileries

24. Assembly of the Champ de Mai

25. Wellington on the Road to Quatre-Bras

26. The Battle of Ligny

27. The Duchess of Richmond's ball on the eve of Waterloo

28. The Battle of Waterloo

29. The last advance
of the Imperial
Guard

30. On the evening of the Battle of Waterloo

31. Napoleon on board the Bellerophon

most elite formation in the army, was laid low with a bout of sciatica so painful that he was obliged to take to his bed. Napoleon replaced him with General Drouot. This was a relatively minor matter but the incompetence of Soult was not. He had very little experience of his important role and he bungled it. Napoleon had instructed him to order Vandamme to lead off the offensive at 2.30 in the morning. The Marshal's orders were not received at Vandamme's headquarters in Beaumont until 5.00. Thus for some reason impossible to determine two and a half valuable hours had already been lost. Worse was now to occur. When the messenger finally arrived Vandamme himself could not be found. An officer was sent out to look for him but the anxious man, riding his horse hard in the dark, felt it stumble before it fell on him. The weight broke the man's leg and he was left in the middle of nowhere blinded with pain and unable to move. Vandamme himself eventually returned to his headquarters still in ignorance of what was expected of him, and it was only when he heard that the VI Corps was now marching up the road in his direction that he realised to his horror that he should have set off hours before. He believed there was only one thing he could do. He requested that the 11,000 advancing men be halted while his own 18,000 troops set off at a quick march. Other massive divisions were now being despatched at ninety-minute intervals, however, and with the inevitable result: tens of thousands of men, cannon, horses and equipment cluttered the road to Charleroi and slowed things down appallingly.

The town was nonetheless captured and a furious Napoleon appeared at midday. At 3.30 Marshal Ney arrived. He wore his history in his troubled face. This was the man who had threatened to bring Napoleon back to Paris in an iron cage, 'the bravest of the brave' whose deeply troubled conscience had not healed from the dark night of agony and self-doubt he had endured when switching his allegiance back from the Bourbons to Napoleon. That Ney had turned his twice hardly boded well. He was, nonetheless, a great soldier and a necessary one. For all his doubts, Napoleon greeted him affably and gave him the vitally important command of the left column, the I and II Corps. He would be reinforced by the light cavalry of the Imperial Guard and would be joined the following day by Kellermann's cuirassiers. Ney was then told to push the enemy up the road towards Brussels and take his position at Quatre-Bras. The course of events was soon to show that the disillusioned marshal was now incapable of the speed and determination Napoleon's plan required, but an equally serious error of judgement was the second appointment Napoleon now made. Grouchy was promoted to lead the right wing of the army and advance on the Prussians gathered around Fleurus and Sombreffe. His subordinate commanders, Vandamme and Gérard, rightly thought he was unsuited to such a responsibility. They protested to no purpose and satisfied themselves by holding him in contempt. Grouchy too would show that he was inadequate to fulfilling Napoleon's demands. Now, however, as Napoleon settled himself in to a small chateau on the banks of the Sambre, he could afford to be pleased at the fact that, despite incompetence and disloyalty in his army, he had captured Charleroi if not with the speed that he had wanted then at least in a way that would surprise his enemy.

## The Duchess of Richmond's Ball

In this latter purpose he was helped by the slowness of certain of the Prussians. General von Ziethen had withdrawn his men after his encounter with the advancing French just as Blücher had ordered but he was painfully slow in sending his news of the capture of Charleroi on to Wellington. It did not arrive in Brussels until eleven hours after the event. It was three o'clock in the afternoon when a sweating and dusty Prussian officer finally arrived with it, closely followed by other messengers sent by Blücher and the Prince of Orange. For Wellington the news was desperate, the surprise humiliating and the information he was given inadequate. He had spread his steadily arriving soldiers over an area west of Brussels which was where he thought he might catch the French in a net. They were not concentrated together and, while they could be moved, this would take time. And time, it seemed, was what he did not have. Nor did he have all the intelligence he needed to react quickly and in an informed way. For all he knew Napoleon's descent on Charleroi might have been just a diversion. Or was it the main thrust of the French army? How large were the forces? How were they deployed around Charleroi?

Wellington needed to know urgently but it was impossible quickly to gather the necessary facts about the disposition of the enemy from the eighty-mile front along which the Allied forces were ranged. He had to do something, however, and at five o'clock he gave orders for his troops to gather at their prearranged assembly points. The greater part of Wellington's army was thus deployed somewhat to the west of Brussels and so away from Blücher who had moved his field headquarters to Sombreffe. To the east of the city, the line through Mons, Ath and Ghent would be kept under observation, but the centre and the cross-roads at Quatre-Bras would for the moment see no more soldiers than the Prince of Orange's men stationed nearly seven miles away. And still the Duke waited for a despatch from Mons. He had long considered it highly likely that Napoleon's main thrust would be launched from there. Mons was on the main Paris to Brussels highway and was nearer to the Belgian capital by ten miles than Charleroi. It was essential to establish that the French presence at Charleroi was not a feint. By midnight he knew it was not. 'I have received a report from General Dornberg at Mons,' he said, 'that Napoleon has moved on Charleroi with all his force.' As a consequence of this, orders were speedily issued for the Allied troops to redeploy and concentrate on Nivelle and Quatre-Bras to the east of the city. It seemed that there was nothing to do now but wait and, since the Duchess of Richmond was throwing her ball that night, Wellington would attend it.

The apparent insouciance of Wellington's decision was, of course, a calculated move. Now more than ever it was necessary for him to appear as the splendid and unshakeable pinnacle of high society and the embodiment of British sangfroid. The ball was, besides, where every young officer of rank would be found and, while he needed to talk to some of them, his presence would encourage them all. Wellington arrived around midnight to find high society delighting itself in the elegantly redecorated impromptu ballroom on the ground floor of the Duchess's rented house. Rose-trellised wallpaper, sumptuous tented hangings of crimson, black and gold, beribboned pillars and abundant flowers were everywhere, while, in Byron's phrase, 'the lamps shone o'er fair women and brave men'. There was nonetheless an undertow of deep concern as the music played and the guests danced. As Wellington entered, young Lady Georgiana Lennox broke off from her partner and ran over to the Duke. Were the rumours of impending battle true? 'Yes, they are true, we are off tomorrow,' he said. The Duke's tone was grave and the chatter in the ballroom turned to a buzz of serious alarm. The Duke of Brunswick felt such a shudder run through him that the little Prince de Ligne fell off his lap. Wellington himself went imperturbably to sit on a sofa beside Lady Dalrymple-Hamilton. They chatted, but she noticed how serious he was under his affability. Wellington would break off in mid-sentence and issue an order to senior officers like Brunswick or the Prince of Orange.

A despatch now arrived for the latter. He handed it straight to the Duke. Wellington opened it and read the desperate news it contained. The Prussians had been repulsed from Fleurus which was barely eight miles from Quatre-Bras. The Prince should return to his headquarters immediately, he said. His carriage horses were summoned but the young man had barely left the room before he returned, his concern evident on his handsome face. He went across to Wellington, who was now eating his supper, and whispered in his ear. A look of utter disbelief flashed across the Duke's face but it was now more than ever essential that he did not show his dismay at what he had heard. For twenty minutes more he sat at the table apparently enjoying his food and the conversation of Georgiana Lennox and Lady Wedderburn Webster. Finally, he turned to the Duke of Richmond and said: 'I think it is time for me to go to bed.' The party rose from the table. Farewells and thank yous were exchanged, and Wellington leaned over to whisper in Richmond's ear. Did he have a good map in the house? Wellington was taken into the study and a map was spread before him. He looked at it intently until his eye lighted on Quatre-Bras. The French, with that incredible speed and surprise the Emperor insisted on, had apparently advanced towards the cross-roads that gave the place its name. It was dreadful, shocking, the way the man could move his troops. An incredulous Wellington looked across at his host:

'Napoleon has *humbugged* me, by God! He has gained twenty-four hours' march on me.'

'What are you going to do?'

'I have ordered my army to concentrate at Quatre-Bras; but we shall not stop him there, and if so I must fight him *here*.'

The Duke's finger moved over the map and stabbed down just south of a small village called Waterloo.

## Quatre-Bras and Ligny

The speed of the French had indeed been terrifying but it was not the speed Napoleon himself required – the speed that had always been essential to his success. A deep, disabling malaise was settling like a fog into the minds and hearts of many of his most senior officers. Both Ney and Grouchy had been given the clearest of orders: the one was to advance to Quatre-Bras in preparation for sweeping on to Brussels, the other was to advance on the Prussians around Sombreffe. Neither man followed his orders adequately. Grouchy's progress was dilatory at best, slowed perhaps by the weight of responsibility placed on his inadequate shoulders. Napoleon had to send orders chivvying him along but these seem to have had little effect. Grouchy had not even made his goal by nightfall when some of his men camped on the bank of the Sambre and others on the road leading to their supposed destination.

Ney's performance was even worse. Napoleon had ordered him to capture Quatre-Bras. Ney again refused, settling his troops instead along a line from Marchienne to Gosselies, where he himself spent the night. Such slackness was almost incomprehensible in a soldier of his standing. In the past Ney's feats of endurance had been prodigious. It had been Ney who brought the remains of the shattered *Grande Armée* back to France after the Russian defeat. He had been the last man to leave that bitter country. Now he was apparently unable to advance a few miles to a crossroads. What had happened to him? The fact was that the fracture which had opened in him during his dark night of the soul was widening, and his unstable enthusiasm for Napoleon's grand scheme was disappearing into the void. Throughout his career Ney had helped Napoleon realise his belief that the impossible was a phantom to frighten the timid and a refuge for fools. Now he began to see that simply wasn't true. It was not fear that crippled him – he was 'the bravest of the brave' – but the exhaustion of a broken spirit that was sick and tired of endless Napoleonic warfare.

Even as dawn rose and the Emperor's written instructions confirming his orders of the previous day arrived, Ney remained where he was, thus giving the Allies time and safety in which to start reinforcing Quatre-Bras. Another message came from Napoleon at eleven o'clock. It was the Emperor's 'express desire' that Ney be ready to march from Quatre-Bras to Brussels on command. The plan was very clear. Napoleon himself would be moving up to Fleurus to support Grouchy's offensive against the Prussians which, he reckoned, would be a small thing for he was confident the Prussians could not muster more than 40,000 men. In the meantime Ney was to reinforce his hold on Quatre-Bras, keep his troops there just in case they were required in Napoleon's battle and then 'start marching for Brussels this evening, arriving there at seven o'clock the following morning'. The two parts of the French army would then meet up in the capital. Speed, as always, was of the essence. 'Therefore do not lose a moment since the faster our objectives are achieved the better the rest of the operation will go.' But Ney had not even got as far as Quatre-Bras. He had lingered where he was for thirteen hours and it was only at noon that he finally broke camp.

Wellington, in the meantime, was vigorously active. He had allowed himself barely more than three hours' sleep after the Duchess of Richmond's ball. Five-thirty the following morning saw him bestirring himself and by 7.00 he was mounted on his favourite charger, Copenhagen. By 10.00 he had reached Quatre-Bras. There he approved the disposition of the newly reinforced troops guarding the place and, having done so, rode off with his aides-de-camp to have a meeting with Blücher at a windmill eight miles down the road. They met up at 1.00 in the afternoon. It was at once obvious to the Duke that Blücher's army of 76,000 infantry, 8,000 cavalry and 224 guns was, for all its impressive size, ranged in a way that was far too dispersed and exposed. The Prussian front extended for seven miles and, as Wellington himself observed, this meant that the French 'had it in their power to cannonade them and shatter them to pieces'. Besides, the Prussians could not easily advance and attack because of the large boggy area that lay between them and the enemy. Wellington suggested that Blücher withdraw the scattered columns and get more of the troops under the shelter of the rising ground. This was not well received. 'However, they seemed to think they knew best, so I came away very shortly,' Wellington declared huffily. When the Prussians asked him to bring his forces over to support them nonetheless he agreed 'provided I am not attacked myself'.

The weakness in the Prussians' position had also been observed by Napoleon. He was, at the same time, painfully aware that his estimate of an enemy numbering merely 40,000 had been woefully optimistic. This was clearly going to be a major battle but, if he was unfamiliar with the terrain and had only just acquainted himself with the disposition of the enemy troops, Grouchy's army was at least assembling, albeit slowly, and he believed that he could always call on Ney's reinforcements supposedly stationed at Quatre-Bras. By the close of the morning Napoleon had marshalled his men into a right wing consisting of 58,000 infantry, 12,500 troopers, two cavalry corps and 210 pieces of artillery. The opening stages of the battle showed the unexpectedly large Prussian army defending themselves with unlooked-for vigour, however, and, by two o'clock, Napoleon was sending orders for Ney to join him and make up his left wing. If they marched up the Namur road Ney would find Blücher's totally exposed right flank standing before him an easy prey. The Prussians would be trapped, enveloped and annihilated. The forthcoming Battle of Ligny would not be an easy victory. 'The outcome of the war can be decided within three hours,' Napoleon told one of his officers. 'If Ney executes his orders thoroughly, the Prussian army will be taken completely by surprise, not a cannon will escape.' Here was the old supreme confidence, a confidence heedless or ignorant of the forces threatening it: the lethargy, the less than total commitment, the inefficiency that were all subtly infiltrating Napoleon's ranks and had even begun to affect even the Emperor himself. He had been uncharacteristically slow in sending out his written orders that morning instead of the night before. He was badly misinformed about the Prussian army and the terrain on which he was to fight. He believed Wellington's troops were spread out across Belgium and he thought that Ney was quietly holding Quatre-Bras.

In fact battle was raging there and when Napoleon's order to Ney finally arrived the harassed Marshal exploded with anger. 'Do not lose a minute,' the note read. 'The fate of France is in your hands.' It was unbearable. 'Tell the Emperor what you have seen here!' Ney shouted at the astonished young officer who had brought the order.

Ney was now confronted with a constantly enlarging enemy army reinforced by contingents of Wellington's best men, including Picton's 5th Infantry Division. Ney had split his own men into three columns in his late attempt to secure Quatre-Bras. They had advanced steadily but by 3.00 in the afternoon Wellington's reserves from Mont-Saint-Jean had arrived and these included an elite infantry division. Ney's early success in rebuffing the Prince of Orange's men was not to be easily repeated now. The Duke of Brunswick's troop of 7,000 men arrived and Ney was desperately awaiting the arrival of some 19,000 men led by General d'Erlon. How could he possibly leave the field to support Napoleon at a time like this? 'I will hold on where I am but nothing more!' he thundered. It was while he was in this exasperated state that a message arrived from d'Erlon informing Ney that he and his 19,000 men had been ordered to offer their support not to Ney himself but to Napoleon at Ligny. Apoplectic now, a desperate Ney counter-manded d'Erlon's instructions. He was to come to Quatre-Bras with all possible speed. The action suggests Ney's state of mind and he now led a furious cavalry charge against the enemy. When this was repulsed, he ordered Kellermann's elite troopers to take the crossroads come what might. It was now 5.00 in the afternoon and the order was suicidal.

Half an hour later d'Erlon and his men dutifully arrived on the battlefield at Ligny as Napoleon had ordered only to cause utter consternation among the embattled French. Reaching the crisis of their offensive, they thought d'Erlon was a battalion of the enemy against whom they had now been struggling for about two hours, an enemy who appeared to have fallen into a delighted Napoleon's trap and who, without reinforcements and with men and munitions now running low, seemed ready for the Emperor's principal attack of the day. This now had to be delayed for an hour and it was at 6.30 that a third imperial messenger was despatched to the General informing him that he was in the wrong place and must at once manoeuvre towards the Prussian right where he would be able to inflict crushing damage. D'Erlon was about to do this when Ney's messenger arrived ordering him to take no notice of what Napoleon had said. D'Erlon was to return at full speed to Quatre-Bras. It was chaotic but, balancing the command of an Emperor against what he guessed was the desperation of a Marshal, d'Erlon sensed that the needs of Ney were greater than those of Napoleon and so returned whence he had come.

Back at Quatre-Bras itself, Ney's decision to take part in the attack he had ordered Kellermann to make proved to be a desperate matter indeed. Kellermann himself was furious that it was to be made at all – to expose an elite reserve like this was unprofessional in the highest degree – but Ney insisted and 4,000 fabulously uniformed cuirassiers, protected as they hoped by their brilliant breastplates, charged with drawn sabres towards Picton's infantry now deployed in squares. They were within thirty yards of each other before Wellington ordered his men to fire. The glorious French fell in their hundreds, their cries and their horses' cries only partly drowned by the merciless pounding of the five batteries of field artillery against which they stood little chance. 'A most destructive fire was opened,' wrote one Scots sergeant, 'riders cased in heavy armour, fell tumbling from their horses; the horses reared, plunged, and fell on the dismounted riders; steel helmets and cuirasses rang against unsheathed sabres as they fell to the ground.' The French were beaten back, their brief heroism plummeting into despair as they picked their way back through their own dying men. Kellermann's horse was shot from under him, but so formidable had the charge been and so heavy the Allies' use of munitions that it seemed unlikely, victorious though they had been, that the British could withstand another attack. He scrambled together what cavalry he could and, even though the Allies were still being reinforced, thundered towards them a second time until stopped once again by Picton's men. Wellington forced the French back once more as yet further British reinforcements arrived. It was now 6.30. Wellington had 36,000 men and with them he launched his counter-attack. Two and half hours later the battle was his, for all that he had lost a thousand more men than Ney.

By 7.30 that evening it was obvious to Napoleon that he could not expect d'Erlon's reinforcements to arrive and he ordered the final attack on Ligny. It was already raining hard and by 8.00 the storm was torrential as two columns of the Imperial Guard fell on the Prussians defending the village. The carnage was terrible. Blücher, leading the counter-attack, had his horse shot from under him, leaving him unconscious in the mud from which he was only dragged by a loyal aide-de-camp after two French cavalrymen had ridden over him. Entire Prussian regiments were obliterated. They suffered in all 18,772 casualties. The state of those still able to quit the field of battle was terrible. 'In the great heat,' wrote a Westphalian captain, 'gunpowder smoke, sweat and mud had mixed into a thick crust of dirt, so that their faces looked almost like those of mulattos, and one could hardly distinguish the green collars and facings on their tunics'. The sixteen-year-old had killed his first man and was cockahoop. 'All I had feared,' he wrote years later, 'was that I should not have the honour of assisting in a thorough battle.'

It was not until the following morning, however, that Napoleon would order the pursuit of the fleeing Prussians. The growing sense that something was amiss, the feeling that the ruthless speed and efficiency which usually characterised a Napoleonic campaign were not functioning as they should, continued into the next day when the Emperor reviewed his troops.[2] His face had a stern expression as he walked along the lines with short steps, his hands behind his back.

'I know you,' he said to one of the men. 'You used to be in my Guard, didn't you?'

'Yes, sire, I had that honour, and I owe you all the steps in my promotion.'

The speaker was Colonel Fantin des Odoards, he who had once rejoiced in the thought of the Russian campaign, survived its disasters and spent a night of agonised self-doubt in Gap when Napoleon was passing through on his return to Paris. He had come to his decision and now the colonel was commanding the 22nd of the line in Vandamme's III Corps. He had fought with distinction at Ligny.

'Good,' Napoleon said. 'How many on parade?'

'Eighteen hundred and thirty, sire.'

'How many did you lose yesterday?'

'Two hundred and twenty.'

'I watched your conduct . . . You repelled the enemy's charges very gallantly. Excellent. We shall meet again. The Prussians abandoned a great many muskets on the battlefield. What is being done with them?'

'Sire, we are making *jambons* of them.'

Napoleon was suddenly angry. Reducing the muskets to 'hams' meant destroying them by removing their butts.

'You are wrong, quite wrong,' the Emperor said fiercely. 'I gave orders for these muskets to be collected with great care so that our National Guards in the interior of France could be armed with them. And the artillery has instructions to allow the soldiers three francs for each weapon collected in this way.'

'Sire, this order has not reached me yet.'

The Emperor turned to his aides, the 'gilded group' standing behind him, and barked out: 'Do you hear that? An order of this importance not yet known. Have this put to rights as soon as possible. Goodbye, Colonel. I am pleased with you and your regiment.'

The pervasive sense of inefficiency and inertia among the French deepened and it spread down from the top. Partly from ignorance and partly from a combination of apathy and arrogance Napoleon assumed that Wellington had been routed and that the defeated Prussians were fleeing in panic-stricken chaos. He was wrong on both counts. Wellington remained in possession of Quatre-Bras, but the news of Blücher's defeat, the 'damned good licking' he had received not altogether to Wellington's surprise at Ligny, meant that Wellington himself was apparently isolated and outnumbered. He had had the bitter satisfaction of being proved right at Quatre-Bras when numerous of his foreign troops deserted in the heat of battle. What was worse, as and when Napoleon and Ney joined forces he would almost certainly be defeated by their superior army. At noon he ordered his remaining men to Mont-Saint-Jean, having told the Prussians that he would only fight the French again if they sent him at least one corps. Gneisenau, the anglophobic Prussian Chief-of-Staff, was against this for he believed that Wellington had betrayed the Prussians at Ligny. The arrival of the redoubtable old Blücher, stinking of onions and gin, changed all of that. He liked Wellington. He had given him his word. His troops, who were far from fleeing in chaos as Napoleon believed, were now ordered to march to Wavre, a point about ten miles from the Duke's new base. There they would regroup in order to help him fight on.

It was just such eventualities that Napoleon should have foreseen and prevented but he did not even try to ascertain the direction of the main Prussian retreat and thus allowed a still mighty army to escape. He assumed on the basis of misinformation that the Prussians were making for Liège. Urgent requests from Grouchy that he be given orders to pursue his enemy of the day before did not appear to rouse Napoleon. He snubbed him and then squandered valuable time riding round the battlefield and talking politics to his high command. It was after 11.00 before he finally despatched Grouchy on an essential mission which the incompetent man, as might have been expected, fouled up. Truly dynamic leadership might have made up for the time and opportunity already lost, but Grouchy did not possess this quality. He should have seen that his major priorities were to ascertain where Blücher's main contingent was and then place his 30,000 troops between it and Napoleon's right wing. Instead, he dawdled. Admittedly the rain was torrential and the roads appalling but the conditions which meant that the French covered a mere ten miles and stopped to make camp two hours before nightfall were precisely the same conditions through which the heroic Prussians trudged on their way to Wavre and Wellington. And still Grouchy believed they were making for Liège.

If Napoleon was dilatory in pursuing Blücher he was astonished when he learned that Ney had not defeated Wellington, but it was only an hour later that he issued orders telling Ney 'to take up your position' and try once again to destroy Wellington's army. Ney was not minded to do any such thing. After the heroic if ultimately futile exertions of the previous day the Marshal's precarious temper was now swinging between anger and inertia. He was already smarting from a letter he had received from his old enemy Soult (himself far from the most efficient of men) telling him how the Emperor looked 'with grave dissatisfaction' on his recent conduct at Quatre-Bras. Faced with such rebuffs, Ney's spirits sank further, and his response to Napoleon's new orders was to do nothing. Thus, when the Emperor himself finally arrived at Quatre-Bras he found neither an army nor a battle. Ney had merely moved his men a few miles south and was having his lunch in peace while Wellington, like Blücher, was falling back unmolested to the north to fight another day. The dressing-down Ney received in front of all his men was yet another humiliation, after which the pursuit of the Allied–British army was ordered to begin at once, Napoleon himself leading the Imperial Guard as they went after Wellington at full gallop.

The British could not understand why the French had taken so long to act. Captain Cavalié Mercer who, with the rest of the Royal Horse Artillery, had marched so gleefully to war from the barracks in Colchester was at a loss to explain it. He, Lord Uxbridge and an aide-de-camp were observing the French from the brow of a hill. Through his telescope Uxbridge could see the smoke rising from the fires that were cooking Ney's lunch. 'It will not be long now before they are on us,' the aide declared, 'for they always dine before they move.' And indeed almost at once the French were marching, urged forward by a furious Napoleon. Mercer saw them swarming towards them 'in three or four dark masses, whilst their advanced cavalry picket was already skirmishing with and driving back our hussars'. Simultaneously with the sinister and sombre enemy, however, came the dark clouds of a torrential storm. As Mercer and his fellows fired at the French so the clouds burst and lightning rent the sky. 'The sublimity of the scene was inconceivable,' he wrote. 'Flash succeeded flash, and the peals of thunder were long and tremendous; whilst, as if in mockery of the elements, the French guns still sent forth their feebler and now scarcely audible reports – their cavalry dashing along at a headlong pace, adding their shouts to the uproar.'

The torrential rain soon put a stop to that. 'The tracks were so deep in mud . . . that we found it impossible to maintain any order in our columns,' wrote a French soldier. Men, horses and the wheels of the heavy cannon all got stuck. Still the rain fell and, as Wellington and his men settled down in the vicinity of the little village of Waterloo, so the French bivouacked alongside the Brussels road. Napoleon had failed to catch his prey and even the weather, it seemed, had joined in a conspiracy against him. Nonetheless, despite the rain, he spent much of the rest of the day on horseback conferring with his commanders and inspecting what would tomorrow become the field of battle, a field chosen by Wellington and not by him. This was a considerable psychological disadvantage for the Emperor.

And still the stultifying inertia and incompetence that seemed to have gripped his army was at work. Napoleon himself was trying to sleep in his temporary headquarters at Le Caillou farmhouse when, about three o'clock in the morning, a letter arrived from Marshal Grouchy informing him that, far from fleeing in disorder towards Liège, the Prussians were in fact advancing on nearby Wavre. It had taken him all day to find this out. Now he promised he would pursue them and prevent them from either reaching

Brussels or meeting up with Wellington. He would start at 8.00 the following day. It did not occur to him that time was of the essence, nor did it occur to Napoleon that he should order Grouchy's troops – almost a third of his entire army – to manoeuvre into a position where they could shield him from a Prussian attack. It did not even occur to him to reply to Grouchy's note. He seemed unaware too that, by failing to recall the Marshal, he was breaking one of his own cardinal rules: 'the army must be kept assembled and the greatest possible force concentrated on the field of battle.'

It was a wise maxim in view of the fact that Napoleon's strategy for the following day was to launch a massive frontal assault on the enemy. It seems that for the moment, however, the Emperor's principal concern was that Wellington should not leave the field during the night and so deprive him of his battle. It did not cross Napoleon's mind that Wellington would stay not only because he was utterly resolved to remove the Napoleonic menace from Europe once and for all but because he now knew that the Prussians were on their way to help him do it. Despite his drubbing, Blücher would honour his promise.

For his part, Napoleon was smugly content in his belief that Wellington had chosen for himself a very disadvantageous position from which to fight tomorrow's battle and he believed that the dense trees of the Soignes Forest would ensure that retreat was impossible for him after the inevitable French victory. There was much else that might have justified such optimism. Napoleon had a sizeable number of veterans in his army, far more than Wellington possessed, the Allied army being a polyglot mixture with a high percentage of raw recruits in its ranks. Many of Napoleon's senior officers were seasoned campaigners. He was also able significantly to outgun the enemy and gunnery was Napoleon's particular expertise. The British were provided with 9-pounders but among Napoleon's arsenal were a quantity of massive 12-pounders – his so-called '*belles filles*' – which were capable under the right conditions of wreaking dreadful havoc. It was not without reason that

Napoleon could mutter: 'Now I've got those English.' A lifetime's ambition was about to be fulfilled.

## The Battle of Waterloo

The atmosphere over the breakfast table in Le Caillou on Sunday, 18 June was nonetheless tense and bitter. Only Napoleon, for all that his night had been disturbed by the unpleasant necessity of having his haemorrhoids attended to, appeared confident. When the imperial silver salvers had been removed and the maps were spread, he addressed his senior officers, telling them that Wellington 'has thrown the dice and they are in our favour'. This was the speech of a man who had not fought the British personally since encountering them at Acre during the Egyptian campaign more than a decade and a half earlier, and its bravado brushed aside matters altogether more telling, in particular the fact that during his Peninsular campaign Wellington had defeated eight imperial Marshals including Ney and an even larger number of generals including some such as d'Erlon and Reille who were to see action that day. His views were wholly untouched by the bitter respect that seasoned Peninsular veterans like Marshal Soult had for Wellington, and Soult now had the temerity to mention that he thought it inadvisable that Grouchy was still away from the field chasing the Prussians. Napoleon was furious. 'Just because you have been beaten by Wellington, you consider him a great general,' he barked. 'Well, I tell you now that Wellington is a bad general, that the English are bad soldiers, and that the whole thing will be a picnic – *l'affaire d'un déjeuner.*'

Soult, suitably abashed, simply muttered: 'I earnestly hope so.'

General Reille, who had just entered the room with Napoleon's young brother Jerome, would surely back the Emperor up. After all, he had had much experience in fighting the British. Napoleon turned to him for support and Reille delivered his opinion with all the portentousness he thought became the occasion. 'Well posted,' he began, 'and Wellington knows how to post it, and attacked from the front, I consider the English infantry to be impregnable, owing to its calm tenacity, and its superior aim in firing.' This was exasperating. Napoleon had just beaten Blücher by mounting just such a direct frontal assault and he was determined to do the same with Wellington. After a heavy bombardment the French cavalry, the Imperial Guard and his all-important reserves would sweep the shattered remains of the Anglo-Allied army before them. It would indeed be *l'affaire d'un déjeuner*. So blindly confident of his strategy was he that Napoleon simply would not consider any other, although Reille offered one.

'The English army is less agile, less supple, less expert in manoeuvring than ours,' he said. 'If we cannot beat it by a direct attack, we may do so by manoeuvring.'

The Emperor merely shrugged his shoulders.

General Foy also had experience of fighting the British. He had lost to Wellington eight times and knew what he was talking about. 'Wellington never shows his troops,' he said, 'but if he is out there, I must warn Your Majesty that the English infantry in close combat is the very devil.'

The advice was sincere but it should not have been given in this way. It was a cardinal rule of Napoleon's that one never talked up the enemy. Now his own brother Jérôme was doing it too, saying how he had heard that a Belgian waiter at the nearby inn had reported Wellington's men talking about the Prussians joining up with the Anglo-Allied army. Napoleon considered that to be absurd. After such a defeat as the Prussians had suffered at Ligny, he told Jérôme, 'the junction between the English and the Prussians is impossible for at least two days; besides, the Prussians have Grouchy on their heels'. But that was quite enough loose talk. Napoleon began to give his orders for how the battle was to be fought. 'Gentlemen,' he concluded, having made perfectly clear that their experience counted for nothing, 'if my orders are carried out well, tonight we shall sleep in Brussels.' With that, he went to review the troops, postponing his attack for three hours so as to let the ground dry after the previous night's rain.

The rain had ensured that many in the British ranks had passed a wretched night. William Leeke, just seventeen years old, had spent the dark hours of torrential rain sleeping fitfully under a cloak and a bundle of straw he shared with a fellow officer.[3] His dreams were of battle and glory, his waking memories of kissing his mother goodbye just six weeks earlier. Now he was saturated and cold to the bone. Very early that morning he and the other men had been ordered to prepare themselves for action. Now they stood about waiting, some of the officers smoking cigars and occasionally shivering as they tried to warm themselves by watchfires that gave out more light than heat. It was all very tense and tedious, and some of them at least were anxious to be off if only to get their blood circulating. Others wished it was all over. Yet more merely got on with things. Cavalié Mercer, who had hardly eaten for two days, was happy to feast on a 'stirabout' of beef, biscuits and oatmeal laced with rum which had fallen off the back of a supply wagon.[4] Gronow in the meantime, having found that he was superfluous to Sir Thomas Picton's needs, rejoined his old regiment and was welcomed in by the ebullient young men he found there downing cold ham and pie with bumpers of champagne.[5]

Gronow had just passed Wellington and staff. Amid the glittering uniforms of the grandees – Uxbridge, whom Wellington disliked because he had eloped with his sister-in-law, General Muffling the Prussian liaison officer, the Prince of Orange, eight aides-de-camp and numerous peers and baronets, including Sir James Kempt, the man who had shared his last ginger biscuits with William Leeke – Wellington looked plain and dignified. He wore a cloak over his dark blue coat, white cravat and leather breeches, Hessian boots and a cocked hat with four cockades. Fastidious about such matters, he was immaculately shaved. He was also alert, well informed and ready for the battle. He had a map of what was for him ideal terrain:

relatively flat but crisscrossed with indentations deep enough to conceal men in safety and rising to the ridge on which his men were deployed, the infantry standing twenty-one inches apart and the cavalry spaced every three feet. British forces were regularly interspersed with foreign regiments to give the latter heart but, because Wellington had chosen to employ his familiar reverse-slope manoeuvre, the bulk of his infantry were for the time being kept on the gentle incline behind the ridge and thereby safe from Napoleon's gunners. Further over on the battlefield were three buildings: a farm called Papelotte, a second farm called La Haye Sainte and a small isolated chateau known as Hougoumont. Napoleon's strategy for the forthcoming battle consisted of seizing La Haye Sainte and the crossroads behind it, thereby cutting off the Allied army's possible retreat to Brussels. D'Erlon in the meantime was to attack Wellington's left flank and ward off a Prussian attack in the unlikely event of such a thing occurring. The whole plan was to be directed by Ney and would be put into operation as soon as the ground was dry enough.

By around 11.30 the waiting was over. Napoleon ordered a diversionary attack on Hougoumont, hoping to draw Wellington's men into a fight for the chateau, thereby weakening the Allied centre where Napoleon's main thrust would later be launched. The feint, which was led by Jérôme Bonaparte, achieved neither result. It took Jerome an hour to clear the wood near the place, fighting from thicket to thicket against soldiers from Nassau and Hanover. Ensign Leeke was carrying the regimental flag of the 52nd Foot at Hougoumont. He later said he was given the task because he was too inexperienced to do anything else, but he had been entrusted with the symbolic heart of his regiment. A man would give his life to defend his regimental flag. An enemy capturing it would have filled his highest ambition. To lose it meant disgrace on all the men. When shot to tatters the flag would be hung up in a cathedral or chapel, and even now the first cannonballs were flying overhead, each of Prince Jérôme's pieces firing two shots a minute.

But the outnumbered defenders inside the building itself were beyond his powers to subdue. Although the struggle for Hougoumont raged all day, the building itself was set alight and a giant Frenchman nicknamed '*l'enforceur*' managed to smash in part of the great wooden door, the men stood firm. Carried away by the thought of the glory he might win for himself and *la patrie*, Prince Jérôme foolishly launched wave after wave of troops at the building. He incurred dreadful losses as the British soldiers inside fired three-quarter-inch iron balls from their Brown Bess muskets and stood to reload, biting the ends off their paper cartridges before pouring powder into their guns' pans and down their barrels and then ramming home yet another ball and more wadding. The skilful could fire two shots a minute, and they did so now with such persistence that Wellington was not called upon significantly to weaken his position by sending large numbers of reinforcements. He could concentrate on the main battle instead. Napoleon's hopes of inducing Wellington to weaken his centre thus failed while his own losses were significant.

Meanwhile the terrible sound of the Grand Battery opening fire could be heard miles away. It was heard, for example, by General Grouchy who was just then enjoying a plate of lunchtime strawberries. A furious disagreement at once broke out between him and one of his fellow generals as to whether they should make for Waterloo or pursue the Prussians at Wavre. They went to Wavre. There the sound of the French cannon was also heard by the suspicious Gneisenau who was only then ready to admit that Wellington was indeed prepared to fight the French again. The Duke himself had been waiting on the Prussians since around noon but they were slow to arrive. Bulow's corps had been despatched first, leaving Wavre about two hours after daybreak. They had been held up first by a fire breaking out in the buildings around them and then by the poor staff work which entangled them in the path of another Prussian corps. A promise from Blücher was a promise, however – he said of himself that despite his painful fall at Ligny he would be tied on his horse rather than miss Waterloo – and by 2.30 the Prussian forces were visible to Wellington. 'The time they occupied in approaching seemed interminable,' he recalled several years later, 'both they and my watch seemed to have stuck fast.'

Napoleon's staff had glimpsed the approaching 30,000 men at about 1.00. At first they had hoped they might be Grouchy's troops (who by now had been recalled) but a captured Silesian hussar soon disabused them of that fantasy. However, the stark reality of the situation – the fact that he was now seriously outnumbered – seems to have made no impression on the Emperor. Certainly, he did not consider a strategic withdrawal necessary but instead determined to hold his ground with what Clausewitz was later to describe as 'foolhardy stubbornness and audacity'. He was now in his element. The ghastly, constant roar of his cannon rained down death on the enemy. Smoke hung heavy in the damp air, but the cannonballs themselves, terrible though they were, could not ricochet with their familiar deadly confusion but, instead, sank into the sodden earth. Yet still the great 12-pounders hurled death into the air, round after round. Perhaps Napoleon assumed that in this way he could mop up the battle before the Prussians were fully in place. Speed and force had always been his principal strengths, and force he could certainly use. Around 1.30 he made the catastrophic decision to release d'Erlon's infantry – more than 18,000 men – on an Anglo-Allied army who were very far from being demoralised by what had been going on simply because many of them had been protected by their lying behind Wellington's favoured reverse slopes. Now d'Erlon, the man who had missed the encounters at both Ligny and Quatre-Bras through the folly of his commanders, was to find out what it meant to face Wellington at Waterloo.

With a frenzied cry of '*Vive l'Empereur!*', d'Erlon's columns moved off in phalanxes, twenty-four ranks deep and with 160 to 200 files in each rank. It was the largest French infantry assault ever launched against a British army but its foolish formation (which no

French commander tried to correct) made it an easy target. Part of this force was to occupy the farm at La Haye Sainte (which it failed to do) while another division was to take Papelotte which they did if only briefly. The main mass of men in the meantime was to advance over uneven ground and then begin the ascent to the enemy ridge. The distance involved was not great – a matter under normal circumstances of a five- or six-minute walk – but d'Erlon's men were proceeding over soft, rain-soaked ground, much of it planted with tall rye, and in the face of heavy enemy fire. The casualties mounted terribly and fast, impeding the slow advance. Advance they did, however, and at last, with more wild cries of '*Vive l'Empereur!*', they rushed at the batteries. Suddenly their path was blocked. Picton had seen his chance. He ordered Kempt's brigade to fire and then charge. Picton himself was killed in the attempt but, despite terrible British losses, the enemy were driven back and Napoleon's hope of annihilating the Allied centre with an overmastering infantry assault failed with terrible slaughter as its only achievement.

Now the Allied cavalry advanced under Lord Uxbridge's personal command, shattering and driving back the enemy cuirassiers. The bloody confusion was dreadful as French officers bellowed uselessly at the men to re-form and the Anglo-Allied cavalry advanced. But the French ranks had been broken and were now being penetrated. Resistance was useless. While Uxbridge and Somerset drove off the cuirassiers others moved in and slaughtered the enemy at almost no risk to themselves. French bayonets could not reach to the cavalrymen on their mighty horses. Their musket shots were as fatal to themselves as their foe. The French found themselves swept back in disorder as the battle-crazed cavalry slaughtered even their drummers and fifers, and captured two eagles and 3,000 prisoners before sweeping on over the 1,000 dead towards the enemy guns. It was terrible. To his lasting chagrin Uxbridge had been unable to contain his men who now suffered appalling casualties from the French response. 'Well, Paget [i.e. Lord

Uxbridge], I hope you are satisfied with your cavalry now,' Wellington said acidly. The sarcasm was unfair for at whatever cost the French attack had been routed, the Anglo-Allied forces had not been shattered before the Prussians arrived and Wellington himself could concentrate on his centre especially.

Ney believed that this was now crumbling. Smoke billowed thickly across the field and he mistook the departure of some prisoners, a number of the wounded and some ammunition wagons for a British retreat. This was a ghastly mistake for his response – carried away as he was by the heat of battle – was to launch 5,000 of his cavalry at fifteen enemy infantry battalions. It was an astonishing blunder. For an hour they charged and for an hour they were resisted. More cuirassiers were called up and still the Allied-British squares stood firm, despite the decimating shot that rained down on them. Gronow was in the middle of it all and described the French attack. 'The horses of the first rank of cuirassiers, in spite of all the efforts of their riders, came to a standstill, shaking and covered with foam, at about twenty yards' distance from our squares.' They resisted all their officers' attempts to force them to charge and thus 'unwilling to retreat, they brandished their swords with loud cries of "*Vive l'Empereur!*" and allowed themselves to be mowed down by the hundreds rather than yield'. The smoke and the smell of spent cartridges were suffocating. Gronow also recalled the terrible suffering of his own men. 'It was impossible to move a yard without treading upon a wounded comrade, or upon the bodies of the dead; and the loud groans of the wounded and dying was most appalling.' So terrible was the rain of bullets that, by a terrible irony, the charging of the cuirassiers seemed almost a relief, and Gronow remembered the eerie sound of British bullets falling on the enemy breastplates as being like a hailstones on a windowpane. Eventually, Lord Uxbridge launched his second counter-attack of some 5,000 mounted men. They drove the French back in disorder only to see them re-form. They charged over the slope with such fury that the mud-churned earth seemed to shake beneath them. And still the dreadful cannon roared. The Allied losses were so terrible that some began to think the French would win the day.

But now, at around 4.00, the Prussians were attacking Napoleon's right flank. The Emperor's urgent message to Grouchy would not find him for six hours and Lobau's corps was thrown against Blücher who was not yet able to deploy his full force. The Prussians turned to menace Lobau's right and seemed to drive him back. Napoleon called out two battalions of his elite Old Guard to reinforce his counter-attack. They charged with bayonets advanced and forced the enemy back nearly half a mile. It seemed as if the Prussians were done for but, even as they were driven off, two more Prussian corps were approaching. Meanwhile Ney's battle fury was approaching its ecstasy. Reinforcing his attack, he launched 9,000 horsemen on the thousand-yard line between Hougoumont and La Haye Sainte. The carnage was dreadful, but the sheer number of dead horses on the field made the advance difficult and when he brought up his infantry it was too late and they were obliged to retreat. Mercer watched the terrible scene. 'Every discharge was followed by the fall of numbers,' he recalled, 'whilst the survivors struggled with each other, and I actually saw them using the pommels of their swords to fight their way out of the melee.' There was worse to come. 'Some, rendered desperate by finding themselves thus pent up at the muzzles of our guns, as it were, and others carried away by their horses, maddened with wounds, dashed through our intervals — few thinking of using their swords, but pushing furiously onward, intent only on saving themselves.'

But Ney persisted. Gathering up what was left of d'Erlon's force, he renewed the assault. This could have been the climax of the battle. Hundreds of British soldiers fell. Those remaining had little ammunition. They were exhausted and exposed to close-range musketry. French mounted artillery began to arrive and it seemed that at last the centre might crumble. 'We were in peril,' wrote one officer in his memoirs, 'at every moment the issue of the battle became more doubtful.' Ney saw his chance and sent urgently to Napoleon requesting more troops. He wanted the Imperial Guard. The besieged Emperor, believing that Ney had already destroyed the cavalry, denied them to him, spitting out with brutal sarcasm: 'Some troops! Where do you expect me to get them from? Do you want me to make them?' His hasty denial lost him the moment of possible victory and contradicted yet another of the maxims that had brought him so close to the mastery of Europe. 'In war,' he once said, 'there is only one favourable moment; the great talent of the commander lies in grasping it.' Napoleon had let it slip as the Prussian artillery rained down about him. And what Napoleon let slip Wellington grasped. The Duke, ubiquitous on the field, energetic and in iron control, now had half an hour in which to reform his line of defence. Brunswickers, German troops and a Dutch–Belgian division were summoned to fill the gap. Then, at last, Zieten's Prussians arrived on the left flank. The centre could thereby be strengthened. The line would stand against the might of the French Empire. The end was in sight.

It was 7.00 in the evening and only now and too late was Napoleon prepared to release the Imperial Guard. It was his last great order on a battlefield and its execution was riddled with the lies and that increasingly catastrophic incompetence which had characterised the entire campaign. Napoleon personally led forward twelve battalions of the Guard, marching them down the road, the triumphant music of the hundred and fifty bandsmen fighting with the monstrous pounding of the Allies' guns. Platoon after platoon advanced. Men fell, wounded and dying. Corpses and grapeshot littered the road. A sense of triumph was essential to morale and officers were now despatched along the line to tell the men that Grouchy had finally arrived on the field with his 30,000 men. '*Vive l'Empereur! Soldats! Voilà Grouchy!*', the officers shouted. The cries of the newly enthused men rose above the music and the cannon. '*En avant! En avant! Vive l'Empereur!*' Grouchy, of course, was nowhere to be seen, but the thought of the victory he would bring raised spirits to their height. The enthusiasm became fanatical. Men found the will to go on and the wounded spurred their efforts. A veteran of Marengo, his legs shattered, cried out from the side of the road: '*En avant! Vive l'Empereur!*' The hypnotic spell of the old imperial language, the grammar and the vocabulary which had been shouted across the length and breadth of Europe, was rising to a final, tragic crescendo invigorated by a lie.

And now the most elite part of the nation in arms, that war machine with which Napoleon had terrorised the entire Continent, was being readied for its last encounter. It was a machine that relied on the genius of the man who had fashioned it, and that genius was unravelling like a broken spring. The tactical dispositions Napoleon insisted on were catastrophic, suicidal. 'A man such as I does not take much heed of the lives of a million men,' he had once boasted. Anyone who did not realise that simply did not know 'what goes on in the mind of a soldier'. This was the ghastly, vainglorious boast of a man who was now sending his elite corps to certain death. Five battalions of the Middle Guard – some 4,000 men – were to form the first wave of the attack. They were to march in columns that made up a crude arrowhead formation. Nothing could have been more disastrous. The outnumbered men were being obliged to advance uphill without the momentum a brigade formation would have given them, without the relative safety of an advance in line, without cavalry protection, without artillery support and with their own firepower reduced by the formation imposed on them by the Emperor whose praises they were shouting and who had lied to them. Nothing showed more clearly how fatigue, inertia, cynical and unthinking arrogance, and perhaps even a wish for death itself, had corroded Napoleon's military genius. Once the fiery young officer at the Bridge of Lodi had been transformed into an eagle by the discovery of his ability. For years he had hovered in the skies above Europe, darkening it with his wings. Now those wings were feeble, broken even.

There were some at least among his men who knew this. Ensign
Leeke was holding his position when an officer of the cuirassiers
came galloping up to his commander crying, '*Vive le Roi!*' The
man's loyalty had suddenly switched to the fat figure sitting many
miles away from the battle that was being fought for him and
eagerly expecting his supper. The French officer was at once
despatched to Wellington, escorted by a sergeant. A little before
eight the Duke himself appeared near to where Leeke was standing.
Leeke himself had heard what the Frenchman had said 'about the
attack of the Imperial Guard, and not long after we heard them
advancing with continued shouts of "*Vive l'Empereur!*" away to
our left front'. And still the Guard advanced, terrible in their blue
greatcoats with their red epaulettes and cross belts, their awful,
grim professionalism made the more fearsome by the great
bearskins that gave them gigantic stature. 'Wait a little longer, my
lads,' came the imperturbable voice of the Duke. 'You shall have at
them presently.' Shells were falling all around him. His own men
on his flanks were being blown to pieces but, apart from them, the
advancing French could see no others. Still they pressed on up the
rise at the *pas de charge*, furiously crying, '*Vive l'Empereur! Vive
l'Empereur!*'

They came within sixty paces, then fifty. Only now were the men
concealed behind the slope ordered to stand up. Their fire was
devastating. Three hundred French soldiers fell in less than a
minute. The rest wavered. The French right was repulsed. The
British Guards advanced after their terrible volley and forced their
opponents into a retreat downhill. Leeke's 52nd then came over the
ridge, wheeled to face the French left and, with devastating fire, sent
the enemy reeling back to their fleeing colleagues. The Imperial
Guard had never failed before. Now they were in full retreat. Those
who were to have formed the second wave were overcome with
shame as Wellington let fly his cavalry which roared down the slope
inflicting terrible carnage on the helpless men. It was no longer '*Vive
l'Empereur!*' but '*Sauve qui peut!*' as, on the raising of Wellington's

cockaded hat, his whole army swarmed towards the broken French who were now fleeing the field. The Young Guard held out until nightfall. Three squares of the Old Guard held out just long enough against the Prussians to cover Napoleon's ignominious flight from the field of Waterloo. His hopes of empire were at an end.

# 6

## ST HELENA

### 21 JUNE 1815–5 MAY 1821

## Napoleon Retreats to Paris

Napoleon had wanted to die, had wanted to throw himself among those members of the Imperial Guard still fighting the Prussians. Soult dissuaded him. 'Oh! Sire, the enemy has already been fortunate enough.' For once Napoleon did as he was asked but, as he made his way towards Charleroi, the tears were running down his pained, exhausted face. Through them he could see the ghastly sights that witnessed to his wrecked ambition. When he arrived at Quatre-Bras the corpses of 3,000 of his soldiers lay in huge rows. The moonlight played gently over their hideous wounds all of which were exposed to view for the scavengers had stripped them naked. It was for this that Napoleon had fled Elba. It was for this that the people of France had cheered him from the Mediterranean coast to Paris, for this that the groaning country had been mobilised and was now faced with who knew what vengeance from the Allies. Yet even now Napoleon would not accept defeat. As he neared Genappe at about one in the morning he determined to fight on. He would try to reassemble the remains of Grouchy's army. Added to the 40,000 survivors of the battle and the 140,000 soldiers posted in France it might be possible to wage another campaign. Surely he could at least prevent the Allied army from sweeping down on Paris and then – who knew? But it proved impossible even to reorder Grouchy's men. Genappe was in pandemonium. So many thousands of soldiers and so many hundreds of wagons clogged the streets that the place was barely passable. Besides, the Prussians were swarming everywhere, gimlet-eyed with their passion to slaughter every Frenchman they could find. They began to fire on Genappe itself. Panic seized the French artillery there who cut the traces of their horses and overturned their guns in order to barricade the road. It took Napoleon himself an hour to pass through and he was in constant danger. His great campaign carriage had finally been recovered, but he had no sooner got into it than the Prussian cavalry rattled by and he had to take to his horse again in order to get to Charleroi, fantasies of vast armies massing and remassing still thronging through his head.

The facts were altogether more brutal. The Prussians had lost 7,000 men, the British 15,000, but there were 25,000 French casualties while a further 8,000 men had been taken prisoner. The lot of the French wounded was ghastly in the extreme. In Brussels the British naturally looked after their own first. The city became a giant hospital and so desperate were the shortages that the Mayor was obliged to appeal to 'anyone who has old linen and lint . . . to deposit it at once with the priests of the parish to which he or she belongs'. Every available vehicle in the city was commandeered for five or six days to carry the wounded from the battlefield where the stench of corpses lying in the June sunshine was so oppressive that the horses pulling the carts screamed at it. The dead horses on the field swelled to a revolting size while the human dead were tossed into huge pits by men using the longest pitchforks they could find.

Those of the French wounded who were eventually returned to Brussels were in a terrible state. The novelist Fanny Burney laboured under appalling conditions to bring what comfort she could. Hers was dangerous work for 'the blood that dried upon their skins and their garments, joined to the dreadful sores occasioned by this neglect, produced an effect so pestiferous, that, at every new entry, eau de Cologne, or vinegar, was resorted to by every inhabitant'. Many of the men were in ghastly pain. They were laid out virtually naked in rows of a hundred or so. They cast their wild eyes on the doctors and nurses who trudged to and fro. A doctor amputating the thigh of one of the victims found himself with thirteen other men huddled in agony beside him and all beseeching to be operated on next. His own clothes were stiff with blood, his arm numb from the unceasing use of the barbarous tools of his trade. The vista of such pain was almost unendurable and as the doctor looked round at the long lines of human agony he noticed how there was 'a resentful, sullen rigidness of face' about the men, 'a fierceness in their dark eyes as they lay half covered in the sheets'.[1]

Thus the price of Napoleon's ambition and still, as he passed through Charleroi and on through the night to Philipeville, he was summoning up phantom armies in his mind. There, in Philipeville and in the morning light, his fantasies spilled over in a letter to his brother Joseph who was acting as his regent in Paris. 'All is not lost,' he told him. 'I believe that when I have assembled my forces I shall still have 150,000 men.' The mad arithmetic went on and on. The fédérés and the National Guard would provide him with another 100,000 men. Fifty thousand could be found in the regimental depots. 'I shall thus have 300,000 men ready to confront the enemy at a moment's notice.' And he could conscript 100,000 more. He could arm them with muskets taken from the royalists just as he could equip the artillery with carriage horses. 'I will organise a mass levy in the Dauphine, Lyonnais, Burgundy, Lorraine and Champagne. I will overwhelm the enemy.' Grouchy's 50,000 men would keep the enemy occupied and out of Paris while the ministers and civil servants in the capital went about their proper business of exhausting the country to feed its Emperor's ambitions. 'The British are making slow headway,' Napoleon continued. 'The Prussians are afraid of the peasantry and dare not advance too far.' This was arrant nonsense, but 'the situation may still be saved'. Paris was the key. 'If I return to Paris,' Napoleon told General Bertrand, 'and I have to get my hands bloody there, then I'll shove them in up to the elbows!' Early on the morning of 21 June Napoleon's dusty carriage drew up outside the Elysée Palace. Napoleon would save his Empire yet again.

## Abdication

Fouché was also busy. Having prophesied the fall of Napoleon with eerie accuracy, he was now determined to profit from it. So complex were his plots and so devious were his methods that he handed over his official role of Minister of Police to two chief inspectors while he got on with his self-appointed task of spreading fear and rumour while making overtures to all sides. He sent to the Chamber of Representatives reports on the state of the army and the nation. The latter, drafted by himself but signed by another, was so alarming that Fouché suggested it might be better if he himself took over all ministerial responsibilities rather than letting things go on as they were. He then organised the next set of elections to ensure that the Chamber was not servile to the Emperor but had a generous sprinkling of men of the stamp of La Fayette in it. These people would help to do Fouché's work of removing Napoleon for him. Next it was a question of appeasing the royalists. The measures against them ordered by Napoleon were checked, and such was M. Fouché's apparent enthusiasm for the Bourbon cause that Louis XVIII let it be known that he would gratefully recognise any service he might do him. Now, as news of the defeat at Waterloo began to reach Paris, Fouché set about organising alarm and despondency. Paris pullulated with rumours to the effect that Napoleon was returning to assume full dictatorial powers, that the Chambers were against him, that the Allies would favour the accession of his son. With such damage done, Fouché went off to attend the meeting of ministers assembling in the Elysée Palace.

Napoleon, exhausted by ten days of unremitting effort, excitable and sometimes on the edge of reason, talked to Caulaincourt as his bath was got ready for him. The defeat at Waterloo, he said, was inexplicable. The army had performed prodigies until it was suddenly gripped by panic. The worst of it was, all of France's matériel was now exhausted. There was only one thing to do. He would summon an extraordinary session of the two Chambers, describe the state of the army and ask for the means with which to save *la patrie*. A fearful Caulaincourt tried to disabuse him of his fantasies. The Deputies were now so hostile to Napoleon that they would never respond as he wished them to. Caulaincourt even ventured to suggest that Napoleon should never have quitted his army. It was the source of his strength and ultimately of his safety. Napoleon for once honestly replied that he had no army left. Yes, he could find men, but how could he arm them? The Chambers must help. It was only a handful of men like La Fayette who were determined to bring things down and that for their own ends. Napoleon vowed he would set a national movement for the redemption of France in motion and then leave Paris immediately to further its aims.

Other ministers began to arrive as Napoleon took his bath, his bitterness against Ney's conduct on the battlefield becoming ever more vehement as he relaxed. Davout said such criticism of a brave man was grossly unfair and that their priority must be to prorogue the Chambers to stop feeling against the Emperor finding too powerful a voice. Soon all the ministers had assembled. An exhausted Napoleon told them to start their meeting under his brother Joseph's chairmanship. They refused, and Napoleon was obliged to go in and address them. 'Our misfortunes are great,' he began, finding something of his old vigour. He had returned to right them, to initiate a great and noble patriotic movement. 'If the nation rises to the summons, the enemy will be crushed,' he declared.

'However, if to the contrary, exceptional measures are not taken . . . all is lost.' The enemy was already trespassing on French soil. Napoleon must be given temporary powers of dictatorship to throw them out. He could seize such powers if he wanted to, he said, but it would seem altogether more patriotic to have them given to him by the Chambers. His audience were divided in their view, some favouring an outright dictatorship, some the support of the Chambers. M. Fouché was getting worried. The support of the Chambers was vital to his plans.

It was only when one of those present, Napoleon's trusted advisor Regnault de Saint-Jean-d'Angély, spoke up saying that 'a great sacrifice' would be necessary that the dreadful word 'abdication' was spoken. 'Tell me honestly,' Napoleon said. 'It's my abdication they want, isn't it?' The counsellor replied with polite circumlocution. However painful it might be he felt it was his duty to inform His Majesty that, under the present circumstances – and always provided that His Majesty did not oppose it – that he should offer to abdicate of his own accord before the Chambers demanded that he did so. Napoleon did indeed oppose it. So did his brother Lucien. The good of France was the first law of the land. Since the Chambers did not seem minded to help the Emperor secure this he would have to do it alone. Napoleon would indeed have to assume the powers of a dictator, put France under martial law and summon all patriotic people to come to his assistance. He was himself the idol of the army and of the people. Everything was not lost. The forces of patriotism and the burning desire to see that *la gloire* remained untarnished would ensure that. With his energies rising with his fantasies, an impassioned Napoleon now spelled out his plan. The forts of the east and north could hold out for three months. Toulon and Lyons could be defended. An army of 100,000 men could be conjured up. Paris could be strengthened. Conscription would raise 160,000 recruits – fresh men to march against the Allies who were already exhausted from their long marches.

The force and passion of this exposition, its seeming clarity and sense of hope, ensured that the ministers were again swept up in the old Napoleonic fervour. M. Fouché became seriously concerned. It seemed to him very likely that the whole ghastly business of Napoleonic absolutism was going to begin all over again. He listened with his usual sepulchral passivity as plans were laid to put Paris under martial law and for the government to be moved to Tours. It was now a question of whether Napoleon should go to the Chambers to explain all this in person and, if so, whether he should wear his uniform. While these matters were being discussed a message arrived from the Chamber of Deputies itself announcing that, because of the national crisis, they were now in permanent session. Any attempt to dissolve them would be deemed high treason.

'I should have got rid of those people before I left,' a furious Napoleon hissed. 'It's all over and they'll be the ruination of France!' It appeared that there was only one thing he could do – lie. Ministers were to go to each of the Chambers and inform them that their Emperor had returned, that there had been a great victory at Ligny and that this had very nearly been followed by another one. The British had been all but beaten. Six flags had been captured and it was only panic created by mischief-makers that had caused the temporary setback that was Waterloo. They were to say that Napoleon himself was now on his way to discuss the situation with the Chambers and that he was also taking the necessary measures to ensure public safety. All would be well. Even now the army was reassembling. It was indeed. Exhausted couriers were just arriving at the Elysée with terrible, detailed information about the suffering of the French troops as they retreated through Belgium, and about the barbaric misery inflicted by the Prussians as they advanced in unrestrained vindictiveness towards Paris itself.

The Chamber of Representatives in the meantime was buzzing with expectation. Bonapartists from before the days of the Empire, increasingly vocal royalists, a large body of liberals and a band of fiery republicans all urged their views. All, in their different ways, were opposed to despotism, La Fayette most fiercely of all. He was Vice-President of the Chamber of Representatives, where he now hurried. Elegant, embittered, utterly confident of his own integrity, La Fayette rose to address the Chamber with what appeared as all the dignity of some ancient Roman, a Cincinnatus come from his farm to save his nation. 'If, for the first time in many years, I raise a voice which the old friends of liberty will recognise,' he began, 'it is because I feel it is my duty to speak to you of the perils threatening our country, which you alone at this present time have the power to save.'

Silence fell as the oratory rose, stirring old memories that ran deep and were, the Deputies supposed, the voice of the people at large. The country should return to the days of 1789 – the days, so La Fayette alleged, of liberty, equality and public order. The deputies should vote to say that *la patrie* was in crisis, that the soldiers had all fought bravely, that their commanding officers should be summoned to Paris to discuss the safety of the state and that the ministers for War, Foreign Affairs and the Interior should come to the assembly at once. There was thunderous applause. La Fayette believed he could steal a march on both the Emperor and the Allied army. The glory days would return to *la patrie*. He was horribly wrong.

Napoleon, when he heard what La Fayette had proposed, was scarlet with fury. Thoughts of what he had once achieved through 'a whiff of grapeshot' flashed through his mind. He would send in the Guards. He would carry the rebellious corpses from the Chambers and throw them in the Seine. He had done such things before and built himself an empire. He would do it again. Davout calmed him down and Napoleon eventually resolved that the ministers whom the Chambers had requested attend them should indeed go with Napoleon's brother Lucien leading them. They were to appear as an imperial delegation come to urge the best interests of France. Lucien, who was opposed to any compromise, told his brother that he was losing his grip. The Deputies would surely announce Napoleon's deposition. The Emperor was contemptuous. They were only talkers. They would not dare do such a thing. They would dare anything Lucien replied. So would Napoleon – for the sake of France, as he claimed. Napoleon was, in his view, hesitating, temporising and wrecking his chances by going to the Chambers. Swift, decisive action had always been Napoleon's way and it had been the way to unparalleled success. But now? The smoke of Waterloo had clearly gone to his brother's head. He was a lost man.

It was evening now and Lucien arrived at the darkening Chamber with the requested ministers of War, Foreign Affairs and the Interior, and M. Fouché, the Minister for Police. The imperial message was read out to the assembled company by the light of the two torches burning on the tribune. Lucien begged the Chamber to rally round the Emperor in the sacred name of the country. They could not abandon him to his enemies without destroying *la patrie* itself. Everything depended on the union between the Chambers and the imperial crown. To rupture this would be to sully the nation's honour forever. There were loud boos and catcalls as La Fayette rose to his feet and shouted out that it was precisely because they had indeed been so loyal to the imperial crown that three million Frenchmen lay dead across fifty battlefields. If Napoleon would leave France the country might yet be saved.

It was eventually agreed that five of the deputies along with a similar number of peers should act with the gathered ministers to agree what should be done. Napoleon himself in the meantime was still vacillating. While the commission was meeting in the Tuileries he was discussing matters with Benjamin Constant.[2] If France gave him up, he said, then she would be surrendering herself too, admitting her weakness, acknowledging her defeat, encouraging the Allies to do with her what they would. Besides, the Chamber was acting beyond its remit if it sought to make him abdicate. It was his right – his duty even – to prorogue it. And what about the great mass of the ordinary people? They, propertyless and easily led, could be whipped up into any form of enthusiasm. As he and Constant strolled in the garden, the murmuring of the crowds could be heard in the Champs-Elysées. What did they owe him? the exhausted Emperor asked. He had found them poor and left them poor and yet 'the instinct of the nation' spoke through them. He could still rouse them as they had been roused at the time of the Revolution. A new Reign of Terror might indeed save the reign of Napoleon. 'But no, it is too great a price to pay for one man's life; I did not return from the island of Elba to drench Paris in blood.' The Chambers meanwhile were in a state of frenzy and some were loud in their demand that Napoleon step down from his throne. If he did not do so of his own free will then they would depose him cried an angry La Fayette. Eventually a messenger was sent to the Elysée to tell Napoleon that he had an hour's grace in which to surrender his crown.

As the messenger made his way, Davout mounted the rostrum and tried to press on the delegates the urgency of the fact that the British and the Prussians were now marching on French soil and towards Paris. The terrible Prussian forces in particular, coming by way of Charleroi, Guise, St-Quentin and Compiègne, were inflicting remorseless damage. Their British allies were appalled. Whole villages were devastated, the livelihoods and well-being of the inhabitants destroyed, even if they themselves were spared. Gronow was revolted. He had seen 'the brutality of some of the Prussian infantry who hacked and cut up, in the most savage manner, all the cows and pigs that were in the farmyards; placing upon their bayonets the still quivering flesh, and roasting it on the coals'. Wellington, marching by a more westerly route, was determined to prevent his own men from doing the same. 'My troops must be well kept and well supplied in camp, if order and discipline are to be maintained,' he wrote to a Prussian major-general. 'It is better that

I should arrive two days later in Paris, than that discipline should be relaxed.'

Meanwhile, the message informing Napoleon that he was to abdicate arrived in the Elysée. His petulant fury was terrible. 'Since they want to force me, I will not abdicate. The Chamber are all Jacobins, ambitious men whom I should have denounced to the country and sent packing. It's still not too late!' Lucien urged him to restage the coup of 18 Brumaire when Napoleon had stormed the chamber of the Deputies after Lucien himself had sworn to the soldiers he would run his brother through 'if ever he interferes with the freedom of Frenchmen'. Napoleon realised this was impossible now. Regnault de Saint-Jean-d'Angély begged him to remember another scenario. The Allied forces were moving towards Paris, time was running out. Napoleon should not give either the people or the Chamber the opportunity to say that he alone had been the great obstacle to peace. 'In 1814 you sacrificed yourself for the good of everyone,' he said. 'Repeat that grand and generous sacrifice today.' Napoleon was to act as if the Hundred Days had never happened. 'Very well,' the Emperor replied, infinitely weary and disillusioned, 'let it be as they wish.' He asked Fouché to write to the Deputies telling them to keep calm as they would soon have what they wanted.

It was now midday and Napoleon bade Lucien take up his pen. He then dictated to him his 'Declaration to the French People', his letter of abdication. In this recent war of 'national independence', as he described it, he had counted on a united effort but now circumstances had changed and 'I offer myself as a sacrifice to the hatred of France's enemies'. He hoped that the Allies were sincere in their protestations that their enmity was directed only at him personally. 'My political life is over,' he continued, and now his only concern was for his son, for whom the Chambers were to organise a regency. This they would not do. It was both impossible and distasteful that they should try to negotiate with the Allies as the delegates of what Napoleon still presumed was his dynasty. They decided instead that executive power would be handed over to a commission of three Deputies and two Peers who would negotiate on behalf of the French people. The commission was, of course, to be headed by M. Fouché. 'We've done quite a lot of work in the last twenty-four hours,' he declared, satisfied that he was now the most powerful man in France.

## At Malmaison

It was now a question of where Napoleon should go. Fouché was perfectly clear that he must be got out of the way as soon as possible. The presence of even a fallen Emperor was a menace to the security of the land he so newly controlled. Among both the military and the civilians there were numerous people still loyal to the imperial dream and in the army especially that loyalty was fanatical. Fouché was perfectly well aware that Marshal Soult was rallying what was left of the Waterloo divisions, which he was even now marching in the direction of Soissons where he would meet up with Grouchy and his men. The same thought had surely occurred to Napoleon too. There was still the remains – albeit the shattered remains – of a Napoleonic army in France and this was as dangerous to Fouché as it might prove advantageous to Napoleon. The army was Napoleon's base and now the *grognards* were grumbling all too loudly about the fate of their beloved general. For all Soult's efforts to let them know that Napoleon had abdicated voluntarily they simply refused to believe it. He would never have done so, they said. He had been ousted by faceless, unknown civilians – politicians. Large crowds of civilians seethed through Paris too, shouting for the man who had ruled the country through what was for many of them the greater part of their lives. They did not want a return of the Bourbons. They did not want a return of the priests. But they did want their Emperor.

Fouché (who knew that Napoleon had applied for passports to the United States) sent Davout to the Elysée to test the nature of his victim's intentions. He was already having a crony prepare a resolution that Napoleon be asked to leave Paris in the name of the people and was now spreading rumours of an assassination plot so that he could reinforce the palace guard. Meanwhile the cries from the people in the street rose up into the gilded splendour of the palace rooms. Napoleon turned furiously on Davout as he entered them, Davout the man who had apparently abandoned him with such alacrity. 'You hear those shouts,' he said, waving his arm towards the windows. 'Had I wanted to put myself at the head of all those people, who instinctively feel their country's true needs, I could soon have been done with all of these men who only have the courage to act against me when they see me down.' Davout turned and left the room.

And still it was a question of where Napoleon should go. The possibilities were played over endlessly. The United States appeared to be one option, after all she had been at war with Britain from 1812 to 1814. Were there other places? Austria? 'Never; they've wounded me too deeply by keeping my wife and son from me. As for Russia, I should be surrendering to one man. In Britain I should at least surrender to a nation.' But this last wild idea seemed, for the moment, equally impossible. 'Every fog would be suspected of tempting me to the coast.' A short-term decision had to be made quickly, however. The Allied advance and the possibility of a royalist uprising in the capital both posed dangers to Napoleon's safety. He turned to Josephine's beautiful daughter, Hortense. She had inherited Malmaison and he would very much like to go there for the night, he said. She agreed and went to ready the chateau while Napoleon himself set about preparing last details: money for his family, for his journey and his future establishment wherever that should be. He said farewell to his mistresses, burned various confidential papers and requested two frigates to take him to America. When all this was done he left discreetly for Malmaison.

The unregainable happiness of the chateau and its garden with its swans and fabulous roses where Napoleon had teased Josephine in his rough and even callous way haunted him. He seemed to see her everywhere and longed to have a portrait of her painted for a locket. Meanwhile, as Napoleon indulged these dreams, M. Fouché continued as busy as ever. He wrote to Wellington requesting a safe-conduct for Napoleon as he made his way to the coast before embarking for the United States. It would be highly undesirable for Napoleon to be killed on French soil but, out at sea, matters might be different. The Royal Navy could do what it was ordered to. A pass was then made out allowing Beker himself and 'his secretary and a servant' unrestricted passage to the Atlantic port of Rochefort.

And now the thundering of the Prussian guns told of the arrival of the victorious and vindictive enemy. It was accepted by all that they would murder Napoleon if ever they found him. Blücher himself had written that he wanted Napoleon dead and he regretted that he would probably be allowed to do no more than shoot him. Fouché knew that such an assassination would cause untold difficulties in an already highly volatile France and he now issued orders to say that the frigates Napoleon had requested – *La Saale* and *La Méduse* – should be put at his disposal. Meanwhile, the fallen Emperor must be removed to Rochefort with all speed. The messengers arrived at Malmaison at dawn on 29 June. Napoleon received them in his dressing-gown and was told that for the good of the state he must leave as soon as possible. He promised to leave that day.

As the day wore on, however, shouts of '*Vive l'Empereur!*' were heard outside the gardens of Malmaison and stirred the fallen Emperor to the depths of his being. 'France ought not to submit to a handful of Prussians!' he exclaimed. He would indeed halt the Prussians and then retire to the United States. He rushed up the concealed staircase from the library to his bedroom and re-emerged a few minutes later in the uniform of the Imperial Guard. His orders were brusque, his ardour unquenchable. The enemy would reach Paris tomorrow. All was not lost! Give him command of the army, make him a mere general again, and he would crush the mighty forces pitted against *la patrie* at the very gates of her capital. It was a gesture as futile as it was glorious. The Prussians were virtually in Paris. When Wellington's troops arrived two days later their combined force would be 120,000 men. Other armies altogether more vast were also on their way. Prince Schwarzenberg was advancing with 250,000 men drawn from Austria, Bavaria, Wurtemburg, Saxony and Hesse-Darmstadt. The Bavarians had already taken Nancy. Soon the Russians would be in Rheims. Meanwhile, from the south, 60,000 Austrians and Sardinians were marching in various columns for Lyons. The fantasies of *la gloire* offered by Napoleon were a lethal snare, a lure to draw the horsemen of the Apocalypse down on France with all their fury. Fouché wrote a stiff, impersonal reply to Napoleon's note turning down his offer of another war and urging that he leave Malmaison as quickly as possible.[3]

'I have no alternative now but to leave,' Napoleon declared as he read the note. He went upstairs to change out of his uniform and into a chestnut-coloured frock coat and a pair of blue breeches. He was anxious to be off. He bade goodbye to a tearful Hortense, to his stoic mother and to the emotional soldiers guarding him in Malmaison. He went to Josephine's apartments and gazed for a last time on her bed with its fabulous golden swans. He had loved her, he had divorced her and she had died. After a few moments he shut the door and went to his study where, at five o'clock, Beker announced that they were ready to depart. Napoleon left the palace of his youthful glory disguised as a mere general's secretary, a humble factotum.

They travelled on in silence, Napoleon as preoccupied with worries about attacks on his person as he had been during the flight to Elba. There was no knowing what Fouché might organise, no knowing what the hostility of the people might lead to. They spent the night in the grim security of the old chateau at Rambouillet, leaving the following morning around eleven o'clock. The day grew hot and Napoleon chewed on some cherries to ease his thirst, throwing the pips out of the window of his modest coach. They reached Tours where an exhausted Napoleon, still anxious about his personal safety, questioned the Prefect who satisfied him that he knew of no threats on his life. They then moved on to Poitiers where Napoleon despatched a note to the Maritime Prefect of Rochefort asking for details of the promised frigates moored off the Île d'Aix. At last they reached Niort, where the Prefect invited Napoleon to spend the night in his residence. The townspeople, realising who he was despite his disguise, again raised cries of *'Vive l'Empereur!'* as he left the following day. It was 3 July and, for the last time in his life, Napoleon was being publicly hailed as an Emperor.

## The Allies Enter Paris

As the townsfolk of Niort cheered Napoleon on, the Allied powers in Paris were deciding how to wind up his empire. It seemed at first that Marshal Davout would try and resist the Allied advance on Paris. He had an army of some 60,000 troops, in addition to 30,000 National Guardsmen – a body of veteran conscripts. He also had a large supply of guns. On the night of 2 July the British and the Prussians were entrenched in the woods around Meudon and Versières. The following day they advanced on Vanvres and Issy in preparation for a general attack. The atmosphere in the capital itself was grim with expectation, tense and silent crowds gathering in the fear of terrible events. Resistance would in fact have been futile. The south side of the city was undefended and whatever short-term gains might have been won would inevitably have been overwhelmed by horrific bloodshed and loss of life. Davout made the only realistic choice available to him and capitulated.

The Convention of St-Cloud signed on 3 July made arrangements for the decommissioning of the French army, which was to withdraw south to the Loire. These terms were vastly unpopular and so many men were reluctant to obey them that discipline was in danger of breaking down. The mood of intense anger and disillusion in the ranks was expressed by Fantin d'Odoards – that veteran of Austerlitz, Corunna, Moscow and the Waterloo campaign – some ten days later. 'I was not fortunate enough to be killed during the brief and fatal campaign which has brought the enemy to Paris,' he wrote, 'and I have survived in order to witness the funeral of our poor unhappy land.' The defeat was total, he felt. *La gloire* and *la patrie* lay humbled in the dust. 'Cowardice, incompetence, treachery, apathy – they all contributed to our downfall,' he continued. He felt he could die of shame and grief. The French people, he thought, were ripe for enslavement.

The Prussians felt much the same. The savagery they had inflicted on their way to Paris was, they hoped, to be inflicted on the capital itself. The very name of the Pont d'Iéna was a standing reproach to their acute sense of national identity and Blücher was determined to destroy the bridge. This was in direct contravention of the St-Cloud agreement but Blücher was not the slightest bit interested in the legal niceties of the matter. He tried to mine the bridge but only succeeded in damaging it, Wellington having placed sentries on it with orders not to leave it under any circumstances. A frustrated Blücher then turned his attention to the monumental column Napoleon had erected in the Place Vendôme as part of his plan to glorify both himself and his capital. Once again, it was Wellington's exertions that prevented vandalism. Indeed, the great soldier had now turned diplomat and politician. The Prussians not only wanted to despoil Paris but were determined to dismember France herself. They had their eyes on Alsace and Lorraine, and it was only the strenuous efforts of the British and the Russians which prevented this. Punishment would be inflicted, however. The

French people had welcomed Napoleon back and had therefore, in the Allied view, made themselves complicit in his crimes. They would have to be shown the error of their ways. An indemnity of 700 million francs was exacted from them. One hundred and fifty thousand Allied troops were also to be stationed in the country at the expense of the French.

The British troops who made their triumphal procession into the city on 7 July were in an exhausted condition. As Cavalié Mercer noted they had marched, slept and fought in the same uniforms for months.[4] These were now of 'a dusky brick-dust hue'. Their shakoes were battered and the appearance of the men generally was 'dirty, shabby, mean, and very small'. Their hearts were quite otherwise, however. It was the proudest moment of Ensign Leeke's life when he entered Paris by the Barrière de l'Etoile and marched with his regimental colours under the still uncompleted Arc de Triomphe and down the middle of the Champs-Elysées.[5] In the Hundred Days of the Napoleonic terror he had come a long way from the rather frightened boy who had to be cheered up with a ginger biscuit. Now he was a seasoned and victorious soldier, a veteran of Waterloo. The most generous tribute to Leeke and his comrades was paid by a Frenchman barely older than Leeke himself. Leaning against a tree in the Champs-Elysées as the British troops marched past, the young man known only as Labretonnière noted how dishevelled the British troops looked but he also saw how very few of them were wearing medals.[6] There was no flashily obvious sense of military splendour about them, nothing of the conspicuous finery of the Napoleonic war machine. He wondered how and why it was that these men had proved themselves victorious. Eventually he came up with his conclusion. 'Love of country, the glory of old Albion – that is what has to suffice for British troops to make them fight with such admirable courage.' It was a generous observation.

## The Bourbon Revenge

The day after the triumphal entry Louis XVIII was returned to his throne. The Hundred Days had been an interlude only, its strains and horrors concluded by the eighteen articles that comprised the Convention of Paris. This was signed by all the parties at 6.00 on 4 July on the Pont de Neuilly. The following day M. Fouché had his moment of triumph. As president of the French delegates to the treaty commission it was his duty to inform the country that France should stand united and put all her ills behind her. 'The peace of Europe is identical with your own,' he declared. 'Europe wants your tranquillity and happiness.' That was true, but there were many among the royalists who thought that France was not quite ready for these things yet. Vengeance on Napoleon's followers seemed a psychological if not a political necessity and in this they were encouraged by their newly returned king. The 'white terror' was released on the country. Civil disorder broke out in nearly all the major towns and cities of France. Senior army officers and government officials were charged with having aided and abetted the sometime Emperor, and two leading figures – Marshal Brune and General Ramel – were murdered. A list of the most important offenders was drawn up by the King himself, but many of these men escaped and were condemned to death in their absence. Only five were actually executed. The real butt of the royalists' revenge was, however, Marshal Ney, and a show trial was prepared for 'the bravest of the brave'.

France needed a scapegoat and Ney was the chosen victim. He was arrested and made to appear before a court martial. When this was found to be incompetent to try a French peer (Napoleon had made Ney Prince of Moskva) it was agreed that he should be brought before the Chamber of Peers. The charge that echoed across the courtyard of the Luxembourg Palace where the trial was held accused Ney of high treason and trying to undermine the security of the state. He stood no chance and was swiftly found guilty by men determined to set an example to the nation. The majority vote for his judicial murder was overwhelming, and when his wife went to appeal to Louis XVIII for clemency there followed a little scene of terrible if wholly typical cruelty. The King was unavailable, she was told. He was having his breakfast and could not be disturbed. Twenty minutes later Ney stood before the firing squad. He told the men to fire straight at his heart. The order was given and he fell as the drums thundered and the members of the firing squad itself cried out: 'Vive le Roi!' France now had her sacrificial victim who had paid for all the horrors inflicted by Napoleon during the Hundred Days.

## The Bellerophon

Of altogether greater interest to the Allies was what should become of Napoleon himself. The British in particular were determined that Napoleon should never again cause havoc across Europe. The Prime Minister, Lord Liverpool, wrote to Castlereagh about the matter. 'I am desirous of apprising you of our sentiment respecting Bonaparte,' he began. 'If you should succeed in getting possession of his person, and the King of France does not feel sufficiently strong to bring him to justice as a rebel, we are ready to take upon ourselves the custody of his person, on the part of the Allied Powers.' The criminal Napoleon was to be a British responsibility and it seemed best to Liverpool at least that the British 'should be at liberty to fix the place of his confinement'. The Lords of the Admiralty already knew that the government had 'returned a negative answer' to the request that Napoleon be given a passport and safe-conduct for the United States, but they were firmly convinced that Napoleon would still 'endeavour to effect his escape, either to England, or what is more likely to America'. As far as they were concerned he was a criminal on the run and they were determined to catch him. To this end the Royal Navy was even now besieging the French coast and Napoleon's every move was being watched from the *Bellerophon* stationed off Rochefort under the command of Captain Maitland.

Napoleon himself was probably unaware of the irony that this British ship had played a significant part in the defeat of his navy at the Battle of Trafalgar, but he was painfully aware of the difficulties she caused him now. Maitland had been lucky. At the beginning of July he had made contact with a ship out of Rochefort and heard that *La Saale* and *La Méduse* were being readied to sail, and that various members of Napoleon's entourage had already arrived at the Île d'Aix. 'Upon the whole there was little doubt,' he noted, 'of its being his intention to effect his escape, if possible, from that place in the frigates.' Here was a golden opportunity for Maitland to win fame and advance his career, and he made his moves accordingly. He anchored the *Bellerophon* as close as he safely could to the two French vessels and then planned what he would do should they attempt to force their way out of the port. One of the frigates would be boarded by a hundred of his best men and be put in charge of his first lieutenant while he himself would pursue the second ship in the *Bellerophon*. Maitland had barely done this when a letter arrived from his senior officer ordering him to 'keep the most vigilant look-out for the purpose of intercepting' Napoleon, 'and if you should be so fortunate as to intercept him, you are to transfer him and his family to the ship you command, and there keeping him in careful custody, return to the nearest port in England (going into Torbay in preference to Plymouth) with all possible expedition'.

The two captains of the French ships, Philibert and Ponée, had also received top-secret instructions from their government. These informed them that they were to transport Napoleon to the United States of America, that he was travelling incognito and that the greatest secrecy should be maintained. Once he was aboard they should put to sea within twenty-four hours at the most, provided that neither the winds nor the enemy cruisers should prevent this.

Once at sea they were to sail as quickly as possible either to Philadelphia or Boston. If they became involved with the enemy during their passage then the frigate that was not carrying Napoleon was to sacrifice itself by engaging with the enemy in order that the other should escape. Napoleon himself was at all times to be treated with the utmost courtesy and the respect due to the fact that he had once been the Emperor of the French. Full honours were to be accorded him.

None of this came about. The *Bellerophon* blocked the way. It was clearly essential that Napoleon and those around him make contact with Maitland to apprise themselves of the situation as fully as they could and, under the cover of a flag of truce, a boat was sent to the *Bellerophon* with a letter asking Maitland whether he had any knowledge about the fallen Emperor's safe-conduct 'or if you think it may be the intention of the British government to impede our passage to the United States'. A meeting was arranged and Napoleon's emissaries asked Maitland whether it would be possible for the Emperor to leave in his frigates under a flag of truce. They were told it was not. Could he then travel in a neutral ship? No. Every neutral ship would be searched. Indeed, Maitland now tried to squash the plan for Napoleon's going to America as firmly as he could. 'Supposing the British government should be induced to grant a passport for Bonaparte's going to America,' he said, 'what pledge could he give that he would not return, and put England, as well as all Europe, to the same expense of blood and treasure that had just been incurred?' The emissaries protested that Napoleon's political ambitions had died away. He would never regain his ascendancy and longed now to live in retirement. Maitland, a cunning man presented with an extraordinary opportunity, suggested that Napoleon might find just the asylum he sought in England and affirmed that he would not be ill treated there. Maitland was clearly playing for time and he dwelt on the mercy that the British would extend to Napoleon in the hope that he would surrender without a fight.

Such temporising was highly unsatisfactory to the French and various other plans were considered. It was suggested for example that *La Saale* should go ahead and, under cover of darkness, take the *Bellerophon* by surprise, grapple her broadside on and so prevent her from moving, thereby allowing Napoleon to escape by force. Philibert, the senior of the two French officers, refused to countenance such a suggestion and Napoleon, distinctly uneasy now and suspicious that the captains might all too easily declare their loyalty to the newly returned Bourbons, gave up all hope of using their frigates.

It was perfectly clear now that Napoleon was not going to fight for his freedom and he installed himself on the Île d'Aix. While he himself took refuge in the gloomy house of the commandant there, various members of his entourage discussed crazy plans for getting him to America. Six young naval officers, for example, suggested that they arm a whaleboat in which they would take Napoleon out to the open sea and there hail the first merchant vessel they met and persuade her captain to take Napoleon to the United States. Napoleon himself expressed some small interest in the plan and the chosen vessel was being readied when, the following morning, Joseph Bonaparte arrived with the suggestion that he should pose as the Emperor, give himself up to the British and thereby give his brother just sufficient time to escape. Napoleon did the only thing he could and rejected the scheme. He was coming slowly to face the inevitable. He would have to surrender to the British in person. When he was told that the little vessel prepared for his escape was now ready he rejected the plan and declared that he would spend the night in the commandant's house. Tomorrow he would hand himself over to Maitland. 'It is always dangerous to trust to one's enemies, but better to take the risk of trusting to their honour than to be a lawful prisoner in their hands.' He now began to draft a letter to the Prince Regent informing him of his decision. 'Royal Highness,' it began, 'exposed to the factions which divide my country and to the enmity of most of the great powers of Europe,

I have concluded my political career.' So historical a decision seemed to require that an analogy be drawn from the classical past. 'Like Themistocles I come to take my place at the hearth of the British people.' It was necessary to give them due tribute. 'I place myself under the protection of their laws, which I now claim of Your Royal Highness, as that of the most powerful, most consistent and most generous of my enemies.'

When he received a copy of this letter Maitland, for all he was cock-a-hoop, was also circumspect. He said that he would indeed receive the fallen Emperor aboard the *Bellerophon*, but in order that 'no misunderstanding might arise, I have explicitly and clearly explained . . . that I have no authority whatever for granting terms of any sort, but that all I can do is carry him and his entourage to England, to be received in such a manner as His Royal Highness may deem expedient'. Preparations to receive Napoleon were at once put in hand. All was expectation and excitement. 'The first lieutenant was engaged seeing all the belaying-pins got an extra polish, and that every rope was coiled down with more than usual care, while every hush from the shore, or speck on the water, was listened to and watched with intense anxiety, lest our prey should escape us.'

By dawn the following day Napoleon was ready to quit the Île d'Aix. Dressed now in the legendary green soldier's jacket and wearing a hat with a tricolour cockade, he emerged before the silent population of the island as he got into the little boat that was to row him across to the *Épervier* which was in turn to convey him to the *Bellerophon* under a flag of truce. General Beker, who had been with him since his last days at Malmaison, now came forward and, with tears in his eyes, asked Napoleon if he would like him to escort him as far as the British ship. 'Do nothing of the kind,' Napoleon said. 'I am going aboard of my own free will.' If Beker came with him then it would be said that the General had handed him over to the British and 'I do not want to leave France under the weight of such an accusation'. Once aboard the *Épervier* the vessel battled its way towards the *Bellerophon* against wind and tide and, as she neared the British ship, so Maitland ordered his men quickly to hoist out the boat so that he should indeed have the honour of securing Napoleon's person rather than losing this supreme moment to Rear-Admiral Sir Henry Hotham, whose ship the *Superb* had just hove into view. Maitland's boat eventually came alongside the *Épervier*. Napoleon made his way down to it and, once aboard, he looked up at the great hull of the French ship, sprinkled it with water as if in benediction, and murmured to himself, 'All my life I have sacrificed everything – tranquility, advantages, happiness, to my destiny. I am a man condemned to live.'

## *Aboard the* Bellerophon

Aboard the *Bellerophon* a general guard of marines had been ordered aft on the quarter-deck. The boatswain stood ready with his whistle in his hand, while Maitland trudged anxiously up and down between the gangway and his own cabin. As his ship's boat came alongside so he leaned over and asked, 'Have you got him?' The answer was strongly in the affirmative. Napoleon slowly climbed up the extended ladder, panting a little. The boatswain's whistle shrilled and Maitland saw Napoleon advance towards him, raise his hat and then heard him say: 'I am come to throw myself on the protection of your Prince and laws.' Rather than arrest him immediately, Maitland bowed and offered to show the fallen Emperor his cabin, which he had set aside for his use. Napoleon looked round it and declared it to be handsome.

'Such as it is, sir,' Maitland replied. 'It is at your service while you remain on board the ship I command.'

'Who is that young woman?' Napoleon asked, glancing at a portrait on the wall.

'My wife.'

'Ah, she is very young and very pretty.'

Napoleon exercised an extreme royal politeness throughout and showed himself interested in all aspects of life on board an English ship. He asked Maitland about his career, and there followed many questions concerning British naval officers and their conditions of service and about the ordinary seamen too whose fine bearing made a deep impression on Napoleon. He even asked Maitland if he thought he would have succeeded had he tried to force a passage past the *Bellerophon*. Maitland courteously replied that 'it must have depended greatly on accident, but the chances were much against it'. At 9.00 breakfast was served. The meal consisted of cold meat with a choice of tea or coffee but so unpalatable was this to the Frenchman that Maitland gave orders that his cook should work for Napoleon and prepare for him the hot dishes in the style he was used to.

An hour and a half later Hotham's *Superb* dropped anchor near to the *Bellerophon* and Maitland, going over to greet his senior officer, was told that Hotham greatly wished to see Napoleon. Returning to the *Bellerophon*, Maitland announced that the Rear-Admiral would visit the Emperor that afternoon and he duly arrived with his flag captain and his secretary. They discussed tactics and other such matters, Napoleon afterwards proudly displaying his travelling library. Unaware that these people were really his captors he invited the senior officers to dinner at five that afternoon. The meal was served on the imperial silver plate and, when the company sat down to dine, Maitland allowed Napoleon to 'play the Emperor' since 'under the circumstances I considered it would have been both ungracious and uncalled for in me to have disputed' so pathetic an illusion. The meal was over by half-past seven and Napoleon took his leave, having accepted an invitation to breakfast with Hotham the next day.

Before departing for the *Superb* the following morning, Napoleon amused himself by inspecting the marines drawn up on board the *Bellerophon*, examining the arms they presented and once again talking battle tactics. Hotham received Napoleon aboard his ship with manned yards but without a salute from the guns. For all his affability, Napoleon was anxious to be off and barely touched his breakfast, and it was with some relief that he returned to Maitland's ship a little after midday and watched while the crew lowered her sails and raised her anchor. Soon, under the press of full sail, the *Bellerophon* was making her way out to sea and the flat wooded coasts and headlands of France began to fade into the distance. The journey from the Basque Roads to Torbay lasted a week during which Napoleon continued to play the part of Emperor, often inviting Maitland to dine at his table and even complementing him on the skill and courage of the Royal Navy. 'If it had not been for you English, I should have been Emperor of the East; but wherever there is water to float a ship, we are sure to find you in the way.'

Yet there were moments of melancholy such as when they were passing Ushant. It was four in the morning. Mr Midshipman Home had just come up to take the morning watch, the crews were swabbing the decks, and Home was amazed to see the Emperor come out of his cabin and make for the poop ladder. The washing of the decks had made them extremely slippery and Napoleon was in danger of falling at every step. The young man went over to him, hat in hand, and offered him his arm. Napoleon took hold of it, smiled and allowed the young man to help him up the poop ladder. When he had gained the poop deck he again smiled in thanks for the attention he had received, pointed to the land and said: 'Ushant? Cape Ushant?' Home told him he was correct and tactfully withdrew. He then watched Napoleon take out his telescope, put it to his eye and look eagerly at the land. 'In this position he remained from five in the morning till nearly midday, without paying any attention to what was passing around him, or speaking to one of his entourage, who had been standing behind him for several hours.'

As the day wore on the English coast became just visible on the horizon. Maitland thought he should inform Napoleon of this. He went to his cabin, where he found Napoleon going to bed. He got up, threw on his greatcoat and came out to stare at the cliffs he had never been able to conquer. By dawn the following day the *Bellerophon* was off Dartmouth and later in the morning was approaching Torbay. Napoleon was impressed by the reddish soil and the semitropical vegetation that luxuriated in it. He was reminded of Portoferraio on Elba. Exile in England might yet prove agreeable. As he had said earlier: 'I must now learn to conform myself to English customs, as I shall probably pass the rest of my life in England.' But this mood was very rapidly to change.

The presence of Napoleon off the English coast posed a considerable problem for the government. 'We are all decidedly of opinion that it would not answer to confine him to this country,' wrote Lord Liverpool. 'Very nice legal questions might arise upon the subject, which would be particularly embarrassing.' There were also other considerations. As Liverpool told Castlereagh: 'you know enough of feelings of people in this country not to doubt he would become an object of curiosity immediately, and possibly of compassion, in the course of a few months: and the circumstances of his being here, or indeed anywhere in Europe, would contribute to keep up a certain degree of ferment in France.' It was also obvious to Liverpool that a now-fallen Napoleon would be an even greater hero than he had been before to those liberals gathered together in Holland House and elsewhere. As Byron's friend Hobhouse noted: 'I find Bonaparte's surrender to the *Bellerophon* has made ten times the sensation here it has in Paris . . . The curiosity to see him here is unabated.'[7]

All of this was clearly undesirable and even dangerous to the government, but altogether more difficult to resolve was Napoleon's legal position as their prisoner. He had abdicated so it was difficult to see how he could be treated as a captive sovereign and it was perfectly possible that he might have to be liberated once peace negotiations with France had been completed. The highest legal authorities in the land were consulted. The Lord Chief Justice gave it as his opinion that peace was being concluded with France but not with Napoleon himself and that he could therefore be considered an enemy and, as such, be held as a prisoner of war. This definition of him could be made the stronger, the experts argued, because he had been defeated in a legitimate war that had been fought against him alone and not against the people of France as a whole. If such were the justifications for making Napoleon a prisoner it was nonetheless clearly undesirable that he should be held a prisoner in Britain. He might easily stir up trouble, and there was ferment enough in the country in Liverpool's opinion. Besides, his proximity to France might also be an inspiration for the defeated Bonapartists still living there.

The Prime Minister had conversed with John Barrow, Second Secretary of the Admiralty, on the difficult issue of where Napoleon might be sent and he told Castlereagh that Barrow 'decidedly recommends St Helena as the place in the world the best calculated for the confinement of such a person'. There were several reasons for this. There was 'a very fine citadel' there in which he could live. The island was healthy but, more to the point, 'there is only one place in the circuit of the island where ships can anchor, and we have the power of excluding neutral ships altogether, if we should think it necessary'. On St Helena Napoleon could be completely isolated. 'At such a distance and in such a place, all intrigue would be impossible; and, being withdrawn so far from the European world, he would very soon be forgotten.' It seemed better to Lord Liverpool at least that action should be taken as swiftly as possible and that the other Great Powers be excluded from it so that there should be no squabbling among them which 'might seriously embarrass the safe custody of the prisoner'. All possible information about St Helena was now gathered together and Lord Bathurst was instructed to open negotiations with the East India Company to transfer the rocky little island far out in the Atlantic to the Crown for the period of Napoleon's detention there. Sir Hudson

Lowe was to be made Governor and Commander-in-Chief of St Helena and thus Napoleon's warder.

In the meantime, Napoleon himself remained an object of intense curiosity to the crowds of spectators who were rowed out in little boats to the *Bellerophon*. Among the first to arrive were the girls who had plied Mr Midshipman Home with tea and buns when he had come on shore with despatches from Maitland. Silly for gossip, they wanted to know if the Emperor was a normal man. Was his coat covered with blood? Could they see him? Young Home, enraptured by the attention, told the girls that if they once glimpsed the Emperor they would fall in love with him. He would take them across to the *Bellerophon* in his cutter. He was as good as his word but the sea turned so rough that strong, seasoned sailors had to return the now frightened little party to the safety of the shore. Others came, more and more of them. Sometimes Napoleon gratified their interest by looking through a porthole, appearing on deck or even raising his hat. At other times the spectators had to content themselves with the system of placards devised by the sailors which were held up to inform them that the Emperor was 'lunching' or was 'in his cabin'. The grotesque charade was completed by an orchestra playing French tunes, but if Napoleon was sometimes amused by it all he also spent much of his time pacing the deck in morose self-absorption.

Further humiliations were now to deepen his sense of gloom. It was resolved that he should neither be allowed to go on shore nor have any communication whatsoever with the mainland and those who might have supported him there. He was not to be told that his final destination was St Helena but, while he waited for an unknown future, he was to be pettily humiliated by the measures taken to ensure that he was safely isolated. His entourage was to be diminished. There was talk of guard boats being manned to keep the spectators at bay. He was to take his exercise on the quarter-deck only where he would not be easily seen. It was also considered desirable to move the *Bellerophon* away from Torbay and on to

Plymouth Sound where he could be watched altogether more closely.

They set sail for Plymouth on 26 July, escorted by the *Myrmidon* and the *Slaney* as they made their way against adverse winds. Once arrived in Plymouth, the *Liffey* and the *Eurotas* were anchored beside the *Bellerophon* and the threatened guard boats were brought out to keep visitors at a distance. As for Napoleon's 'playing the Emperor', a stop was to be put on that. Admiral Lord Keith was firm in his conviction that 'the reptile', as he chose to call his prisoner, should be allowed no more privilege than exactly became his present status. He wrote that 'he has been allowed to assume a great deal more state, and even authority, and has been treated with more submissiveness than belongs to his station as a prisoner of war, or to his rank as general officer, which is all that can be allowed him in this country'. The night watch guarding Napoleon was doubled, the patrolling guard boats were kept constantly on the move and at night his cabin door was locked. There were good reasons for these moves for it was now known that Napoleon had heard unofficially of what his fate was to be. 'He read in the papers that he was to be sent to St Helena,' wrote Keith, 'which idea was dreadful.' Throughout his career Napoleon had always read the British press, always regarded it as a source of trustworthy information. Now, in this cruelly unofficial way, he had glimpsed his likely future and was thrown into despair. The Tower of London would have been better and 'he would prefer death'. Who knew what Napoleon, reduced to such a state would do? Bribery, violence, desperation, any or all of these things could easily lead to a repetition of the Elban debacle and that simply could not be allowed to happen again.

That Napoleon was indeed a prisoner was made clear when he was eventually visited by Lord Keith and Major General Sir Henry Bunbury, Permanent Under-Secretary of State for War. They were to read him the letter apprising Napoleon of his fate, but that letter was addressed not to Napoleon himself but to Keith, his jailer and only legal means of contact with the wider world. Napoleon received the two officers alone in his cabin. As he entered, Bunbury looked at the man who had terrorised Europe for a quarter of a century, quickly taking in the appearance of this jaded, middle-aged colossus. He noticed his double chin. He saw that Napoleon was going bald about the temples and that the hair on the upper part of his head was long, thin and ragged, looking as if it were rarely brushed. Napoleon's movements were ungainly but, for all the pallid, puffy nature of his complexion, the carriage of his head had an unquestionable dignity. His teeth, however, were bad and dirty and he tried to show them as little as possible.

Lord Keith began to read the letter but Napoleon, apparently dissatisfied, took it from him and gave it to Bunbury to translate aloud. Thus he learned officially that he was to be transported to St Helena on the *Northumberland* and there remain for the term of his natural life. When Bunbury had finished, Keith asked Napoleon if he wished for a written translation. He did not. He had very well understood the contents of the letter which was now handed to him. He put it down on the table. Then he replied. Even now he refused to lose his dignity, and Napoleon's response was a long and ruthlessly self-controlled expression of his indignation laced with lies, half truths and special pleading. The whole was borne on an undertow of despair. As Bunbury noted: 'his expression was serious and almost melancholy, and showed no sign of anger or strong emotion.'

The British government had no right to treat him in this way, Napoleon began. He appealed to the laws of the country and its people. 'I came here voluntarily,' he said, 'to place myself in the home of your nation.' He claimed the privileges of hospitality. He was not even, in his own view, a prisoner of war. If he was, he had rights under the law. No, he had come to Britain as a passenger aboard one of her warships, having previously negotiated with its commander. This claim was unfair. For all that Maitland, desperate to keep a hold of his prisoner, had said he thought the British would treat Napoleon well, he had been perfectly clear about being unable to give a firm assurance to this effect. Such things were nothing to Napoleon now. He had been betrayed, he said. If Maitland had told him he was going to be a prisoner then he would never have come at all. As for being sent to St Helena, such a decision was his death warrant. He protested vehemently against going there. He demanded instead to be received as a British citizen. He knew perfectly well that as a refugee he could not claim full rights immediately but he was perfectly prepared to let the Prince Regent place him under surveillance until the proper time had come for a greater measure of freedom. 'Let me be put in a country house in the centre of the island, thirty leagues from the sea.' He would have no objections to the authorities placing a commissioner close to him so that his correspondence could be read and all his actions reported. In a quiet country house he could at least have a certain degree of liberty and find the time to read. On St Helena he would not last three months. It would be death to him. 'What am I to do on this little rock at the end of the world?' No, he would prefer to go to Botany Bay where the British transported their convicts.

He changed his tack. If the government really wished to kill him they could do it here and now. There was no point in sending him to St Helena. But what good was his death to them anyway? 'I can do you no harm. I am no longer a sovereign, I am a simple individual.' Times had changed. The Empire was no more. 'What danger could result from my living as a private person in the heart of England under surveillance, and restricted in any way the government might imagine necessary?' It was all desperate and pitiful, the futile squawking of an eagle fatally maimed. By treating him as they proposed, Napoleon continued, the British government would shame itself irreparably in the eyes of the whole of Europe and its own people. 'If you kill me, your reputation will be lost in France and Italy, and it will cost the loss of many Englishmen.' Veiled but empty threats now followed. Napoleon had not, he averred, been obliged to the step he took. Men were still loyal to him in Bordeaux, in Nantes, in Rochefort. The army had not

surrendered at the time he boarded the *Bellerophon*. He could have
joined them. He could have chosen to remain in France. 'What
could have prevented my remaining concealed for years among a
people who were all attached to me?' But no, he had forgone such
things. 'I prefer to settle as a private individual in England.'

He had made an honourable choice and he expected to be treated
with honour in return. Surely Keith could see what an eternal
disgrace would fall on the Prince Regent and the British government
if they killed him. 'It would be an act of unparalleled cowardice.'
The feckless and futile figure of the Prince was hinted at. By
surrendering to his mercy Napoleon had offered him 'the finest
episode in his history'. What a contrast was implied between them!
'Remember what I have been, and how I stood among the
sovereigns of Europe.' He was a monarch and a soldier still. Look
what he had achieved when he landed in the France of the newly
restored Louis XVIII. 'I had six hundred soldiers, and he had two
hundred thousand; all the same I made war on him; I beat him, I
drove him out of the country, and off the throne.' All this he had
done and he would not now be sent away illegally and in humiliation
to some ghastly and remote island in the middle of the Atlantic. 'I
will not leave here, I will not go to St Helena, I am no Hercules, but
you will not be able to take me there. I prefer death here.' He had
been shamefully fooled. He had come to them as a free man.
'Replace me in the state you found me.' If they would not or could
not do this then at least let him go to the United States. 'But I appeal
to your laws, and I throw myself on their protection to prevent my
being sent to St Helena or being shut up in a fortress.' The two
British officers listened with quiet and absolute self-control.
Napoleon turned his desperate eyes on them for a last time. 'I will
give my word of honour that I will not hold any correspondence
with France, and that I will not engage in any political affairs
whatever.' Above all, he would not go to St Helena. The pitiful
outpouring had at last come to its end and Lord Keith and Sir Henry
Bunbury 'made our bows and retired'.

As the tedium and isolation of waiting began to mount intolerably Napoleon's thoughts turned once again to suicide. 'Sometimes I feel a desire to leave you, and it would not be difficult,' he said. The member of his entourage who was with him, the Comte de Las Cases, tried to comfort him by reminding Napoleon of the Stoic fortitude of the ancients. 'But what can we do in that awful place?' Napoleon asked, his mind fixed on the prospect of St Helena. Las Cases suggested that they live in the memories of the glorious past. This seemed to stimulate him and Napoleon was suddenly excited by the thought of writing his memoirs. 'Yes, one must work,' he said. 'Work is Time's scythe.' He would present an image of himself to the world that he himself would create. Meanwhile, the British cabinet determined to give legal weight to their decision about his future, the document they drew up eventually being signed in Paris by the representatives of the Great Powers on 2 August. Then, quite suddenly, a threat to the plan to remove Napoleon from the coast of Britain and, eventually, the civilised world, suddenly made itself known. The fallen Emperor might yet be saved by a shrewd exercise of British law. The newspapers were suggesting that he might be 'brought out of the ship' by a writ of habeas corpus. If that were indeed to happen then there was only one thing to do. What was for the authorities at least a desperate situation required a desperate remedy. Under no circumstances whatsoever should the writ be served or Napoleon be allowed to set foot on land. The *Bellerophon* would have to be moved out to sea.

The following day Keith received orders from the Admiralty to that effect. Despite their Lordships' wish that Admiral Hallowell take responsibility for this, Keith (who hated the man) was determined to act on his own account. He wrote back to London saying: 'I have decided on embarking in the *Tonnant* and proceeding off the Start with that ship, the *Bellerophon* and the *Eurotas*, for the purpose of meeting the *Northumberland* and more effectually executing their Lordships' directions respecting General Bonaparte.'

Maitland was then given orders to sail but so surprised was he that he was determined to check matters with Keith himself. He was promptly told that 'a Habeas Corpus has been taken out for the purpose of bringing Bonaparte on shore' and that 'a lawyer is on his way down to serve it'.

The ships weighed anchor at once for the Whig lawyers had been busy. They would not see their hero hurried into ignominy in what they considered to be a flagrant defiance of the law of the land. They made their position clear in the newspapers. Writing to the *Morning Chronicle*, the radical Whig Capell Lofft expressed his opinion that Napoleon could not legitimately be described as a prisoner of war, and that even as an alien he had rights under habeas corpus because he was within territorial waters. 'Deportation, or transportation, or relegation, cannot legally exist in this country, except where the law expressly provides it on trial and sentence.' But there had been no trial nor, in Lofft's view, could there legitimately be one. And, if this theoretical approach failed, another was to hand. It was now arranged that Napoleon would be served a subpoena to appear as a witness in a libel trial concerning an international incident that had happened off the North American coast as far back as 1806. Napoleon would have to be put on land to attend the court and, once on British soil, all the protective intricacy of the law could be brought into play on his behalf.

These were clever if desperate plans, and they very nearly worked. Even now the subpoena was on its way, and it was only by dint of escaping through the back door of his house, being rowed across to his ship and then scrambling into another one that Keith avoided having to receive the subpoena on the part of his prisoner. The ships were then ordered out to sea. As they battled against the waves the lawyer vainly waved his papers at the disappearing bulk of the *Bellerophon* and Napoleon penned his mighty protest against all that had recently happened to him. 'I appeal to history,' he wrote, 'it will say that an enemy who for twenty years waged war against the British people, came voluntarily, in his misfortunes, to seek an asylum under their laws.' He could hardly have showed more esteem or more confidence in their legendary justice. But what did the British do? 'They feigned to stretch forth a friendly hand to that enemy; and when he had delivered himself up in good faith, they sacrificed him.' Perfidious Albion indeed.

## HMS Northumberland

The *Northumberland*, captained by Sir George Cockburn, appeared off the stormy horizon around nine o'clock on the morning of 9 August. By noon she was alongside the *Bellerophon* and was waiting to have Napoleon hurried ignominiously aboard. Much to Captain Maitland's relief Napoleon himself had 'at last' made up his mind to quit one prison ship for another 'without force being used'. He was nonetheless still protesting at what he saw as the injustice of his treatment. Two days earlier he had written a long and forthright letter to Lord Keith. He continued to insist that he was not a prisoner of war and he now demanded to see the signed document that said that he was. He also wanted to read the paper which 'directs that contrary to the laws of the country and of hospitality I should be taken from the *Bellerophon* and exiled two thousand leagues away, on a rock lost in mid-ocean, and in the heat of the tropics'. He reiterated that this last would kill him. Once again Napoleon was insisting in vain that everything should be done by due process of law and he now said that he needed the signed documents so that he could both appeal to the courts and make a public protest. The letter was ignored and the only concession granted to him was his being allowed to wear his sword as he transferred to the *Northumberland*. All the rest of his entourage were to be disarmed.

These people spent much of their remaining time removing their money and papers from their luggage before this was subjected to the inevitably thorough and humiliating search. A quarter of a million francs in gold was sewn into belts which were then distributed around the various members of the entourage. Only 80,000 francs remained for inspection, money that would later be given to Napoleon's jailer, Sir Hudson Lowe, in order to cover additional expenses. Very precise instructions had been sent for the ordering of Napoleon's personal effects especially. 'The Admiral will allow all the baggage, wine and provisions which the General may have brought with him to be taken aboard the *Northumberland*,' they read. This included his dinner plate 'unless it be so considerable as to seem rather an article to be converted into ready money than for real use'. Actual money, diamonds and other valuables were to be surrendered, however. 'The Admiral will declare to the General that the British government by no means intends to confiscate his property, but merely to take upon itself the administration of his effects, to hinder him from using them as a means to promote his flight.' The principal derived from realising Napoleon's effects would then be used for his maintenance. Cockburn duly carried out the inspection but he and his men 'seemed surprised how little luggage there was for them to examine; probably measuring the Emperor's fortune by the heights of his glory, they expected to find piles of riches, whereas only a few odds and ends, hardly worth showing, were spread out.'

The inspection was over by eleven o'clock. Keith went aboard the *Bellerophon* where Napoleon again protested that he was not voluntarily leaving the English coast. Then, as a last act, he distributed money to his followers, each of his servants receiving the equivalent of a year's wages. There were tears and earnest conversations of farewell that lasted for nearly two hours. Then, at around half-past one, Napoleon emerged from his cabin to tell Keith that he was ready and at the Admiral's orders. He thanked Maitland and his crew for the treatment he had received and descended to the boat that was to take him to the *Northumberland*. He allowed no trace of tragedy or strain to cross his face and instead, sitting on Lord Keith's left, he talked about his Egyptian campaign and a host of other subjects. He even managed to make jokes about being seasick.

Once aboard he made a last, brief speech to those of his entourage who were not to follow him to St Helena. 'Be happy, my friends,' he said. 'We shall never see each other again, but my thoughts will always be with you, with you and with all those who have served me.' Napoleon remained composed throughout and ended his speech by declaring: 'Tell France that I wish her well.' With that, he watched those who were to leave depart, doing so through dimmed eyes.

Napoleon declared that his living arrangements aboard the *Northumberland* were satisfactory, consisting as they did of two cabins, one of which was occupied by Cockburn and his flag-captain and the other by Napoleon himself. There were, in addition, a dining room and a drawing room. Cockburn was determined that his passenger was not to be treated with the respect due to an Emperor and, to emphasise this, it was made clear to him that the saloon was a place where all the gentlemen aboard might gather when they chose. Even now he propelled the Honourable William Lyttleton, the ardently Whig Member of Parliament for Worcestershire, Lord Lowther and Sir George Bingham into the drawing room and bade them sit down. As Cockburn withdrew to attend to last-minute details a rather stilted conversation took place between Napoleon and the others. He asked them who they were, about their political interests and showed himself well versed in British affairs of state. Eventually Napoleon began to complain about the state of the *Northumberland*. It seemed, he said, to have been fitted out in great haste. The men agreed that this was so but 'on the other hand it is one of our best ships, and sails particularly well'. The answer did not satisfy. There were far better ships moored in Plymouth. One of those should have been chosen. Napoleon's temper was beginning to fray and a bitter exchange took place between him and Lyttleton, who spoke excellent French.

'You have tarnished the flag and your national honour by making me a prisoner like this,' Napoleon burst out.

'Any agreement with you has been broken, and it is vital to the country's interests that you should not be in a position to return to France.'

'You are behaving like a small aristocratic state, not like a great free nation! I came to take refuge on your soil, and only wanted to live in England as an ordinary citizen.'

'Your party in France is still too powerful; affairs might take such a turn that you would be recalled to the throne.'

'No, no, my career is ended.'

'You used the same words a year ago, in Elba.'

'Then I was a sovereign, I had the right to make war; the King of France did not keep his word to me. I made war on him with six hundred men!'

The whole history of the Hundred Days flashed briefly before the minds of those gathered aboard the *Northumberland* and, with it, the bitterness of defeat. Napoleon claimed he would have done better to have surrendered to either the Emperor of Austria or the Tsar. Alexander in particular loved France, he said, and if he had surrendered to him then he believed he would have been able to rejoin the Army of the Loire and been at the head of 100,000 men today. It was a pitiful fantasy, the only way of warding off thoughts that the only army he was associated with now were the 2,280 British soldiers who were to guard him on St Helena.

'You do not understand my character,' he continued. 'You ought to have trusted my word of honour.'

'Will you permit me to tell you the truth?' Lyttleton interposed. 'Tell me.'

'From the moment you invaded Spain there was hardly an individual in England who trusted your word.'

Napoleon defended himself as best he could, saying it was necessary to counterbalance the enormous power Britain had by sea. He was asked if he had wanted to destroy England. 'Why yes! During twenty years of war. Or rather not to destroy you, but to humble you; I wanted to force you to be just, or at least less unjust . . .' The great myth of Napoleon as the embattled liberal force in Europe – a myth first fashioned by Napoleon himself – was here in the making. The years he spent on St Helena would be much devoted to elaborating it.

## St Helena

On 8 August, as the *Northumberland* pitched and rolled on the heavy seas, Cockburn hoisted his signal flag to order the departure for the remote and wretched little island that lay more than 1,000 miles off the west African coast and some 5,000 miles from France. Here Napoleon was to remain. Here was the personal price he would be made to pay in boredom, frustration and humiliation for the failure of the Hundred Days.[8] His first impressions of St Helena were dismal indeed. 'This is a shameful island,' he declared. 'It is a prison,' he continued, adding that he would need much strength and courage to survive there. That St Helena was indeed the prison the British intended it to be was evident to Napoleon day and night. The coastline was continuously patrolled by two brigs. Sentries in red uniforms were on constant guard duty outside Longwood House, the damp, unhealthy, rat-infested wooden farmhouse that became Napoleon's home. The cruelly unimaginative and petty-minded Hudson Lowe who was responsible for Napoleon at all times epitomised the ghastliness of it all. 'They have sent me more than a jailer,' Napoleon opined. 'Sir Lowe is a hangman.' Terrible boredom deepened the desolation. Napoleon devised a routine for himself, tried to keep up his health through exercise, wrote his memoirs, read in the evenings and conducted a long war of psychological attrition with his warder. The meanness of Hudson Lowe's spirit became daily more evident. Constantly riled by Napoleon, he instructed an orderly to snoop in at the shutters during the evenings and even meditated having a peephole cut in the ceiling of the salon so that he could watch him at all times unobserved.

Despite periods of lassitude, Napoleon kept up his spirits, feeding them with fantasy and hope. Perhaps there would be a change of government in England and he would again be a free man. What would he do with his freedom? America still beckoned and Napoleon vowed that he would join the wars for freedom even then being fought in Chile, Peru and Venezuela. 'I shall mould Latin America into a great empire.' He was confident, too, of the immortality of his reputation and the lasting nature of much of what he had achieved, the Code Napoleon especially. He thought often about his son and, as the dynasties of the old regime tightened their grip on Europe once again – Russia and Prussia dividing Poland, Austria reannexing parts of Italy, the Papacy reintroducing the Inquisition and the British slaughtering and wounding those who dared campaign for parliamentary reform on the field of Peterloo – Napoleon believed that his son might yet be called to the French throne to continue his father's work. In fact the boy was frail and was to die of consumption when barely into young manhood.

Gradually Napoleon's own health began to fade. At first he suffered pains in his liver which were like the jabs of a penknife. He blamed these on the climate, saying: 'I should have lived to be eighty if they had not brought me to this vile place.' He started to be regularly sick and the pain got worse. He lost weight and the emetics administered to him made him roll on the floor in agony. He began to sweat profusely and sometimes his bed linen had to be changed seven times a night. Eventually he realised that he had stomach cancer and faced the prospect of intense and ghastly suffering. He would inevitably grow weaker and weaker as he was able to ingest less and less food. The pain could only grow worse for the only known analgesics had to be taken orally. He began to get horribly thin and to grow exhausted from regular and terrible vomiting. On 29 April 1821 he was sick eight times. This left him exhausted and thirsty. As he was served a little orange-flower water his servants wept at the sight of a man who had mastered Europe now begging for a spoonful of coffee and being denied it. The end was clearly approaching and Napoleon, whose thoughts had turned more to religion during his five and a half years of exile, was eventually offered extreme unction. By the night of 5 May he was delirious and at 5.49 that evening he died. When the news reached Paris, Talleyrand was taking tea in the fashionable salon of Madame Crawford. The polite chattering fell quiet. 'What an event!' someone said. Talleyrand's voice rose above the excitement. 'It is no longer an event,' he said, 'merely a piece of news.'

# NOTES

## 1: Vienna, 1815

1. For Talleyrand's machinations at the Congress of Vienna see Duff Cooper, *Talleyrand*, Chapter 10, *passim*.
2. See Anthony D. Smith, *National Identity*, pp. 85–89.
3. The genesis of Napoleon's myth of self is discussed in Philip G. Dwyer, 'Napoleon and the Drive for Glory: Reflections on the Making of French Foreign Policy' in Philip G. Dwyer (ed.), *Napoleon and Europe*, pp. 118–135.
4. For the economic and industrial development of Britain in the nineteenth century see Eric J. Evans, *The Forging of the Modern State: Early Industrial Britain*, *passim*.
5. Details of Napoleon's routine are given in Vincent Cronin, *Napoleon*, pp. 179–186.
6. For the Continental System see D. G. Wright, *Napoleon and Europe*, pp. 52–55, 65–67, 74–75 and 109–110.
7. For details of Wellington's early military career see Richard Holmes, *Wellington: The Iron Duke*, Chapters 1–4, *passim*.
8. For the rise of nationalism see Wright, pp. 71–73 and Smith, Chapters 3 and 4, *passim*.

## 2: Elba, 1814

1. For Napoleon's attempted suicide see Alan Schom, *One Hundred Days: Napoleon's Road to Waterloo*, pp. 2–3.
2. For details of the journey to Elba see Norman Mackenzie, *The Escape from Elba: The Fall and Flight of Napoleon*, Chapter 4, *passim*.

3. For the restoration of Louis XVIII see Henri Houssaye, *1815*, Book One, Chapter 1, *passim*.

4. Napoleon's government of Elba is described in Mackenzie, Chapters 6 and 7, *passim*.

5. See plate 3

6. The Napoleonic court is described in Isser Woloch, 'The Napoleonic Regime and French Society' in Philip G. Dwyer (ed.), *Napoleon and Europe*, pp. 60–78.

7. See Michael Sibalis, 'The Napoleonic Police State' in ibid., pp. 79–94.

8. For the social and political impact of the *Grande Armée* see Alan Forrest, 'The Military Culture of Napoleonic France' in ibid., pp. 43–59.

9. Napoleon's sexuality is discussed in Theo Aronson, *Napoleon and Josephine: A Love Story*, Chapter 14, *passim*.

10. See Houssaye, pp. 26–76.

## 3: The Flight Of The Eagle, 27 FEBRUARY–20 MARCH 1815

1. For Colonel Girod de l'Ain see Anthony Brett-James, *The Hundred Days: Napoleon's Last Campaign from Eye-witness Accounts*, pp. 7–8.

2. For Coignet see ibid., p. 6.

3. For Ney during this period see Henri Houssaye, *1815*, Book Two, Chapter 4, *passim*.

## 4: Paris, 21 MARCH–12 JUNE 1815

1. See Henri Houssaye, *1815*, Book Three, Chapter 1, *passim*.

2. For Constant see ibid., Chapter 4, *passim* and Vincent Cronin, *Napoleon*, pp. 283–286.

3. The political divisions in France are described in Houssaye, Book Three, Chapter 5, *passim*.

4. See ibid.

5. For Fouché's part in these events see R. E. Cubberley, *The Role of Fouché in the Hundred Days*. For his career generally see Alan Schom, *One Hundred Days: Napoleon's Road to Waterloo*, Chapter 6, *passim*.

6. Contemporary newspaper coverage is described in Houssaye, pp. 457–463.

7. See Cavalié Mercer, *Journal of the Waterloo Campaign Kept through the Campaign of 1815*, vol. I, pp. 2–17.

8. See Rees Howell Gronow, *Reminiscences and Recollections*, vol. I, pp. 64–65.

9. For Leeke's background see Davis Howarth, *A Near Run Thing: The Day of Waterloo*, pp. 8–11.
10. See Brendan Simms, 'Britain and Napoleon' in Philip G. Dwyer (ed.), *Napoleon and Europe*, pp. 189–203.
11. For Carnot see Schom, pp. 136–149.
12. For Davout see ibid., pp. 161–171.
13. See Houssaye, Book Three, Chapter 3, *passim*.
14. See plate 24.

## 5: Waterloo, 12–21 JUNE 1815

1. See Anthony Brett-James, *The Hundred Days: Napoleon's Last Campaign from Eye-witness Accounts*, pp. 24–25. (I would like to record my indebtedness to this work, its admirable commentary especially.)
2. For Fantin des Odoards see ibid., pp. 71–73.
3. For Leeke see David Howarth, *A Near Run Thing: The Day of Waterloo*, p. 8.
4. Ibid., p. 21.
5. Ibid., p. 25.

## 6: St Helena, 21 JUNE 1815–5 MAY 1821

1. See Anthony Brett-James, *The Hundred Days: Napoleon's Last Campaign from Eye-witness Accounts*, pp. 196–203.
2. For Napoleon and Constant see Gilbert Martineau, *Napoleon Surrenders*, pp. 27–28.
3. For Napoleon at Malmaison see ibid., Chapter 4, *passim*.
4. For the Allied advance on and entry into Paris see Brett-James, pp. 204–216.
5. For Leeke see ibid., pp. 212–213.
6. Ibid., pp. 214–215.
7. For Napoleon off the English coast see Martineau, Chapters 9–13, *passim*.
8. For details of St Helena and Napoleon's life there see Vincent Cronin, *Napoleon*, Chapters 26–27.

# BIBLIOGRAPHY

Aronoson, Theo, *Napoleon and Josephine: A Love Story*, John Murray, 1990.

Asprey, Robert B., *The Rise and Fall of Napoleon Bonaparte*, 2 vols, Little, Brown and Company, 2000.

Brett-James, Anthony, *The Hundred Days: Napoleon's Last Campaign from Eye-witness Accounts*, Macmillan, 1964.

Chandler, D., *The Campaigns of Napoleon*, Weidenfeld and Nicolson, 1967.

*Correspondance de Napoleon Ier*, 32 vols, Paris, 1855–1870.

Cooper, Duff, *Talleyrand*, Jonathan Cape, 1932.

Cronin, Vincent, *Napoleon*, Collins, 1971.

Cubberley, R. E., *The Role of Fouché in the Hundred Days*, Wisconsin University Press, 1969.

Dwyer, Philip G. (ed.), *Napoleon and Europe*, Longman, 2001.

Evans, Eric J., *The Forging of the Modern State: Early Industrial Britain*, Longman, 1993.

Fisher, H. A. L., *Napoleon*, Oxford University Press, 1912.

Ford, F. L., *Europe 1780–1830*, Longman, 1970.

Geyl, P., *Napoleon: For and Against*, Jonathan Cape, 1949.

Glover, M., *The Peninsular War 1807–1814*, David & Charles, 1974.

Gronow, Rees Howell, *The Reminiscences and Recollections of Captain Gronow, being Anecdotes of the Camp, the Court, and the Clubs, and Society at the Close of the Last War with France*, 2 vols, 1900.

Hartley, Janet M., *Alexander I: Profiles in Power*, Longman, 1994.

Holmes, Richard, *Wellington: The Iron Duke*, HarperCollins, 2003.

Houssaye, Henri, *1815*, 59th edn, Paris, 1911.

Howarth, David, *A Near Run Thing: The Day of Waterloo*, Collins, 1971.

Keegan, J., *The Face of Battle*, Jonathan Cape, 1976.

Longford, Elizabeth, *Wellington: The Years of the Sword*, Weidenfeld and Nicolson, 1969.

Manceron, Claude (trans. George Unwin), *Napoleon Recaptures Paris: March 20, 1815*, W. W. Norton, 1968.

Markham, F. M. H., *Napoleon*, Weidenfeld and Nicolson, 1963.

Martinau, Gilbert (trans. Frances Partridge), *Napoleon Surrenders*, John Murray, 1971.

Mercer, Cavalié, *Journal of the Waterloo Campaign Kept through the Campaign of 1815*, 2 vols, 1870.

Schom, Alan, *One Hundred Days: Napoleon's Road to Waterloo*, Michael Joseph, 1993.

Mackenzie, Norman, *The Escape from Elba: The Fall and Flight of Napoleon*, Oxford University Press, 1982.

Palmer, Alan, *Napoleon and Marie-Louise: The Second Empress*, Constable, 2001.

Pericoli, Ugo (with additional material by Michael Glover), *1815: The Armies at Waterloo*, Seeley, Service and Company, 1973.

Roberts, Andrew, *Napoleon and Wellington*, Weidenfeld and Nicolson, 2001.

Smith, Anthony D., *National Identity*, Penguin, 1991.

Thompson, J. M., *Napoleon Bonaparte: His Rise and Fall*, Blackwell, 1952.

—— (ed.), *Napoleon's Letters*, Dent, 1954.

Thornton, M. J., *Napoleon After Waterloo*, Stanford University Press, 1968.

Wright, D. G., *Napoleon and Europe*, Seminar Studies in History, Longman, 1984.

# PICTURE CREDITS

1. General Bonaparte on the Bridge at Arcola, 17 November 1796 (oil on canvas) by Baron Antoine Jean Gros (1771–1835). Chateau de Versailles, France/Bridgeman Art Library

2. Bonaparte as First Consul, 1804 by Jean Auguste Dominique Ingres (1780–1867). Musée des Beaux-Arts, Liege, Belgium/Bridgeman Art Library

3. Napoleon I on the Imperial Throne, 1806 (oil on canvas) by Jean Auguste Dominique Ingres (1780–1867). Musée de l'Armee, Paris, France/Bridgeman Art Library

4. Napoleon Bonaparte in his Study, 1812 (oil on canvas) by Jacques Louis David (1748–1825). Kress Collection, Washington D.C., USA/Bridgeman Art Library

5. Napoleon on the Battle Field of Eylau, 9 February 1807, 1808 (oil on canvas) by Baron Antoine Jean Gros (1771–1835). Louvre, Paris, France/Bridgeman Art Library

6. & 7. The Consecration of the Emperor Napoleon and the Coronation of the Empress Josephine (1763–1814) by Pope Pius VII, by Edmond-Francois Aman-Jean (1858–1936). Musée d'Orsay, Paris, France/Bridgeman Art Library

8. Portrait of Marie Laczinska (1786–1817) Countess Walewska, 1812 (oil on canvas) by Baron Francois Pascal Simon Gerard (1770–1837). Chateau de Versailles, France/Bridgeman Art Library

9. Marie Louise (1791–1847) and the King of Rome (1811–32) (oil on canvas) by Baron Francois Pascal Simon Gerard (1770–1837). Chateau de Versailles, France/Bridgeman Art Library

10 Portrait of Charles Maurice de Talleyrand-Perigord (1754–1838) (oil on canvas) by Pierre-Paul Prud'hon (1758–1823). Chateau de Valencay, France/Bridgeman Art Library

11. Portrait of Joseph Fouché (1763–1829) Duke of Otranto, 1813 (oil on canvas) by French School (19th century). Chateau de Versailles, France/Bridgeman Art Library

12. Louis XVIII (1755–1824) (oil on canvas) by Baron Francois Pascal Simon Gerard (1770–1837). Hotel de Beauharnais, Paris, France/Bridgeman Art Library

13. Marshal Michel Ney (1769–1815) Duke of Elchingen, c.1804 (oil on canvas) by French School (19th century). Private Collection/Bridgeman Art Library

14. Alexander I of Russia by Baron Francois Pascal Simon Gerard (1770–1837). Apsley House, The Wellington Museum, London, UK/Bridgeman Art Library

15. Field Marshal Prince Von Blücher (1742–1819) c.1816 (oil on canvas) by George Dawe (1781–1829). Apsley House, The Wellington Museum, London, UK/Bridgeman Art Library

16. Portrait of Arthur Wellesley, 1st Duke of Wellington, 1814 by Sir Thomas Lawrence (1769–1830). Apsley House, The Wellington Museum, London, UK/Bridgeman Art Library (Topham Picturepoint)

17. Napoleon in Fontainebleau, 1846 (oil on canvas) by Hippolyte Delaroche (Paul) (1797–1856). Hamburg Kunsthalle, Hamburg, Germany/Bridgeman Art Library

18. The Congress of Vienna, 1815 (pencil & w/c) by Jean-Baptiste Isabey (1767–1855). Louvre, Paris, France/Bridgeman Art Library

19. 'Adieu at Fontainebleau': Napoleon says Farewell to Old Guard at Fontainebleau in 1814 (engraving) by English School (19th century). Private Collection/Bridgeman Art Library (Ken Welsh)

20. Departure of Napoleon for Elba (w/c on paper) by John Augustus Atkinson (1775–1831). Private Collection/Bridgeman Art Library

21. Return from Elba, c.1852 (oil on canvas) by Ambroise-Louis Garneray (1783–1857).Chateau de Versailles, France/Bridgeman Art Library

22. Napoleon returning from Elba by Vasily Ivanovich Sternberg (Wilhelm) (1818–45). Christie's Images, London, UK/Bridgeman Art Library

23. The Return of Napoleon I to the Tuileries, 20 March 1815 (coloured engraving) by Francois Joseph Heim (1787–1865). Musée de l'Armee, Brussels, Belgium/Bridgeman Art Library (Patrick Lorette)

24. Assembly of the Champ de Mai, 1 June 1815 (oil on canvas) by Francois Joseph Heim (1787–1865). Chateau de Versailles, France/Bridgeman Art Library

25. The Duke of Wellington (1769–1852) on the Road to Quatre-Bras, 16 June

# INDEX

POCKET
BOOKS

# DRAKE
The Life and Legend of an Elizabethan Hero

Stephen Coote

'Fascinating . . . reads almost as a novel . . . a vivid
picture of this legendary but flawed hero'
*History Today*

Was Sir Francis Drake a rabid anti-papist, a state-
sponsored terrorist and slaver? Or was he the
embodiment of English sang-froid, an empire-builder
and hero? He was certainly the most dashing of the
many ambitious seamen to serve Queen Elizabeth I, in
an age when the world seemed there for the taking. For
a God-fearing Protestant of good yeoman stock,
turning the high seas into an English lake seemed
nothing less than a birthright – especially if the only
people in one's way were Catholics. In this new
biography, Stephen Coote shows how Drake's
reputation was made and challenged, and eventually
manipulated in the centuries following his death. This
brilliant re-evaluation of the self-made Elizabethan hero
is a fascinating portrait of the man and his era.

ISBN 0-7434-6870-8
PRICE £8.99